The Craft of Rehearsal

PETER LANG
New York • Washington, D.C./Baltimore • Bern
Frankfurt am Main • Berlin • Brussels • Vienna • Oxford

Anatoly Efros

The Craft of Rehearsal

Further Reflections on Interpretation and Practice

Translated by
James Thomas

PETER LANG

New York • Washington, D.C./Baltimore • Bern
Frankfurt am Main • Berlin • Brussels • Vienna • Oxford

Library of Congress Cataloging-in-Publication Data

Efros, Anatolii.
The craft of rehearsal: further reflections on interpretation
and practice / Anatoly Efros; translated by James Thomas.
p. cm.
Includes bibliographical references and index.
1. Theater—Production and direction. 2. Theater rehearsals.
I. Thomas, James, II. Title.
PN2053.E315   792.02'3—dc22   2006033673
ISBN-13: 978-0-8204-8860-8
ISBN-10: 0-8204-8860-7

Bibliographic information published by **Die Deutsche Bibliothek**.
Die Deutsche Bibliothek lists this publication in the "Deutsche
Nationalbibliografie"; detailed bibliographic data is available
on the Internet at http://dnb.ddb.de/.

Cover design by Lisa Barfield

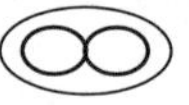

Table of Contents

The Craft of Rehearsal

Translator's Preface

The format and arrangement of this book are identical to Efros's first book, *The Joy of Rehearsal*. Both were written in a continuous stream, much like impromptu notes, although skillfully organized around certain themes. Both have been published without any attempt to alter Efros's mauvist ("bad-ist") writing style. Confident in the reader's understanding, Efros intentionally employs run-on sentences, hesitations, half-finished thoughts, repetitious conjunctions, and other sorts of grammatical "imperfections." The originals did not contain a table of contents or section headings either, only small breaks in the text to indicate a change of topic. To offset some of the demands made on English-speaking readers, I have added section headings and a table of contents keyed to the plays and professional issues involved. Certain passages have been omitted where Efros digresses from the world of theatre or where he discusses plays, authors, actors and other figures not well known outside Russia. I have also inserted a word or comment here and there for extra clarification. The introduction that appears in the first book is not reproduced here, but nonetheless serves to introduce both books. It contains an account of Efros's life and career as well as historical and contextual information. Notes have been inserted where Efros refers to a topic the reader could not be expected to find readily in another source. A foreword, illustrations, chronology, and bibliography give some background to Efros's writing. Most of the Russian spelling employed here is dictated by my personal use rather than phonetic transliteration, but in the notes and bibliography, the names of other authors or their books follow their own spelling.

Acknowledgments

My gratitude is due to Natasha Krymova and Dmitry Krymov, Efros's wife and son, for their permission to publish this translation and for their help and encouragement along the way.

To Tatyana Sherman and Jessica Thomas for editing the translation.

To Anatoly Smeliansky, Rector of the Moscow Art Theatre School, for his influence and support.

To the Wayne State University Humanities Center for important financial assistance.

To my students for their patience while I sought to explore Efros's ideas and methods in the rehearsal hall and classroom.

Foreword

I can only direct the way I feel today.
—Anatoly Efros

Anatoly Efros's first book, *The Joy of Rehearsal,* consists of reflections accumulated between 1954 and 1975.[1] This second book covers the years 1975 to 1979, with some overlap. In this 25-year period of both books, Efros directed at three theatres: the Central Children's Theatre (1954–64), the Lenkom Theatre (1964–67) and the Malaya Bronnaya Theatre (from 1967). In the West, a theatre is simply thought of as a building where plays are produced. In Russia, when speaking about a theatre, what is really meant is a company, an institution. Each theatre comprises a distinctive artistic family with its own genetic code, so to speak, composed of an aesthetic philosophy, an artistic tradition, a special legacy, and socio-cultural resonance. The issue is important here because Efros truly created the identity of each theatre where he worked.

Efros's time at the Central Children's Theatre coincided with the decade following Stalin's death in 1953, an era known in Russia as the "Thaw." Nikita Khrushchev was the new leader of the Soviet Union, and the path was cleared for a rebirth of artistic freedom after a long period of Stalin's ruthless dictatorship. Owing in large part to Efros's productions, the Central Children's Theatre became the epicenter of advanced theatre life in Russia during the Thaw.

Efros's period at the Lenkom Theatre and his first years at the Malaya Bronnaya Theatre corresponded with the end of the Thaw and the beginning of the so-called "Freeze." In 1964, Khrushchev was removed from office and replaced by the neo-Stalinist Leonid Brezhnev, who reintroduced severe control over the arts and ushered in a prolonged period of economic stagnation. The Lenkom Theatre had been rudderless for some time, and when Efros got there, he found himself caught between these two incompatible periods of Russian history. It was an uncertain position for him to be in. He attempted to modernize the repertory by introducing liberal, Thaw-era plays, and in response, the Lenkom Theatre began to flourish. Unfortunately, conservative, Freeze-era authorities increasingly disapproved of the subjects he chose. What seemed to upset them the most was his neo-expressionist interpretation of Chekhov's play, *The Seagull,* in which he emphasized the absurd, dehumanizing elements of Treplev's environment. Even Efros's allies expressed reservations, putting forward dramaturgical arguments against this heretical interpretation of Chekhov, whose plays were traditionally interpreted as warmly humanistic. In 1967, at the end of his third season at the Lenkom Theatre, Efros was dismissed as Artistic Director.

Afterward he was assigned to the directing staff of the Malaya Bronnaya Theatre. Despite the fact that this theatre had also been directionless for a long time, Efros's productions improved its reputation as well. Moreover, almost immediately after he arrived, the Malaya Bronnaya became one of the leading theatres in Moscow. Efros directed there for the next seventeen years, and today his reputation is mainly associated with his time at Malaya Bronnaya.

In 1984, Efros became Artistic Director of the Taganka Theatre, where a promising but brief tenure ended with his death in 1987. He did not live to see the reforms known as "glasnost" and "perestroika" that Soviet leader Mikhail Gorbachev introduced the same year, or the dissolution of the Soviet Union four years later.

The Russian title of this second book is *Profession: Director.* It can be traced directly to Michelangelo Antonioni's 1975 film *The Passenger,* whose European title is *Profession: Reporter.* Efros was impressed by the film and its central theme, which is the nature of the reporter's disposition toward the exigencies of his profession. The book title's reference to the film is somewhat misleading, however. The tone of Efros's book is not world-weary, as was the case with the reporter in the film, but courageous, as clearly seen in more than one of his paragraphs. The Russian title further suggests that this book is only intended for directors, which is also misleading. Efros writes with such enthusiasm and such confidence in the reader's intelligence that everyone from the world of theatre has derived pleasure and profit from reading him. I hope they will continue to do so in this translation. For these reasons, I thought it best to devise a new title that more clearly conveys the general idea of the original, which I also did with his first book. Craft is a synonym of profession, and the English title chosen here, *The Craft of Rehearsal*, is mindful of the unsentimental, craftsman-like point of view that Efros conveys in this book.

As in *The Joy of Rehearsal,* Efros continues to write about the need for reform in an assortment of professional matters, or at least the need to free them from confused thinking. He also retains his "mauvist" writing style, based on respect for the reader and confidence in his or her intelligence. Unlike his first book, however, he confines his explications primarily to two plays: *Othello* and Turgenev's masterpiece, *A Month in the Country* (a plot summary is provided in notes). These two plays provide ideal examples of how Efros meticulously developed modern literary reconstructions from classic works. Conservative critics may have considered them "failures," in the sense that they did not coincide with traditional interpretations. Nevertheless, Efros purposely chose them to establish the perspective of his second book. To underscore the point, he begins *The Craft of Rehearsal* with an account of a sleepless night after a critically unsuccessful premiere, whereas he began *The Joy of Rehearsal* with a statement about the *joy* of rehearsal. In other words, his second book focuses on the courage required to deal with the struggles inherent in artistic life and the constant prospect of failure that goes along with it. Given that Efros held Stanislavsky in high regard, comparing *The Craft of Rehearsal* with Stanislavsky's similarly self-critical analysis of his own "failures" in *My Life in Art* is illuminating.

Anatoly Efros is important not only because he was a brilliant director and rightful heir of Stanislavsky, but even more so because he represents an artistic philosophy. A manifesto is a declaration of principles, and his books are in effect sublimated manifestos of late modern theatre interpretation and practice. The text consists of a variety of thought-provoking theatre narratives together with innovative directorial explications, and the subtext conveys a unified aesthetic point of view. *The Joy of Rehearsal* and *The Craft of Rehearsal* Efros puts Efros into words Efros's vision for the late modern theatre into words and illuminates the ways this aesthetic informed his practice.

The Craft of Rehearsal

At Four O'clock in the Morning

At four o'clock in the morning, in the unpleasant hours after an unsuccessful premiere, it is impossible to sleep, and you remember every trifle with a chill. A ridiculous performance, a ridiculous curtain call, the alienation of old friends. It hurts to think that in so many places today they will curse and ridicule you. Moreover, in the morning, early in the morning, work is already scheduled, and you must show up with *ideas and more ideas.*

Perhaps it is necessary just to select something and think it through for a long time, but I have a different nature, and after many years, my life has formed itself differently.

I have succeeded many times, but many times, I have also experienced shame and fear from the thought that my artistic calculations could prove to be unsound.

All the same, it is impossible to sleep—I write so there might be some semblance of order in my mind. It would be good to be out in public now, to have someone to argue with, not alone, and in the middle of the night.

What my parents probably had to go through for me today is a pity, and then they had to plod the long way home, exhausted.

The hardest thing is to develop in myself a clear attitude toward the facts in the shortest amount of time. In addition, in this clarity, to calm down, or more accurately, to reconcile myself to this clarity. By tomorrow evening, it will come, I hope.

However, tomorrow evening—is far away.

Othello

I am looking at an empty, dark stage, where a lonely ghost lamp is burning. In the theater are only the watchman and myself.

The appearance of a dark stage and an empty auditorium is always pleasant, mysterious. It is possible to sit for a long time, as though waiting for something. It is possible to arrange the future scenery mentally.

For *Othello*, a bench must be approximately this size. Its back should be about this high.

Maybe it will be in semi-darkness, exactly like now. No more than the outlines of those sitting on the bench can be distinguished.

Rodrigo and Iago have the first lines. They sit next to each other, and a microphone is fixed between them. Their secret whispering will reach us with a little amplification.

Next to them, but without hearing their conversation, sits everyone else, and, of course, Othello.

Someone quietly enters, sits down or leaves, but all of Iago's whispers will be still audible.

This beginning will last a long time, and will only change when Iago begins to awaken Brabantio. The knocking and noise will begin, then everyone will disappear, and the Senator will leave.

Out of Iago's whispering grows the *action*

It Is Necessary to Change!

For twelve years in a row now, I have vacationed about a hundred kilometers from Vilnius. When we arrived here for the first time, there were fields and three lakes around the house. Now, where there once were fields, the forest is higher than my tall son is. Once he ran around here trying to catch butterflies in a net; now he seriously sketches costumes for his future degree performance. The young mistress was expecting her first child at that time. The old grandfather was still alive, and in the adjacent house, there was another pensioner as well. Now there are no old men, the mistress has three children and expecting a fourth. Near the house stands their cherry-red automobile. Next to the formerly vacant lake is now a campground—noisy cars, tents, cheerfully speeding boats are all around.

Why haven't I simply written, "Hi, Gang…"? After all, it would be so easy to write. Simply say what comes into in my head.

I used to work at the Central Children's Theatre.[2]

In the literature at that time, a leading question was the problems of youth. I directed many plays like this and was coming close to a dead end.

At that time, I repeated the same thing to myself many times—probably not to forget: *it is necessary to change!* I arose in the morning and thought: what was that good idea that came to me yesterday? Ah, yes! *It is necessary always to change!* In addition, I was right, although who is not familiar with this truth…

However, they do not really know it; I am certain they do not know it.

Because the most difficult thing is precisely to think about changing direction. Moreover, after changing direction, there will be the vision of a "new world."

It is good to travel as long as your feet keep moving. However, we, so to speak, settled people, sit all the time, and then others go ahead, leaving us behind.

After that, I sat here beside these lakes, I sat and suffered because I was losing contact with my former actor-students at the CCT.

I had become intelligible to them in all my weaknesses. However, at that juncture, I required something fresh from them and them from me. One night in a hotel on tour, they called on me and demanded a report. Why did I put on certain plays, why did I cast them in certain roles and not in others? So it goes with people, they grow and begin to look down on you. This is a very difficult moment. I did not know how the next year would begin, how I would once more encounter the actors.

I walked back and forth along this shore and did not feel the pleasure of a vacation.

The next year was beginning to look frightening. Only one thing was clear: it was necessary to change again.

Othello

A persuasive idea: throughout the play, not to dwell on any trifles. The audience must grasp the whole thing as quickly as possible. *It is not the way of life that is important, but the philosophy.*

…Iago indicates to Roderigo that he hates the Moor, and explains the reasons for his hatred. Iago and Roderigo make a noise to awaken Brabantio, Iago and Roderigo tell Brabantio about his daughter's flight. Brabantio departs, and after discovering that Desdemona is gone, he returns to overtake her.

A street scene, someone awakens someone, someone leaves. They report to him about the flight of his daughter. He goes to check and returns *a different man.*

The philosophy is this: intrigue makes a man unrecognizable. It destroys him.

This scene is one small cell of the large future organism.

He entered as a strong, strong man, an imperious Senator. Then we see him *after the impact.* He is weak, helpless, destroyed. All this before our eyes, as though it were a test run.

Intrigue strikes at the heart of a strong and still rather young man. He is about forty years old. A very confident, strong fighter—to strike a man like him is difficult.

Ulyanov should play this role, or, "if worse comes to worst," Marlon Brando...[3]

Intrigue is destructive. It changes a man into nothing.

At the beginning is a Venetian flag. Then another one, a small one. At the end, when Othello stabs himself, the small flag will be lowered.

At the beginning, a scenic turret will swing open. It is, in essence, two large semi-circular benches with high backs. The senators will sit there, or simply curious people or Iago himself will observe his own handiwork. In front of these benches will stand a small cot. All the time someone sits on the benches and watches. Maybe it is even Desdemona, while Iago performs in this "arena." She listens, as though none of this were about her...

When they summoned Desdemona, she dressed quickly and followed the guards. The essence of what is coming is clear to her. However, how this essence will be revealed is unexpected. *In what way* will it be revealed? Certainly, while she was running here, Desdemona thought that they would be judging Othello. Some scandal is unavoidable. Both of them knew this and went ahead anyway. Nevertheless, how will the scandal develop, *in what form* will it appear?

Desdemona runs to the Senate and waits for what will happen *concretely.* She comes running in—everyone is standing in expectation of her arrival. What will happen next? What has already happened? Her father asks a question—who was she with, was she with him or not? Despite all her preparation, this is still a surprise. It could not be otherwise. Now, this sharp question, and in her face.

She is breathing rapidly from her fast run. The Senate. So many faces. Her father, the Doge, Othello, so many people all around. Lots of light. In addition, this direct question—who was she with? Her father even embraces her, seating her on his lap.

How long our adult children remain only children to us.

Desdemona keeps silent, and then, although this action is *the breaking point,* she gets up and walks over to Othello.

Now too will be *that silence. In addition, her father's fit of anger.*

Once again, Iago will explode, having remained with Roderigo.

Hatred, hatred, hatred.

However, what happened here was only the first step.

Iago's war against Othello began openly only after the Moor stole the Senator's daughter. Prior to this, Othello appointed Cassio his lieutenant. Iago was strongly upset. His spite accumulated and accumulated, and now, with the story of Desdemona, his rage has *exploded*!

It is necessary to begin precisely from *hatred, fury.*

It happens that a man cannot suppress his hatred any longer. After this, any sudden accident causes it to pour out. The person who hates suddenly has seizures; he starts to shout, maybe even to shoot. It is impossible to calm down.

Iago probably did not expect a complete victory when he decided to stir up the kidnapping scandal. He indicated that they probably would only reprimand Othello, since the Senate needed him today. It is possible that this entire scandal will end peacefully, but for Iago this open act, this eruption of hatred, this nighttime hysterics, is *necessary.*

...I hate, I hate, I hate, I hate. For this and for that, without any reason. I will aggravate him, I will erase him from the face of the earth, and I will torment him with small and large troubles. I hate!

How could it be otherwise! From his point of view, nothing goes the way it should. People like him are below; people like the Moor are above. They only allow people like Cassio near them. The beautiful woman became the wife of Othello. A kind of order was established that Iago could not accept. In his irrepressible, open antagonism, he is capable of anything. He is violent. He behaves the way very emotional people behave around those they know, after they have had to undergo a humiliation among strangers. The power there was not on their side, and they had to stifle their hatred, but here they are at home, they can rage, groan, threaten, it is hard to reason with them.

Then, when Iago is around Othello, he has to become quiet again.

Then Iago is like a brother to Othello. Iago worries, sensing the nearness of danger, and Othello is even ashamed that Iago is worried.

Othello feels guilty before Iago: he has forced Iago to worry because of his marriage to Desdemona.

When there is danger, a good person does not worry so much about himself, but, for example, about the friend he feels strongly about. A good person does everything to calm his fellow friend, persuading him that there is nothing to worry about, that the danger hanging over him is not so bad.

Idea

The idea of an artistic work is a strange thing. It begins to penetrate through exactly when you cease paying attention to it. You have already finished *all this* [preparation], and improvisation begins [at rehearsal], and then when *life* enters in force, the *idea* appears again, only with a different face.

In directing, everything you say means almost nothing, but not quite. This is only your thinking, even if it is correct. Moreover, the actor, even if he understands it, nevertheless will still not play it. Because an idea cannot be acted, it would be something too general. It is necessary to find a concrete expression of those thoughts and feelings—very *concrete*. It is necessary, of course, not to lose this general feeling and this general thought. You have to carefully consider everything, and then, as it were, forget everything while you build something concrete on stage.

It is similar to how you would prepare a lecture, for example. You finish preparing it. Then you leave and get into a traffic jam. In addition, when you get to the lecture, everyone has left without waiting for you. Now the lecture is rescheduled for tomorrow. However, tomorrow is a whole day that will be filled with a multitude of events. Finally, the next morning you go to the institute. Then some student argues with you the whole time, and ridiculous questions were asked.

In general, you did all you wanted to and planned for; you gave this lecture, only somehow, it was different.

In my opinion, the highest skill in our work is the capability for *improvisation*. You consider everything carefully, possibly for months, even an entire year. Now you enter on stage during rehearsal, and the *concreteness* begins. It is in your partner, in him and no one else, in living dialogue, in some new orientation, quite different from what was only in your head. It is necessary to examine, to absorb what is concrete and real into you. In addition, what you prepared earlier "for yourself" must now be refracted here, "out loud," through what is real.

Classic and Modern Plays

After an interval of about ten years, I am once again looking at the MAT production of Jerome Kilty's play, *Dear Liar*.[4] This time to make a film of it. By this time, the original director, Josef Rayevsky, has been deceased for a long time.[5] The performers are the same, only ten years older. I see how hard it is for them to play these difficult roles. It is no laughing matter for two actors in their seventies to hold the attention of an audience for three and a half hours. However, they hold it. The character of Bernard Shaw-Josef Ktorov climbs onto a table in the same manner as before, taking offense at the character Mrs. Patrick Campbell-Angelina Stepanova.[6] The same straight back of an athlete. Only his voice, perhaps, is a little quieter. Stepanova looks no more than fifty, or maybe sixty. It does not matter, however. They are from MAT, where *Three Sisters* was produced. In addition, this training remains in them. It is not a bit boring for me to sit in the auditorium for several hours listening to the text, even though the play was virtually without action. Ah, what a text! What characters, and what events! I understand why those who came here wanted to see this old production.

This play is a sharp concentration of two enormous lives. Here it is about the love of two people, as seriously as in Shakespeare's plays. Here it is about the death of a mother and the loss of a husband; here it deals with the triumphs of creativity and the poverty of old age. It is about war and the loss of a son. It is about the profound reactions of two people to their entire life. Ah, what reactions! The mother learned that a shell, which fell on top of a bunker, killed her son, and Shaw writes in answer to her letter. Ktorov, playing Shaw, comes down to the edge of the stage and simply shouts that the priest who praised her son is a scoundrel. That this priest probably read a prayer when they sent the same young boys to the front. In addition, another priest will probably read the same prayer when the first priest is also killed by a shell. Shaw shouted and choked up. Then slowly sat back in his chair, collected himself a little, and suddenly, distinctly, terrifyingly, began to repeat, "Devil, devil, devil!" Then he waited half a second and said again, *"Devil!"* Then, turning in the direction of Mrs. Campbell's, he tenderly began to speak, "My dear, dear, dear..."

Yes, this was the *evaluation* of the loss of a *beloved* son.

Still, at the beginning, when a misfortune happened to Shaw, he described it in a letter with terrible details. He described how they cremated the body of his mother, and how the worker extracted the nails from the ashes of her burned coffin. Shaw always jeered at everything, and here he jeered too, but he also *wept*. His "correspondent" did not simply pity him, as one might easily imagine. She joked and became angry too, but in this anger and humor there was so much love...

Why don't they write such plays today? Why don't they write about so many things? Why don't they write now about the fact that Iago is Iago! In addition, precisely *how* Othello killed Desdemona? Moreover, *for no reason?* Why do they write everything "just a little," as if they are afraid to disturb someone? And they do not disturb anyone. Why is a happy ending compulsory? As though *this* public is less intelligent than the one during Shakespeare's lifetime.

We say that Shakespeare was a champion of bright ideals. Yet Othello brutally murdered Desdemona.

There is the concept "what it is about" and there is "what it is for." However, we often deny "what it is about," not believing, perhaps, in the beneficial "give-and-take" power of art. *Richard III*, God knows, is about terrible crimes, but there is so much benefit from this play.

Molière's Don Juan killed the Commander, who subsequently appeared before him at dinner, and from the Commander's handshake, Don Juan suddenly fell through the earth. What opportunities there are here for a play! For the actor's spirit, for the design!

No, thus far contemporary plays are poor.

On the other hand, let us not even talk about Iago or the Commander or Mitya Karamazov;[7] let us talk about a simple apartment with a kitchen and a bathroom, but *with a degree of truth, exposed*, with new questions. With the things that art must speak about.

When you read a [new] play, you find yourself repeating all the time: I already know this; I already know this. However, it should be, I do not know, I do not know, I do not know! In addition, the audience does not know. However, it *will* know.

Othello

Pushkin said that Othello is not jealous but trusting. Why does Othello trust only what is evil, however, and distrust Cassio, Desdemona, Montano, Lodovico, and Emilia? What is behind this one-sided trustfulness? Perhaps this trustfulness (so often directed only toward the bad) is not in itself the original cause of his further troubles, but the result of something that precedes such one-sided trustfulness.

The essence of Othello, I think, is in his weakness, the sensation of his foreignness, a certain feeling of inferiority in comparison with *them, the others.* If he were a strong man, self-assured, *equal,* wouldn't he notice that Desdemona's eyes were more honest than Iago's? Wouldn't he guess that Desdemona's love for Cassio was not real?

They say, of course, that a jealous man does not need a real basis for his jealousy. But then what about Pushkin's well-known observation that Othello is not jealous but trusting?

Yes, he trusts the bad because he feels himself an *outsider*. In this is his vulnerability and weakness.

Aren't the great star actors stretching a point when they portray Othello's composure and rock-like loftiness? The absence of harmony in his soul is what has triggered the misfortunes occurring in this play.

To the Limit

This may be true or not, but I think that sometimes a modern play is not as good as a classic because there is no *intensification* in it. I am speaking not only about Shakespeare, but Molière too is constructed with sharp edges.

Recently I saw a rather lovely play about a scientist who struggles against air pollution. His colleagues betray him, and then realizing the truth, they return to him. This subject is worthy enough, but the plot could be thought up in fifteen minutes, and it would be like all the other subjects where the story, for example, is not about air pollution but about correcting bad manufacturing.

Maybe the author wrote this play in a year, or even two, but the impression from the development of the material is that it was cleverly written in only fifteen minutes. Because nowhere is anything taken *to the limit*. Something extreme. Something that would make us want, for example, to cry bitterly or reflect strongly. Something that would stick in the memory.

This does not come from any absence of diligence or even talent, but because the concept of *taking decisions to the limit is not customary.*

The truth is presented somewhere between zero and, let us say, six on a scale of one hundred. To reach the top of any situation is not permissible.

This is a problem of the modern play in general. We take the topic of the day and then run through it lightly and quickly. Quickly, because it is necessary to get to the ending as soon as possible so that the *moral* will smooth over the virtually invisible sharpness. Without morals of this kind, we think the audience will not understand it. We will understand, but the audience will not understand—that is our favorite saying.

Therefore, *pseudo-realism* is born this way. Alternatively, *semi-realism*, if you will. It is the basic style of our dramatic art.

These plays are comic strips, simplified statements on any subject at hand. In addition, it also happens that the subject itself is too simple. They have forgotten how to write long acts because indeed it is necessary to find *development and growth* in an act. In addition, skipping along in small pictures creates the illusion of growth. That's why we now consider a "unit setting" fashionable—neither concrete nor abstract, but God knows what kind, the actors jump out on this platform for five minutes to fasten on something supposedly significant, and then escape from the stage to continue the conflict "just a little bit" in another locale. Eventually, common diligence, perhaps, arrives at something slightly useful and to some degree touching.

Only *to some extent?* Semi-realism probably also brings some benefit, but in fact it is only relative. Seriously speaking, it does not really bring any benefit. It only develops certain bad habits, both in the theatre and the public.

Daring

On the first of January, the first day of the New Year, one of our premieres took place.

There were many people. In spite of yesterday's celebrations, people were again going to the theatre. Those who love the theatre go even on New Year's, even in the snow, even in the rain, in the heat.

The theatre must have some authority, however, to justify this purpose. Fortunately, our theatre is not empty. Although nowadays, generally speaking, few theatres are empty. Not because of many good performances, but because of the thirst for good shows.

The auditorium has filled, everyone has grown quiet, the lights have been extinguished, and our performance began.

It was quite a good performance, and it did not begin timidly. However, after five minutes I left the auditorium because was everything so *timid*. After all, people come to the *theatre*. This does not mean, of course, that it is necessary to scream falsely and noisily or that there should be magnificent scenery or anything like that. Such things have ended. Today, theatricality means searching for something different from the usual thing, a special atmosphere, whether bold or lyrical, only revealed in extremis, with the meaning openly in extremis. The beginning of our production went like this: a new man was appointed to a post and another man was removed. An office, an official sat behind a desk, etc. Boring. Then I thought up another beginning besides this beginning. A reporter runs in behind the man who was "sacked," literally *photographs* him, and the huge portrait of him hanging on the wall is removed. Then the man who was hired appears. A photograph is taken of him too, and his huge portrait is hung on the wall. The house is lit, and cheerful music is heard in the auditorium.

This beginning is like an overture that sets up the subject of the play. To give it a necessary push. However, the play's opening was done timidly; it was timidly thought out, *small.* Maybe the subject of this play would collapse, however, if it were any bolder. Because a courageous opening must be followed by a courageous continuance. In *Othello,* for example, one could almost shoot cannon off at the beginning, and its effect would still be sustained. However, in the play above we were modest. After all, this is the theatre, and New Year's, and the people have arrived in this snowstorm because they believe in us.

Do not let them think, however, that I need to go out of control contrary to reason. No, going out of control is not necessary, of course, but "reason," my God, this "reason" really gets on my nerves...

Complete truth, grace, subtlety, and daring. Both in the sense of the play and the sense of its illustration!

Growing Stale

For a long time, ten years, I have considered my basic specialty to be the production of contemporary plays. When one of our authors read a new play at the theatre and I liked it, I felt confident and at peace. Isolated ideas were fastened together as though by a single rod. Everything was in its place.

With nervous excitement, but with belief in success, we waited for premieres.

Something noticeable has happened lately, however, some kind of different, most likely temporary, phase. I have felt that the public has developed a greater interest not in contemporary plays, but in classic productions. I can explain this situation in several ways. First, perhaps, consists of the fact that many directors, and myself among them, have used up their artistic stock regarding modern plays.

Writers call these moments, I think, "growing stale." And for directors, naturally, there are moments when their creative energy grows stale as well. Today I can hardly find any new colors, for example, when I produce Viktor Rozov's plays.[8] I cannot conceive of other statements than I have already used for the plays of Alexei Arbuzov or Ignatii Dvoretsky.[9] I feel that my imagination has become a little dull.

In addition, naturally the public feels this immediately. I do not see the same reactions as before to my new productions of modern plays. In addition, I think that audiences have become bored with my artistic interpretations of the statements made by modern plays. It is necessary resolutely to find a new tone, a new style of statement, but, unfortunately, it is not to be found.

In classic productions, on the other hand, something new has arisen, and in them, you can feel that lively interest by the public that I already spoke about. It is very joyful, this interest, there is nothing to compare it with. When it exists, not only the actor but also the stage-hand feels it. It is even seen in how the audience assembles before the beginning of a performance. In the classics, apparently, compared with recent years, something has been seen anew, something new interests the audience. Both from the point of view of the essence of the plays themselves, and from the point of view of their theatrical presentation. Here too, of course, there is the danger of creative work growing stale—it is the kind of work in which, as they say, one must be "on guard." Repetition may be the mother of learning, but not of creativity. We always face the danger of repetition. And here it is necessary to look at things soberly, without self-deception. A sober viewpoint offers hope for new artistic ideas. I particularly would like to think that I look at things without self-deception. I try to avoid repetition in the classics. In any case, to note the moment when this happens in myself, even if I do not have the strength to do something differently.

However, doubt already produces new energy, which should eventually break free. In the interpretation of a modern subject, I think this new energy will also appear. In fact, experience with classical subjects should promote this.

I would still like to say something more, however, not just about our directorial craft, but also about the plays themselves. It seems to me that many playwrights, aside from our dissatisfaction with ourselves [as directors], are not very satisfied with today's plays either. They sometimes take advantage of the leftovers, as it were, from their past successes, they feel this, are tormented by it, and search for new ways. However, unfortunately, like us, they do not always find them. I allow myself to criticize them only to stir up their imaginations. Even if they do not agree with me, some additional positive charge may appear in their disagreement.

Othello

Stanislavsky had a surprisingly clear and vivid mind and imagination.

When I first read his director's plan for *Othello*, I naturally understood his thinking, but not to such a degree.[10] Now, when I open Stanislavsky again after my own rehearsals, you still find the same miracles—his explanations, moreover, are very concrete.

For example, here is how Stanislavsky writes about Brabantio's speech to Othello during their first meeting on the street.

> My advice to the performer: this is a strong monologue, and it is well known that a strong creative monologue incites the actor to give more spirit to it than he can give. As a result, the correct line of action diverts to an unintended line of passionate affectedness. To avoid this error, a very clear and active objective is needed. What is it? Brabantio is sincerely convinced that without sorcery, it would have been impossible for Othello to marry his daughter, and that she must have been kidnapped from her bed. This is his major argument. Therefore, now he is not simply angry and disturbed (this would lead to affected passion), but he vehemently proves to everyone present that Othello is a sorcerer. The more convincingly the actor expresses the execution of his argument, the more vehement his monologue will be.[11]

Only after knowing the play and conducting many of my own rehearsals is it possible really to appreciate this "modest" advice.

True, many years have passed since Stanislavsky wrote this director's plan intended for MAT. In addition, when you attempt to think about the play and perceive it in new way, much imperceptibly varies in your interpretation of the same moment in the play. I will begin with the external side. I will not have a crowd for Brabantio to address as Stanislavsky did. In his director's plan, a whole crowd scene is developed. He writes: "Let every one of the officials say to himself: 'What would I do if I genuinely believed that Othello was a sorcerer and that it is necessary to suppress sorcerers, like vermin, or burn them at the stake.'"

Now there is no crowd scene, and not just because you are unable to compel anyone to participate in a crowd scene. Even an actor, who, according to the rules, *should* participate in a crowd scene, will approach and speak to you, referring to his age, asking you not to humiliate him [by asking him to be a supernumerary]. In addition, you will probably release him. Moreover, the young actor will not ask because he is afraid to, but it probably would be better if he did not ask because he will make a mess of it anyway. It might be better to restore the discipline behind the question, but the issue is not simply that. The issue is the skepticism displayed now about the subject of crowds. Maybe there is no reason for it, but this skepticism is real—a fact. Imagine what the participants of this crowd would do in the present-day conditions of the stage, how they would gape with their eyes, trying to prove to me that they understand my remarks and are reacting to the words of Brabantio. No, I prefer to show the scene without any crowd on stage. I will even throw out Gratiano, if I can find even a small opportunity to do so, because after tormenting myself with important roles still to be cast, I cannot worry about casting Gratiano... Therefore, the heck with Gratiano and the heck with those who do not wish to play him.

In a word, I will have no crowds, and Brabantio will simply address *the audience.* However, to convince today is audience that Othello is a sorcerer—this would be strange. Involuntarily, you begin to look for some different motivations for Brabantio's behavior, or at least for the nuances of these motivations.

In the monologue there is the motive that Brabantio basically cannot imagine how the daughter of a Senator, living in the comfort of *this* home, having *this* family, could fall in love, in his opinion, with someone so terrible to look on. Brabantio, acted well, could incite in the audience a clear enough representation of the unknown risk of Desdemona's deed. Really, for someone in her position, having so many suitors, to leave all of them for the Moor—this is *risky, impudent.* Brabantio will hardly have to convince the audience that Desdemona's act is madness, but in his sincere attempt to convince them of this, he will expose a point of view in the audience that occurs in people, unfortunately, even in the present day. In any case, they will understand what the speech is about.

Therefore, a parental protest erupts, it is not necessary for the daughter to go with the Moor; there are even additional ways to disagree with her choice. In this case, these scenes will be perhaps a sort of extreme symbol of a very understandable situation.

Stanislavsky's directing plan begins with an analysis of the mutual relations between Roderigo and Iago and with a discussion of their first dialogue. With remarkable simplicity, with the utmost social persuasiveness, Stanislavsky presents the objective for the performer of Iago. In the statement of this objective, Stanislavsky recognizes that

Iago needs Roderigo's money as an instrument for further actions. That is why when Roderigo ceases to trust him, Iago uses his utmost power to calm him down and convince him of his truthfulness.

All this is true. And yet... Iago, after all, is neither a profligate, nor a drunkard. He is on a salary, since he holds a definite post. Though Shakespeare wrote that Roderigo squandered all his fortune, giving the money to Iago, I personally do not take this very seriously, probably because for me other psychological reasons are set in motion for this "alliance." I think it is more likely that Roderigo, as he said once, feels like a "dog on a leash."

People like Iago always need a certain environment. True, this time Shakespeare chose a man with money, but it does not seem to me to be of crucial importance. Roderigo is simply a representative of those weak forces that are usually found near an original force and are a necessary part of the environment for this true force—within it, they can feel themselves especially superior. Roderigo is the nonentity whom you can address when you want to, whom you can speak aloud to when you wish, or with whom you could even go into hysterics about what is really bothering you. He is the nonentity that you can notice when you want to and use for the purpose of any villainy. That is why I do not think that the text written by Shakespeare for Iago for the consolation of Roderigo has to be interpreted literally as consolation. It is possible to find other objectives.

Iago tells Roderigo the reasons that force him to hate Othello. He talks about this, we assume, because Roderigo's faith in Iago's honesty has run low and needs new proofs. After all, Iago has not even managed to warn lovesick Roderigo that Othello will steal Desdemona.

Now it is necessary to prove to Roderigo all over again that Iago is honorable toward him, even prove it by resorting to some sort of intimate knowledge.

Therefore, to prove his truthfulness, Iago explains to Roderigo how Othello prevented his promotion.

All this is true, if one trusts normal "everyday" logic.

However, very often you are convinced that each person has his own logic. In addition, that normal logic for a given subject can often be quite abnormal. Iago, it seems to me, does not need Roderigo in the narrow monetary sense. It means nothing for Iago to apologize to him. He makes use of Roderigo's presence only to voice aloud what is inside him. Inside him is more than the fact that Cassio was promoted over him in rank, but also what has just happened to Desdemona, which, perhaps, he did not know about, and which also enrages him by its fearlessness in the face of its possible consequences. "Ah, so you are that kind," thinks Iago, "you are of one class and I am of another; with me it means I must do this and I must do that, I am nothing; but you can do anything! Oh no, you are messing with the wrong person; I will try to prove it to you!"

This is just about how he thinks, and he states it aloud to the non-entity standing nearby.

The second scene between Iago and Roderigo happens after the meeting in the Senate, when Brabantio has lost the struggle for Desdemona.

After that, Iago once more consoles Roderigo, sneering that he takes the loss of Desdemona so hard. If we go by simple everyday logic, Iago would need Roderigo to stop this useless business of being upset, and take him and his money and go with everyone to Cyprus— *to be useful!*

In several precise phrases, Stanislavsky advises the actor playing Iago to be good-natured and cheerful, to keep control of himself, and only after Roderigo leaves to become himself again, spiteful and malicious.

Many playful retorts are available for Iago in the text of this scene, and one could easily imagine that after the tension of the scene in the Senate there would even be a certain release in the behavior of Iago, who in public is not always really who he is.

All this is so convincing that I wanted to do the scene this way. Then I was prevented by the idea that Iago is discouraged that the marriage of Desdemona and Othello has now been legitimized. I don't think Iago can control himself so much that he can completely hide his own shock, even in a short conversation (however, not that short) with Roderigo. In addition, it occurred to me that after not only Roderigo departs but also in his presence, Iago painfully searches for a way out. He has temporarily lost [the battle with Othello], and he needs to consider how to proceed. In addition, regardless of Roderigo whimpering beside him, Iago's own pain prevents him from sneering too much at the weakling, consoling him, and employing the expected tone.

After all, Iago needs this tone because it is not clear to him what he needs to do, and he will think up a new plan when Roderigo leaves. However, *to come up with something,* it is necessary to endure this, and then something acceptable will turn up. It is necessary to force himself *to formulate* what he needs to do. In addition, to do it here beside the whimpering Roderigo. He could simply send him away, so that he does not distract Iago, but it is inconvenient without the right environment—not only because Roderigo is needed for any possible business, but also because Iago's thinking works better when there is someone beside him.

Moreover, there is the complex process of developing a new course of action through a certain pale similarity of consoling Roderigo. Pale because this consolation should not disturb the process of Iago's own thinking, but on the contrary, should somehow prepare his thinking in the necessary direction.

When Roderigo leaves, the tension drops at once, for Iago feels that a moment earlier he discovered something valuable.

"I have it!" he says, exhaling easily, and he relaxes.

Finally, there is a third meeting between Iago and Roderigo, just after a scene on Cyprus. However, to touch upon it, it is necessary to say a few words about how Iago behaves before Othello arrives at Cyprus.

He behaves easily and cheerfully, for he has already thought up something in the earlier scene, and now he only needs to wait for the right situation to present itself.

Cassio kisses Desdemona's hand, and Iago notices it cheerfully, remarking cheerfully to himself: Kiss, kiss, such a little web to catch such a large fly as Cassio.

Incidentally, this little scene should be crafted so that it will be remembered. Stanislavsky writes splendidly about this moment: "Cassio consoles her quietly. Iago observes. Cassio takes her hand, at that moment Iago says 'He is taking her by the hand!' Then, when Cassio smiles, Iago notices the smile.

Now everyone has left, and only Roderigo remains.

Iago, under orders to carry the trunks, sits for some time stiffly silent, then calls Roderigo and gives him his first *objective*—to get Cassio drunk so that he will start a fight. Roderigo does not yet know, however, that Cassio has temporarily become their main target; some explanation is required so that Roderigo understands why Cassio is the main target. Once again, Iago does this not only to persuade Roderigo, but also *to establish the necessary tone.* This long monologue needs to communicate the single idea that, according to the simple laws of life, Desdemona will soon fall out of love with Othello and grow fond of Cassio. Iago imagines this so convincingly that, after Roderigo leaves, even Iago is surprised at how easily he believed in his own fabrication.

In addition, at the end, when Cassio is discharged after the drunken fight, Iago, singing something, stops to watch how the sun is rising. The night was cheerful, and it had not gone badly for Iago.

At the Moscow Art Theatre!

I have been invited to direct at the Moscow Art Theatre![12] This is the very theatre that for some reason always considered me either a "formalist" or "decadent."[13]

Now we understand each other perfectly. The actors speak the same language as I do, and sometimes I even have to remind them what Stanislavsky said. Those standing in front of me, however, are already far from that generation of *founders,* who were accustomed to talking about Stanislavsky. More likely, they are the descendants of the descendants, and the latest descendants are absolutely the same as those who work at the Taganka Theatre or the Malaya Bronnaya Theatre, absolutely the same. In addition, just like those at the Taganka Theatre and the Malaya Bronnaya Theatre, they frequently do not know about their great-grandfathers and great-grandmothers.

Perhaps even more often than they, I can imagine a time when there were several great actors such as Vassily Kachalov here on this stage. Oh, what a time it was for this theatre!

Kachalov had the personality of a true intellectual, but nowadays personalities are generally simpler. Such talents as his are gone, too. As Doctor Dorn said in *The Seagull,* "the sparkling talents are fewer now, it is true, but the average actor has become far better."

However, just as Dorn said of his time, maybe it seems to us also that the modern stage has *declined* in comparison with former times.

No, the stage does not decline. Most likely, the problems change, and the type of actor changes with them. You cannot do anything about that here.

In any case, even though I often think of Kachalov's talent, I have to admit it was interesting to work with Yevgeny Yevstingeev, for example.[14] Sometimes I thought that perhaps Yevstingeev does not concede anything to those great predecessors of his. The difference is not so much in their talent, but in the special conditions in which *those former* actors were placed. However, what about those conditions?

Even now, passing through the back yard of MAT, located between the main building and the shop, I continually imagine that Nemirovich-Danchenko once passed through here, which I did not see in person, but about whom I, by no means his direct descendant, know so much. I know them as though I had worked with all of them; I know them through their remaining productions (now already almost gone), through books and spoken stories. I know them through many legends. But after all, once this memory was *alive,* once this person actually conducted rehearsals, conducted them precisely this way instead of another way, had a certain credo, and the actors became his *students*, they absorbed these riches, this experience, this wisdom and this knowledge of craft and art. They absorbed this *person*. In addition, they became artists from personal contact with this teacher, from individual rehearsal conversations with him.

Such happiness is not given to everyone—to feel yourself a *student*. Many people do not know this happiness. Many people think that they would sooner *escape* their apprenticeship, since it feels like a sharp knife to them. The best years of the original MAT actors, however, were precisely those spent during the lifetime of their teachers, but when it ceased to continue and they had to become independent, perhaps their happiness was less then before.

In art, it is impossible to work without a master—original, of course, and not false. However, there at MAT there were the original masters, and they elevated the talents, integrated the component individualities into a larger unit, and collected everything that was in each person into one fist.

No one knows what Moskvin would have done without Nemirovich-Danchenko, who taught him throughout his entire life. In addition, from this young man, talented of course but inconsistent, materialized Moskvin.

It is a feature of the modern dramatic theatre that *without great directors there are no great actors.*[15] Some will say there are exceptions. However, as everyone knows, they only confirm the rule. In addition, if your actors are not great enough, they are a mirror of you. That is why for a long time by now I have personally stopped becoming angry with actors. It is the same as becoming angry at a mirror. Oh, how empty my eyes are in this mirror; oh, how silly my smile is in this mirror...

Stanislavsky and Nemirovich-Danchenko did all the plays of Chekhov and nearly all of Gorky; they did Maeterlinck, Ibsen, Hauptmann, Dostoyevsky, and Tolstoy.

Moskvin acted in *Tsar Fyodor Ivanovich, The Cherry Orchard,* and *The Brothers Karamazov.*[16]

In addition, what do we feed *our* students...?

It is awkward for me to name the actors who, as it seemed almost ten years ago, would emerge as a Khmelyev or an Ivan Moskvin, but are now famous, maybe even more famous than their predecessors were in their own time.[17] However, today it is only through the benefit of mass communication.

To paraphrase Stanislavsky, there are no small actors, only insignificant theatrical circumstances.

Productive Work

For the year [1975]: two films (teleplays, actually) and three plays—*Marriage, The Evacuation Train,* and *The Cherry Orchard.*[18] Some praise me for my pace; others curse me. It seems to me, however, that it is necessary to work precisely *this way.* Directors work little, by virtue of reasons that often do not depend on them; you might even say they loaf. They direct one play a year, even one every two years. Then, as though preparing their next play, they actually sit around, chatter about art, visit friends, gossip about their actors and others, as though they were searching for a new play, but in effect, they are simply wasting time. Often, it is true, they have to wait their turn quietly, since their theatre produces few plays each year, and there are many directors. However, those for whom the road to new work is always open are not especially in a hurry either. After all, what is the hurry?

There are different views on this subject, of course, but all the same, it is better to prepare new ideas by degrees, while you are continue to work on other plays—then the time isn't wasted.

Time, in fact, moves quickly, simply rushes, and it is necessary to work!

They say you should not produce a play while it is still "damp," and they use this catchphrase all year, until it is as dry as last year's leaves, until everyone becomes tired of the director and he becomes tired of himself. For me, it is better to work lightly and without strain. So what if it does not happen? Make a note of it and move on.

It is necessary to have time to direct Shakespeare and Chekhov, Ostrovsky and Tolstoy, and many new and different plays.

To have the time—this is a very serious issue.

They say they are working away from Moscow, but out there, unfortunately, very often they have a different outlook. For productive speed, an ample artistic environment is necessary, the possibility of comparative analysis, etc. Finally, you need a big audience, interested in the development of this art specifically. Without all this, even a significant amount of productions every year only castrates the artist, devastates him.

However, such an artistic environment exists in many cities, and it is simply preposterous to work only a little there.

We spend time carelessly; squander it on trivia, meanwhile only very productive, powerfully fruitful rehearsal work correctly illuminates our entire day.

Productive not only in terms of efficiency, of course, but in the larger sense—in the sense of artistically fulfilling.

At one time, they designated the Maly Theatre as a "second university," and so—if the rehearsal is not a university, then the theatre will not be a university, neither a second nor a third.[19] It will only be a refuge for people who have no other place to go in the evening.

A genuinely thinking and reading person will not attend such a theatre, where it is boring and embarrassing to sit there, probably as embarrassing as a person with a good ear listening to a bad singer.

Why go somewhere and listen to bad singing when there is a tape recorder at hand or some wonderful record. Why go and watch how people on stage lag behind life, "...they eat, they drink, they love, they walk, they put on coats..."[20] And all this when you are tired after work, and it is possible simply to lie down with a good book.

It is another matter if the theatre is a second university. Or even a third...

Othello

Anyway, let us return to Shakespeare. In his plays, it happens that when you reach for what is most important, you tire yourself and you tire the audience.

That is why you need incredible facility, so that when you reach the moment that is *most important,* it is possible *to slow down.*

The scene of the townspeople talking about the storm, the message that the Turkish fleet has sunk, and the arrival of Cassio. Then Desdemona and Iago arrive on another ship. There is a long scene full of coarse jokes by Iago, with which he tries to entertain Desdemona. Finally, Othello arrives. Only after all this, Shakespeare returns to the all-important intrigue. After all, scenic time is passing. What do we concentrate on now when there are so many details and so little essential for the future?

With horror, I recall the citizens of Cyprus in the performances I have seen, naively shouting about the storm and the sudden end of the war.

In addition, the more serious and more detailed all this was shown, the sillier it seemed, as if the action was left somewhere out-of-the-way, and what was genuinely important was postponed...

For some reason, Iago's intrigue against Othello is linked everywhere with Desdemona. Othello's marriage has apparently produced an impression on Iago no less than it has on Roderigo. Othello has grown fond of one of the most beautiful young woman in Venice. This can hurt. Iago does not want to believe it. It is better to see something bad in it because then it will be easier to believe. Anything extraordinary insults his ordinariness.

Iago stands near this young woman and sees how she worries about her husband. In addition, she is attractive even to him. Therefore, in keeping with his idea about preserving his dignity, he must tell her something coarse, dirty, although as a joke. Yes, I am a soldier, and so I understand women!

Then he sees how Othello arrives, and how he greets Desdemona. Moreover, he will destroy both of them—*even for that.*

The scene in Cyprus can also be interpreted another way. It is possible that since Othello has not arrived yet, Iago "jokes" with Desdemona. Seeing that she is worried about Othello. Naturally, he tries to make her laugh with a few trite little jokes, and Desdemona only affects to become angry. Iago means nothing to her; she is waiting for the appearance of her husband.

Under this apparent easiness, of course, there could be a subtext. In fact, Iago has already informed us that he will slander Desdemona and Cassio. Now, here in this peaceful conversation on Cyprus, there is a certain ominous glimmer. Nevertheless, perhaps I might not be limited to only one of these glimmers. Since I have the bad habit of seeing everything "darkly." In addition, the idea that Othello is still on the way, precisely when *his* ship should be the first to arrive at Cyprus makes me uneasy. Indeed, the wind and the storm have destroyed the Turks. Why should the same wind and storm suddenly spare Othello's ship? Desdemona really loves Othello, and this emotion often incites excessive fear. Because of possible loss.

No person here was as worried as Desdemona was. Iago is not worried at all. This, in fact, is clear, however. Cassio, too, is only a little bit worried. He likes Othello, naturally, but as a good soldier, he knows that the wind is powerless against such a ship. Only Desdemona is truly worried here, alone among these men, strangers, foreigners, who maybe worry too, but not as she does. In addition, this is much more difficult—to worry alone.

On top of that, Iago tells bawdy jokes. He joked all the way back to port, and maybe even drank. The ship was filled with people like him, seamen and soldiers. There was a terrible squall, and they fortified their spirits, possibly, with wine and jokes. It is impossible to think that Desdemona was comfortable with all of this.

Some exaggerate the "male" nature of Shakespeare's young women. Their force of spirit is more often just force of spirit and not the ability to get used to circumstances alien to them. Moreover, Iago, I think, could not have pleased Desdemona along the way. Now, when he has begun again to sharpen his language on the familiar subject of "women," Desdemona replies sharply to him.

Hearing similar banalities, most often an intelligent young woman would simply hold her tongue or even joke in reply so that she does not get a reputation for being fastidious. However, there are also those who will interrupt a shallow person, daring to receive a blow or at least a sneer in reply. Desdemona is like that. Alarm for Othello has kept her aloof from these men, and Iago's crude jokes *wound* her. Turning her back slightly, with silent anger she throws him a sharp reply.

In addition, here, standing before Iago, is *a person with a passion for purity,* a touchy person, the wife of a swarthy animal, an extremely young wife, ever since yesterday the wife of an ape. To Iago, it means her passion for purity is a *pretense*; she has only assumed an air of sanctity. There are no pure persons in the world; there is only hypocrisy. Oh, how pleasant it would be to crush this hypocrite! If only you were not the wife of Othello...! In addition, Iago happily fires off his salacious jokes. God knows how this struggle would have ended if it were not for Othello's arrival. Immediately, everything returns to its rightful place. Iago becomes merely an *assistant*. Now he must go to the ship and fetch the luggage. Moreover, Desdemona does not have to worry and protect herself from an alien environment. Her defender has embraced her and taken her home.

However, what will happen to her when this defender strikes her in the face.

After that, the story becomes almost unbearable as Iago literally bends Othello to his will, and makes him his toy.

Powerful Othello began to faint, became soft, and began to submit to impulses awful to think about. He has surrendered to the belief that he had to eavesdrop and spy, that he had *to renounce trust for revenge*. Othello has become ensnared in Iago's own [cynical] philosophy.

Analyzing the scene between Iago and Desdemona on Cyprus, I imagine, perhaps only for the sake of clarity, a somewhat different picture. A train. A women goes into a compartment, worried about her husband, let us say, who is ill. She is going to meet him. Some men, traveling on the same train, are sitting in the next compartment.

All the time laughter and abusive talk are heard from in there. On one occasion, it is about young women, their faithfulness, etc. The men, as they say, do not waste their time doing nothing—they drink, eat, and amuse each other with "funny" stories.

One of them, however, does not do it merely because it is fun. That women in the next compartment excites him, she will not let him rest. He knows that their abusive talk will affect her.

In addition, indeed, she suddenly opens the door and stops at the threshold. She is cheerful, and with well-concealed anger, she would like to know if her companions could talk about something without abuse. Is there not even one young woman whom they could speak well of?

Their abusive talk bothers her, because she is in love, and now she is *worried*. Moreover, her questions are a certain form of protest or, if you will, a sneer at such vulgar people.

The man who started all this answers her seriously, but also hides behind a joke. He responds that he is *not a poet,* but a most *simple man.* Then the young woman again becomes upset and questions him. She says that even if he is not a poet, he could speak decently all the same.

Five minutes without abuse.

Or even one!

However, those who are laughing answer that they can only swear. The man who started all this is strongly affected by her contempt, nevertheless he laughs, not knowing any other defense.

The only thing remaining for her is to admit they truly are not poets, and leave them to themselves, as though she too is laughing.

This is a small conflict; however, it is capable of saying a lot.

To a Young Director

Having completed his studies at MAT School, my son has set off to design a play in a small town. The young director has also gone with him. Remembering myself at this age and knowing what this director has to do, I advise him only to retain his composure. It is necessary to work a lot, of course, but there should be a sort of "cunning" in his approach to business. It is not necessary to go into it one-hundred percent, but only ninety-five percent. In addition, leave five percent for playfulness, breathing room, so that it doesn't seem like your whole life is being decided *right here*. So many directors break down in their first step because they are not aware of this "cunning." Enormous difficulties are inevitable, but also panic from thinking that you will fail. You lose composure of spirit, you lose the ability to look at what you are doing from a distance, you come to terms with adversity too intimately—and in the end, and you are already broken. Meanwhile, you are already busy with the actors, management, shops, etc., and you do not know how to get out from under the heap of work collapsing on you any more.

A director's work is complicated by the fact that it is only possible to master this profession after having directed many performances. However, they can crush you at the first show, moreover without any sort of malice, simply by making use of the theatre's "truths," using the laws of completely different trades.

A little boy can play a violin ingeniously and do so with success. A young man can paint a remarkable picture or compose a poem. Only a mature person is capable of directing a performance. Because in many respects this profession is built on the ability to subordinate people to "I," and in my opinion there is nothing more difficult than to achieve this subordination.

It is possible to force people to obey commands, but to transmit all the subtleties of feeling to them, all the shades of vision, and to make it necessary for them to believe, to obey all this sincerely—this labor is not comparable to anything else and only feasible for a person who has a great deal of experience.

How to get through all this when actors who are far more experienced can turn you into dust at the first performance? For them there is the artistic director, and even he is not always esteemed, then there is the next in line, still less esteemed, and then here you are, a student, a recent graduate, and a clumsy youth. There will be no success for you, only extra work and less than a first-class staff—the [production] "meat-grinder" has begun to work.

From the very beginning, however, certain young directors have skill, they are able to organize, to put things in order, to achieve subordination, but unfortunately, such unexpected initial skill is not always a reflection of talent. On the contrary, often talent is barely perceptible in a very clumsy beginner. In addition, in the course of time, such so-called skill often changes into banal craft. People grow; they become capable of forcing others to fear them, become strong-willed and consequently able to hammer complete nonsense into an actor's head.

A real talent will eventually develop willpower as well, but more often, it is developed by going through tortures, through very bitter disappointments, through despair.

As a rule, seemingly unending patience is necessary until the director is finally revealed. However, where is this patience obtained? After all, it is not written anywhere on a student that he is talented, that in the future his talent will be revealed. To the actors it often seems that the director standing in front of them is put there completely by accident, and they are severe not from any organic cruelty, but from their need to be rescued, so to speak, from their own possibility of failure. Everyone starts to operate independently, something like anarchy occurs, and the poor director is lost.

All the same, talent will appear even in an inept student—in his unexpected reasoning, in his non-stereotyped character, and so it is necessary, if you will, somehow to examine such a "newcomer" more calmly and more attentively. However, where is this calmness to be found when plans are smoldering, when next to this student is another one who is just as awful?

In addition, the years pass, and so very few new names are sifted through the sieve of time.

This work is difficult: it is necessary to have the endurance of a buffalo, the composure of a chess player, and furthermore of course, even talent, which in itself must be accumulated one grain at a time, until finally you attain attention.

I remember one rehearsal moment, probably fifteen years ago. I have directed Gogol's play, *Marriage*, twice—once recently and the other a long time ago at the Central Children's Theatre. Therefore, I am speaking here about the former rehearsal.

It was not the first year of my work at the Central Children's Theatre, but the eighth or ninth. Therefore I was, so to speak, accepted, they even liked me, since behind me were many plays that had been running successfully for several years.

It seemed to me that the day ahead would not be especially difficult.

Nevertheless, it *was*, this day, and I remember it even now. The day is like a splinter in my brain.[21]

It was some kind of rehearsal run, it was approaching the end, and the actors descended from the stage into the auditorium and prepared to listen to my notes. I was not pleased by anything that was happening on stage, I was in a panic. I saw that the work was bad, but I could not find out what the problem was. The play was falling apart, but I did not have time to figure out *why*.

The problem was hidden deeply somewhere. Detailed analysis was necessary, and after a long rest, if possible, someone's advice was necessary, a conversation. However, the actors sat and waited for an answer right now.

The actors waited, and I walked down the aisle—the silence lasted a long time. To me it seemed that I would simply cry. I had to confess ignorance. At that time, however, I thought this would be disgraceful. With an effort of will, I calmed down and began *to think*. I filtered my words through a tea strainer, trying to find at least a little bit of an answer.

In art, there should be the usual belief that the director knows everything. But at points like this he does not know, he needs to search, to discuss, to have a quiet detailed conversation with someone he is not afraid to reveal himself to.

I thought that I needed a mentor, a friend with whom I could talk "irresponsibly," but the profession of director is one that most often does not have anybody to talk with. Actors at such times are not counselors. The work starts to come apart at the seams. One doubt comes after another.

Oh, the agonizing loneliness! When you believe in yourself and are confident in something—there are many friends and you can *easily* trust them. When you are in doubt—trust is difficult, and even your friends do not seem suitable enough for very open conversation.

My assistant then was Lev Durov.[22] After a poor rehearsal, we often locked ourselves in together for an hour, two, or three and went over the entire play, scene by scene.

We forced ourselves through the scenes so intensively that we came out reeling and barely reached home. Pride didn't worry me, I was confident that he would not run off anywhere, and that he would not use my weakness as an occasion for further destruction later on.

Durov, however, was not the only one. Over the years, I have worked successfully with an entire group of people, so that an unsuccessful rehearsal no longer has such terrible importance. I know that *we would understand each other*.

It is wonderful to sit *among your own group* and quietly think. In addition, not to be afraid that a hidden meaning is concealed behind someone's words. I love the room where we usually assemble, and when summer comes and everyone departs, I go there, want it be autumn again, and to work.

Othello

In *Othello,* it is necessary to insert a pantomime scene in which Iago carries the Moor's trunk under the sounds of solemn music, and then, tormented by vanity, falls down and sobs.

The Herald announces a holiday. Othello asks Cassio to watch the guards so they do not get drunk. Cassio and Iago speak about Desdemona.

Iago teases Cassio's imagination, speaking too lightly about Othello's wife. To endorse such conversation is not in Cassio's nature. Not because he is a faithful lieutenant, but because he actually holds a different opinion of Desdemona. Iago offers Cassio a drink. The people demand it, says Iago, etc. Moreover, Cassio agrees. Iago organizes the drinking bout.

He has arranged everything quickly and even entertains everyone with his singing. Cassio feels that he is getting drunk and hurries to leave. Iago tells the others that Cassio, unfortunately, is a drunkard. Cassio and Roderigo get involved in a fight. Iago instantly signals an alarm. Othello separates the fighters, but Montano is already injured. Othello discharges Cassio from his post. Iago calms down Cassio, advising him to ask for Desdemona's aid tomorrow.

The most difficult thing in this flood of little scenes is *not to linger.* The rapid current should grab us and toss us onto the shore only at the moment when an *event* arrives. Everything before is only a rapid and steady approach to the main event.

Cassio must get drunk during the merriment that unexpectedly arises this evening. Roderigo *must* get into a fight with Cassio, since he believes that "his" Desdemona has fallen in love with Cassio. Iago is necessary only at the moment when all this begins, to have time to strike the alarm so that the fight becomes known, and so that it would already be too late to stop it.

Right here the main event itself arrives, and the current tosses us onto the shore.

Desdemona and Othello bandage Montano, and Iago remains behind with Cassio.

The action will be finished when Desdemona is completely exhausted from all this commotion and curls up and falls asleep again, and Othello settles in next to her. Cassio also goes to sleep and Iago calms down for the night. Everything falls silent in expectation of tomorrow.

A lullaby.

Perspective

People often live only for the present. Let us assume an apartment is being repaired, and it is necessary to finish it. A certain perspective is required here. The workers must live both inwardly and outwardly aiming for a specific day.

In some people, this feature of perspective thinking is connected with a way of life, in others, with work. In one, the prospect is short; in others, it is long. One person is capable of setting himself a task only for tomorrow and no more. Another, for an entire fifteen years. For one, it will be a stroll through the city. For another, the most complex scientific research. The larger the personality, the longer the perspective, and the more significant the goal. All this interests me in this case mainly by way of the actor's skill. A great actor necessarily has the ability to act with a sense of perspective. However, a small actor only knows how to act in small pieces. He does not know what the serious development of a role is, development for the sake of its essential purpose. He does not understand how to aspire to a point that will be somewhere at the end of the performance.

This target should be significant, however, for there is nothing worse than violently spouting nonsense [about something insignificant]. However, it is no less ridiculous trying to strive for a large purpose one syllable at a time, with no perception of movement, to play statically. The sensation of movement gives economy to acting, and this in turn gives birth to clarity of arrangement.

Our [theatre company's] so-called lively manner of acting exposes a number of excesses.[23] We often live through a role and create a certain life on stage as though it is outside of time and space. Such performances "on the move" can fall to pieces; it is difficult to watch them. Pauses should only occur when they are essential. Only the most necessary details should be totally thought out. It is necessary to conserve the actors' and audience's time, and the actors' and audience's strength, to carry out what is necessary at the decisive moment. This is very important.

The ability to act with a sense of perspective should be in an actor's blood, inherent in him, just as it is inherent in people who think and feel seriously.

It is necessary to cultivate a sense of perspective from the first rehearsal.

To learn to sense the development and a worthwhile goal is much more difficult than to learn to analyze an individual scene. For general concepts and feelings, the intellect and entire nervous system must be well developed.

The creative organism must be elastic in the understanding of such issues as perspective. Every moment is a movement toward an important goal. It can be extremely complex, this movement, and twisting. Even more reason why it must be clearly built and experienced. The most complex perspective must be overcome with ease.

For the Critics

I would like to write very calmly, without challenging any of the criticism so often leveled at my colleagues and me about our allegedly incorrect interpretations of the classics. I would not like to debate or defend, but, if possible, to write aloud, to think over what I have been engaged in daily in the course of many, many years.

Only the actors hear my thinking about the classics on a daily basis. Our performances of the classics, usually the result of many complex circumstances, often do not turn out as satisfactorily as they were conceived. Therefore, it would be a good idea to have a talk about our basic positions and to propose these positions, so to speak, for discussion.

I will begin, perhaps, with what is least important. I have noticed that when one or another production of a classic play appears, it often does not meet with unanimity of opinion. This was true even with Stanislavsky's production Alexander Ostrovsky's play *The Ardent Heart*.[24] Some critics at the time even wrote that Stanislavsky had distorted the viewpoint of MAT. Today such opinions seem ridiculous, but they existed. There are people who, as they say, want to be holier than the Pope is. In the same way, there were critics who wanted to be more faithful to the principles of MAT than Stanislavsky was. In addition, this was probably was very insulting to him.

As you can see, the work of even such an indisputably authoritative director as Stanislavsky was exposed to some doubt from the critics. What about us, the modern directors, whose authority is not so absolute?

I remember the fights that went on not so long ago over Yuri Lyubimov's *Hamlet*.[25] We were working together on a television performance at the time, and I saw Lyubimov's emotional condition during the shooting.

However, probably, I thought, such a difference of opinion about the staging of a classic is *natural*, since at one time; even the interpretation of *The Ardent Heart* was subjected to criticism.

When my production of *Romeo and Juliet* opened, the disagreements became frightful sometimes, but again I said to myself, there is nothing to be done—after all, it is probably the rule.

Then a miracle happened! Decades passed and in a review of a new show, you read about the earlier productions of *Hamlet* or *Romeo and Juliet* as though they were almost indisputable. Today the disputes are about newer work. Then a ridiculous, very ridiculous, idea comes to mind: Shouldn't the critics be able to look ahead several years? There would be less unnecessary pain. However, it is probably only an idyllic dream...

We will consider my lyrical digression finished, however, and move on to the, so to speak, basic question.

A dispute is always going on about the fact that a new production is not done the way it was done before and not done the way in which the play was written. In addition, this, they say, is bad. Most often, if it is done in a new way, it is represented as poorly done in comparison with the original version. Undoubtedly, this happens quite often. We are concerned now, however, with another question.

They say that Modigliani once visited Renoir and showed him one of his paintings.[26] Renoir told him that there was no juice of life in the picture, and Modigliani left insulted. In the meantime, in Renoir's pictures, there really is this juiciness, but Modigliani's do not have this same juiciness. However, what can be done if Modigliani is an artist of a completely different sense?

Chamomile, we assume, is not like poppy. Nevertheless, what can it do, poor thing? In spite of all its wishes, it will never be poppy. A pity? Maybe or maybe not, since we would not want to be deprived of chamomile either.

Some will say to me, however, that in the theatre the issue is more complex than even in nature itself. In the theatre, there is the play, and it is necessary for those devoted to it to be accurate. So that's what it is! However, I am always convinced precisely of this—of the fact that I am being accurate with the author. I study plays for years and rehearse them scrupulously. All the same, after a play opens some agree with me and some do not. In addition, all because I cannot think or feel *exactly* as Chekhov or Shakespeare. I interpret in many ways *involuntarily*, for something comes into play that distinguishes *me from them*.

Besides, is a good, profound play really so simple? So indisputable? Can someone really say that Shakespeare said exactly this in *Hamlet* and not something else? If what he wrote was always so clear, then there would no more books about Shakespeare. A play is eloquent—quite true. We also know at the same time, however, that a play is silent. In addition, Hamlet himself can be different. He can be strong or weak. Quiet or loud. He could be acted as though he was mad, or he could actually be mad. What is the truth, and what did Shakespeare tell us himself? Even in his prose, which contains many direct explanations, there are also different interpretations. Moreover, with a whole play—even more! However, added to the ingredients of this sacred mystery, is the personality of another artist. Very rich or not very rich, but *different*.

In spite of critics' fights for the ideas of a writer, the performance would prove to be something different from the play even during the writer's own lifetime. Chekhov wrote about *The Cherry Orchard* at MAT that Stanislavsky probably did not read the play. It means that even this great person did not completely understand *The Cherry Orchard* from Chekhov's point of view.

Then how can a critic say that *The Cherry Orchard* is already completely understood?

Often a critic interprets what is correct and what is not. Then I recollect lines from a certain very good play. A son and father are arguing, and the son tells his father that something will turn out *wrong*. Then the father replies bitterly that the son always acts correctly, but he seldom acts well.

Yes, admittedly, I know that with a certain group of actors I will lose some part of Chekhov or some other playwright, but I will manage to say something different that is precious to others and me today. In addition, I, with all the passion of the actors, will seek to achieve a worthy level of quality in that specific interpretation. The reactions of the audience will help me to understand whether I achieved what I wanted. In addition, the critic is often that same audience, only perhaps with larger experience. However, there are those who only look in a book and tell us that *this* is not done in the manner as it is *there*, and it is not *like that*. As if the whole issue was in that. After all, it will never be *completely* like that. It is only an empty dream that it ever could be exactly as it is set down. One is only impeded by such [baseless] requirements. Something stops. And how many times has something already been impeded. And stopped. Perhaps it is not necessary to do so anymore...

Once they painted pictures with chiaroscuro. Brilliant Rembrandt succeeded in art this way. At another time, perspective was discovered. Then they ceased to notice it or notice chiaroscuro. Meanwhile Van Gogh, it is believed, liked and appreciated Rembrandt, perhaps even more than a certain adviser who wanted Van Gogh to return to the old manner.

Something from the old is lost in the new, of course, even something beautiful. However, in exchange, other riches are obtained. Therefore, it is in our art. A certain depth that we miss is gone. No one can act like Kachalov or Moskvin.[27] Yet in exchange, a new truth comes, new boldness, sharpness, new integrity. However, unfortunately, this is often not appreciated, and after the years pass, they will speak about what has already gone.

I am not writing all this in defense of my own productions—God be with them. However, to the extent that it touches on the general question.

Some will say all this is true, however, yet the argument is not so much about general principles, with which we all probably agree, but about concrete work. And principle plays no part in the abuses of, let's say, your [interpretation of Molière's] *Don Juan*.[28] Simply put, your *Don Juan* had so many mistakes and gaps that the critics were obligated to articulate them. Besides that, what is new and what is simply bad, trite, and superficial?

Naturally, not everything that is different from the old can be considered good. (Although old is not necessarily good either.) Our general *experience* [of the past], however, allows us to think and feel more deeply [about the present]. In addition, the idea of *change* enters into this experience, too. To forget about change is probably as bad as forgetting about experience. A house without a foundation will fall, of course, but a foundation is not yet a house. To make something with depth, where there is a harmony of new ideas, is difficult. Moreover, initially scope is debatable, even when it exists. For it is never like an obvious pattern. This is a serious difficulty in our work.

For example, in *The Cherry Orchard* I wanted to strengthen the moments of dramatic, even tragic nature. Yes, I knew that Chekhov considered this play a comedy. Possibly Chekhov said this, however, because the MAT production was excessively lyrical, maybe even sentimental. From his point of view, of course. Today, reading *The Cherry Orchard*, I can argue that it is a tragedy, although concealed in the form of a farce. However, I particularly placed many accents on the openly tragic. I am not capable of directing *The Cherry Orchard* as it was done earlier. Neither according to the manner of MAT, nor according to the manner advised by Chekhov. I can only direct the way I feel today. *Regardless of all my study of the subject. In addition, my respect for it.* However, to a critic it can seem as though I did not know that Chekhov called his play a comedy. However, how can I explain to him that I did not read any less than he did? In a new performance, however, I am not only a reader but also a living person working on a production. Yes, Chekhov also said they did not need to have gravestones on stage [as ours did], but did he know our entire concept? Moreover, who could say that, knowing all our problems, he would not agree with us? In addition, even if he did not agree, would that really be so awful? After all, MAT did *The Cherry Orchard* a thousand times and Chekhov did not agree with their idea. How good it is that on the shelf is *the book,* and in the theatre is *the production.* Moreover, there will still be a second performance, third, fifth, twenty-sixth. In addition, each one of a special kind. Theatre is a living, active affair, and the spectators feel this. Moreover, the critic is the best, most subtle, spectator, or is he not?

Now I will admit, of course, that some of our plays were bad. Not in comparison with the past, but with what will exist sometime in the future. Because every day we understand increasingly more that it is necessary to work better than we have worked up to now. That is all there is to it. In addition, all directors think this way, of course, not just me alone.

A Month in the Country

Natalya Petrovna is not her usual self today.[29] Those close to her have noticed it. Moreover, are alarmed by it. Today she is anxious, nervous, excited. Some secret is buried here. The first action in Turgenev's play, *A Month in the Country,* is supported by this secret. Then drop by drop, it will be revealed. The new tutor disturbs Natalya Petrovna. The tutor is much younger than she is. He is still quite young. In addition, she is married; she is almost thirty.

However, what happened?

I saw this production at a good, serious theatre in Warsaw. The stage was arranged like a small circus inside the auditorium. Only instead of an arena, there was a platform with green grass, genuine grass. There was a stream and flowers. A cherry tree. Two remarkable dogs ran out from behind the wings, drank water from the stream, and lay down on the grass.

In a word, a little slice of life at an aristocrat's country estate. A wicker chair, cushions on the ground, and so forth.

It was beautiful to look at the platform with its grass, and at the audience, closely sitting around together.

The evening was pleasant. The actors played beautifully, the audience laughed a lot, and I watched the actors and two young people sitting near them in the first row. They smiled wonderfully, watching the stage. They were not delighted, but their attentive half-smiles indicated they *understood*. After this, I tried to understand what *theme* was being expressed here, but I only came away with—*a country estate*. Quiet, peaceful, aristocratic *overindulgence*.

With a shade of lyricism, however, even sadness. For all the same, Natalya Petrovna has fallen in love with a young man who is loved by Vera, her young ward. A moment of light drama.

Returning to Moscow, I leafed through Stanislavsky and found the place where he discusses *A Month in the Country*.[30]

Growing used to hothouse life, Natalya Petrovna reaches out for simple and natural feelings, for nature.

Further, on [in Stanislavsky's notes] there is a lot about the subtle outlines of love that are so masterfully woven by Turgenev.

Then I thought what if this theme could be expressed as *"unexpended feelings"*? A thirty-year-old woman, she does not love her husband, and furthermore there was no love as there should have been when they were married. About *this subject,* however, there can be different opinions, of course. Possibly, there was love once. In addition, possibly, life was quiet then, peaceful, obviously clear, and— boring. However, I repeat, this can also be *love*. Soon the years pass, and then the boundary line of the thirtieth birthday passes. In addition, already it begins to seem that everything is finished. Meanwhile, in the heart there is a storm of feelings, a storm of passion, not yet expended, not experienced.

In addition, here Natalya Petrovna is caught up in the misfortune or the happiness, I do not know which one, which occurs when a person is consumed by love.

She recklessly rushes back to live what she has never lived, to feel young again, to start all over again, but *differently*. To live *strongly,* with something given back in return. It is the theme of a woman growing older; maybe her fear that time has passed her by; that life with all its passions, torments, and strong pleasures does not belong to her anymore, but to others, those who are young. Her destiny is—this boring peace.

Now, a desperate fling in hopes of returning herself to the past and knowing a *different* sort of love.

Reality is strong, however, and she has to become reconciled to it. Everyone departs, and she remains *alone*.

Green-Room Opposition

Once, when I was working at a particular theatre, I ran up against opposition from some of the actors.[31] I proposed something worthwhile, it seemed to me, and almost all of them supported me. However, a certain few interfered very much. Moreover, not overtly, but secretly, behind my back, which spoiled the general working atmosphere.

When I became upset, my friends said, "Don't pay any attention to them. Those people not only interfered with you, they also interfered with the artistic directors who were here earlier, and they will continue to interfere after you are gone. So, don't pay any attention." However, I turned around and performed even more stupidities, unable to restrain my feelings. Since then, the artistic director has already been replaced three times, and so my friends were right. Those actors have continued to behave the same way as they did toward me.

They only looked after themselves, and [with each new play] it seemed to them that their time had come. After all, the theatre must do plays, and preferably good ones. That is why the destiny of these actors nonetheless developed to their disadvantage.

They remained and waited, however, for the arrival of the next artistic director.

"How strange," I thought, "that after such a long period of time they still don't understand that their position is wrong, *false*."

In addition, it was a pity that the artistic directors did not grow any wiser either. Everyone continued to be afraid instead of taking a *decisive* step.

This decisive step is difficult to do, however, not only for "political" reasons, but also for internal reasons. It is necessary to use authority, but often this authority only alters the spirit of the artistic director for the worse. The new qualities, which he notices in himself in connection with this problem, nauseate him.

Sometimes he even prefers to surrender to these actors, if only to win out for himself. Unfortunately, all these seemingly small questions also enter into the larger theme of theatrical production.

However, there is so much happiness, so much freedom when you are completely within your own circle. When you do not have to argue, grow angry, and shout. No, this still happens—but for quite different, artistic reasons.

True, then you begin to think about other dangers. Will you fall asleep creatively within such a "unanimity of viewpoints"? However, no, word of honor, no. In fact, many other difficulties remain. There is an auditorium to be filled with spectators, and you watch to see whether it is filled or empty, and if it is filled, with whom. In addition, there will be many other worries that will not allow you to sleep.

A Month in the Country

A Month in the Country is such a good play! So well written and so subtly written. What is good, however, and what is subtle? All kinds of things might be good and subtle in themselves, but they do not remain in the memory. However, this play remains in memory because it is a serious, subtly written thing. Until recently, it was considered almost a vaudeville piece, a trifle; it was seldom performed, meanwhile it is [actually] about something serious. In addition, it is written so softly, so intelligently. It is precisely the "politeness" of the writing, however, that is often deceptive, and it seems like a well-polished toy. However, there, behind the politeness and charm of the people's behavior toward each other, are greater experiences, essential experiences, which, if discussed from the point of view of life itself, have great significance in the existence of each person. A recent production of this play treated its politeness and emotional experience ironically. However, in vain.

Once, a long time ago, they proposed a play for me to direct in which the central subject was a middle-age woman whom several young people play a trick on, by giving her the impression that one of them had fallen in love with her.

At that time, probably because I was young, this story seemed *amusing* to me, and I imagined a certain comic actress in the main role and a rather cheerful performance.

Then, unexpectedly, I saw the film that was made from this play. It was a Spanish film, I think, and the play was Spanish. The woman was not comical in any way and not very old. She simply was lonely. In addition, the young people laughed cruelly at her.

Maybe it was from this time or maybe it was another, but now I am afraid of evaluating this or that literary situation too cheerfully. Little of life seems charmingly "light" to me now. Moreover, of course, *A Month in the Country* does not seem like that either.

In the first place, as I already said, this play could perhaps be about an attempt to experience love, only it is already too late. Similar incidents, I think, are not the most trivial, so to speak, in human psychology worldwide. Only in the abstract could one think it as trivial. How many tortures a person like Natalya Petrovna experiences, someone who realizes that love came when youth, and the freedom of youth, were gone?

All these disturbances will somehow calm down of themselves, possibly, but the *scar* will remain. After all, this incident will force her to get used to the idea that, in some things, *her time has already passed*. It does not mean that another time will not have its own charms, but who is so wise as to be immediately reconciled to loss of the past, more than that, as though it did not even exist. Possibly, life is remembered in moments of very great happiness or great misfortune. Something average, after all, is not remembered.

However, what exactly happens to everyone in *A Month in the Country* that is not "something average." To understand nothing but this—wouldn't it mean to sacrifice the true basis of the play?

If it were possible to depict along the inner walls of the stage something like a country estate, leaving the entire surface of the stage free, like on a movie set, when they eliminate the general setting and only use that portion of the convention that is needed for filming modern stage settings. To have a wide-open stage space...[32]

To reject immediately any sort of isolation, what we call "intimacy" or "coziness." Open space for the open release of spiritedness, for a greater exposure of the emotional design. Wide open, not traditionally "Turgenev-like," so that the characters will be shouting across the entire space of the stage. Therefore, that it would be possible to create not only internal but also external tension.

I do not know, maybe this is a mistake, but it seems to me that it is always necessary to find some challenge to literal thinking. What about psychological Turgenev's "lacework"?[33] Anyhow, it is certainly not compulsory to weave it standing only half a meter from each other.

Strength of feelings is directly proportional to restraint, no question about it. However, restraint should not deprive a work of art of its *theatricality*. In addition, what exactly is Turgenev's restraint? We have a strange notion about the classics, about Chekhov, for example, or Turgenev. We confine them within a rigid corset. Meanwhile, they are full of fire and merriment, often—*open fire*. The [tsarist] censors used to prohibit *A Month in the Country*, and now we often pass it off as distilled water. However, to break this false tradition of "psychological lacework," maybe it is even necessary to put an end to the "restraint," if, of course, the right grounds are found for this idea.

However, unfortunately, any such ideas have to be expressed carefully, for sometimes the same idea can mean something completely opposed to people's taste. In addition, maybe the "lack of restraint" found in certain other directors disgusts me no less than it does the critics, but for the time being I can't find any other formulation for my idea.[34]

Therefore, Natalya Petrovna is excited today. Naturally, this can be performed in all sorts of ways. It is possible to sit and sit and still be excited. Maybe it is also impossible to conceal this excitement because it is so great. In addition, all sorts of bold colors, sharp colors, and roughness will appear. Today I am in favor of them. Moreover, let the reactions of Rakitin also be a hundred times sharper. And more dramatic. Let us feel they are on the threshold of [crucial] events, and that everyone is capable of understanding them *today*. Therefore, they are not merely incidents from the past. Rigid [behavioral] corsets still exist. If it is true for us, how much more so for them! Naturally, everything should take place *in that period,* but it should be completely accessible to us, understood, near at hand.

Meanwhile, for it to become recognizable, certain *adjustments* are necessary, it is impossible simply to read the roles "like Turgenev." Even he did not enjoy a proper success. Critics condemned it. Therefore, we will not refer to those times. We have our own feelings: can we get rid of them when we read a play? This is not necessary either! If these feelings exist, they should be protected. After all, an ordinary reading "according to Turgenev" occurs not because an actor wants to be faithful to the author, but because he does not have anything of his own. However, when there is nothing of his own, this is not fidelity, but God knows what.

One modern actor has said that Rakitin is an ineffectual person, but in his own time Rakitin was written no better than, and the same as, Natalya Petrovna. With the passing of years, in fact, the work of a great writer becomes a relic. During Turgenev and Chekhov's times, for all the love many people had for them, they were exposed to terrible criticism! Natalya Petrovna seemed a boring and apathetic baroness. In addition, Rakitin dragged right along behind her, drowning in the words of a gentleman. In the *present day,* literature experts, with their "historical perspective," can find justification for each psychological twist [in the text], but when you see some production, on the surface there is still the same inability to see things whole. All those identically shallow appraisals of the events. A boring, apathetic baroness and a man drowning in words, dragging along behind her. Now today I want, dammit, to do something about what Pasternak said, "Oh, if only I could, just a little, I would write eight lines about the characteristics of *passion*."[35] It is possible to subject passion to analysis, passion such as, for example, that of Claudius, who poisoned his brother and married his wife. It is possible to write "eight lines" about the characteristics of this passion. It is also possible to write about another, and a third, a fourth, and my God, how many of them there are! Moreover, Rakitin does not drag along after Natalya Petrovna, he loves her, loves her strongly, but her husband is his friend. In addition, other things happen too, which by all accounts should not happen. It even happened that after the death of Gertrude's husband, "or e'er those shoes were old,"[36] she goes for Claudius, and then, even knowing that he killed her husband, she does not abandon him, but on the contrary, submits to the new way of things.

> O, if only I could, just a little,
> I would write eight lines about the characteristics of passion.

Therefore, Rakitin loves, but he is a man of extraordinary honesty. This honesty does not allow him to overstep the line. Moreover, love compelled him not to go away before all the unpleasant events happened. He is in captivity, he feels *dependent*, and this could be played strongly, without any shades of "weakness." The struggle that occurs in an honorable man in such moments is a strong one and worth becoming acquainted with.

> ...and everywhere are fatal passions, and no protection from fortune...[37]

Natalya Petrovna has many mood changes. In which direction? For what reasons?

For me, what is most interesting of all is the riddle that needs to be solved in the play. It draws me in, I reach for the text every second. I want to carry out its analysis with the actors sooner.[38] Then when the performance is ready, I lose interest. The further creative work of the actors begins—what does it consist of?

What is the essence of the first act? The zigzags of mood?
Natalya Petrovna is excited at the beginning of the play. She compels Rakitin to read aloud to her. Then, having compelled him to read, she jumps up, and she shifts to another subject... She is annoyed by Rakitin, she remembers about her husband, about the usual discontent in him too.

Going on in parallel [in the background] is the excited card game of the old people.

When the acting shifts to the foreground, Natalya Petrovna is gloomily silent, and then she does something excitedly again.

Excitedly, she talks with pleasure about the tutor. (Here the excitement takes the form of a concealed secret.)

—Where is Vera? I haven't seen her since this morning!

She does not want Rakitin to read anymore, let him talk about something.

She *covers up* her nervousness with energy.

Through Rakitin's story, as though in a detached manner, she realizes her position. Naively, like a child.

Rakitin says something about love. She does not even understand, for the word *love* does not relate to him.

Her character is preoccupied—*sharp, frank, erratic,* inclined to take risks.

Once again, the card game rise takes the foreground. Natalya Petrovna is gloomily silent.

She demands that Rakitin describe the changes he sees in her.

Again, she is active. Silence is awful for her.

She quarrels like this, she protests against her hopelessness.

She vents her agitation to Rakitin about Belyayev and Vera being absent for a long time.

How did she first encounter the new tutor, Belyayev? Probably secretly. *She waited* and met him *later on.*

NATALYA (to RAKITIN): "Well, how did he strike you?"

However, Rakitin was thinking about something else. This is called insight!

After she sees Belyayev with her ward, Vera, she feels depressed. Is she tired? Or has she calmed down? Or is she simply deep in thought *about them.* There is an ambiguity in these ideas.

Again the card playing!

The neighbor, Doctor Shpigelsky, has arrived. Once more, she becomes active with the new person so that he can talk about something funny! A painful desire for distraction.

The card players also listen to Shpigelsky's funny story, but she has only taken what concerns herself from what he is saying.

In his little story, Shpigelsky says that it is impossible to love two men.

Does the doctor already know everything and only pretend that he does not understand the reasons for her quarrel with Rakitin? Or not?

The card game is finished.

How impulsive she is, how poorly she keeps control of herself...!

She takes the idea of a possible marriage for Vera cheerfully, without subtext. The idea that Vera's marriage is in her interest, this comes to her later.

She speaks to Vera with open jealousy, with sincere happiness, with interest.

With the feeling of a *murderer*.

...Rakitin again asks what the matter with her is. Her new, soft, quiet mood. Why?

Then once more, she changes to candor.

A thirst for personal contact.

Complex female logic.

Othello

Sometimes a good idea appears suddenly, almost at the twentieth rehearsal. It seems that everything has already been rehearsed and considered, and suddenly only *then* do you begin to understand what is going on.

I knew, for example, that Iago catches Cassio drinking, that Cassio gets drunk, and that Othello discharges him from his post because of the [resulting] fight.[39] Iago knows that Cassio, drunk, is not himself. However, right here an idea came into my head. With Cassio, after all, something *concrete* happens when he gets drunk. What exactly happens to Cassio when he gets drunk? Maybe being a very quiet person, intelligent, kind, honest—when drunk, he might become sick with delusions of grandeur. On the other hand, knowing his own weakness and his inability to hold his liquor, he feels the first signs of dizziness and starts to suspect boorishly that everyone sees him as an alcoholic. Then, becoming more and more intoxicated, he quarrels with everyone, asserting that he is sober.

Maybe analyze throughout Cassio's intoxication precisely *what* is in his behavior that makes Iago so confident it will turn into a scandal. Not to play this scene without justification or "in general"—they say he evidently became intoxicated and everything else—but to discover the secret, to understand it, to find the end and the beginning.

...Iago invites Cassio to drink. It is necessary, by the way, not to make the offer, but only to open the bottles, to prepare the place so that intoxication becomes *inevitable* for Cassio. Cassio should feel that he does not have the power to refuse, since Iago is already preparing something. However, if Iago does not succeed in preparing things, then it might still be possible for Cassio to refuse. There is almost a struggle with the bottle, whether to open it or to put it back. However, Iago points to the door behind which, presumably, their comrades are waiting. In addition, Cassio, weak not only for wine but also for comradeship, gives up.

Strictly speaking, only Montano appears, but Iago has already struck up a song, and Cassio, after drinking, joins in the song. Because he likes poetry, just as he likes comradeship and wine. They sing roughly, beautifully, loudly, improvising, so much so that Desdemona and Othello, who have not yet had time to fall asleep, hear the song.

Othello even sits up a little—are his comrades drunk?

Cassio likes the song very much. He sings it with gusto, and when the song is over, he says thoughtfully, "'Fore God, an excellent song!"

Then Iago excitedly begins to tell how he learned this song in England, and he begins to talk about the English, about how they drink and at what point, they might become intoxicated. "...your Dane, your German, and your swag-belli'd Hollander—Drink, ho!—are nothing to your English," Iago says with zeal. An Englishman, "...he drinks you, with skill, your Dane dead drunk; he sweats not to overthrow your Almain; he gives your Hollander a vomit ere the next pottle can be filled." Of course, everyone laughs wholeheartedly at these jokes. Very good jokes, by the way, if presented to the audience at the "Globe," who were English and heard such stormy praise addressed to themselves.

Noticing they are bellowing and drunk, Cassio suddenly stops when it is necessary to restore order. Moreover, partly to restore things, he lifts a glass to the health of Othello. In addition, everyone drinks to the black general, and Iago once again launches into a song, which, moreover, will be impossible not to join in, because it is even better than the previous one.

Desdemona gets up and listens, but once more settles down and goes back to sleep. Voices are heard and they are drunk, but they are singing a beautiful song, not violent.

"Why, this is a more exquisite song that the other," Cassio says quietly.

Iago quickly turns to him: "Will you hear it again?" Cassio for one moment sees something malicious in Iago's eyes. Like a devil pretending to be an angel, some feature betrays him, and Cassio notices this in a quarter of a second. He is frightened; he saw what was happening from outside [himself]. Moreover, he says that he will stop this idle talk.

However, being already drunk, right here he begins to laugh cynically and assure everyone that he knows both the *rules* and the *loopholes* perfectly, and considers himself a person whose soul must be *saved*.

"And so do I, Lieutenant," adds Iago.

However, ambition has already begun to speak in Cassio. At this point, he is the most important and Iago is the subordinate, and it is necessary for the most important to be "saved" first.

This is a dangerous moment of intoxication, and Cassio has almost controlled it.

"God forgive us our sins!" he says.

In addition, he goes off to organize the sentries, but it seems to him that those remaining laughed behind his back. Then, returning, he conducts an interrogation: do they think he is drunk? In addition, he begins to prove that he is not drunk, to prove it by using the most elementary methods. He stretches out his right hand and says that it is his right, stretches out his left and says it is his left.

Moreover, because all this was true, it became clear to everyone that he was fatally drunk and that this is very serious.

On the way out, Iago manages to tell Montano that this *always* happens with Cassio, and that is the danger of their general situation. He even rushes to Montano with this, as though for help, but when Montano proposes to inform Othello about *this*, Iago jumps back from Montano as from a traitor, reminding him that Cassio is a friend. At the same time he managed to show Roderigo, who had just run in, where Cassio went.

Then Cassio and Roderigo appear on stage again. They are breathing hard and walk around each other in circles, like boxers before the first punch. Cassio becomes terrible. Roderigo has probably managed to say something to him behind the scenes.

Stunned, Montano tries to take Cassio by the arm, plainly not knowing that Cassio is intoxicated. Then he finds out, for Cassio, having thrown off Roderigo, instantly addresses him with the same awful hatred, threatening to attack him if he interferes. Montano does not expect this turn of events. He was simply offended by what was happening. The man who was just drinking in friendship with him a few moments ago now crudely threatens him. After all, Montano is not a boy. He leaves contemptuously, only muttering, "Come, come, you're drunk!"

Then Cassio pulls out his sword, and with his weapon starts to prove that he is not drunk. He proves it to the point where he plunges his sword into Montano. In addition, at that moment Iago manages to take charge and sound the alarm.

This ends it. The thing is known.

Scenic Imagination

Today I was once more convinced that it is impossible to be the slave of any one idea. Let us say, for example, that constructivism is now more modern than realism.

Or, on the other hand, that realism is now more modern than constructivism. I have selected this example at random.

I remember how in *Othello* they used to represent the storm on Cyprus: the thunder rattled, raincoats fluttered. True, this was a long time ago, but it must have been ridiculous to remember it so clearly until now.

And in the struggle against such nonsense, the idea was gradually born that a certain degree of *abstraction* is necessary. That a solid illustration of *meaning* is needed—but it will still be a scene on Cyprus. Moreover, it is not necessary to simulate a ridiculous windstorm, because this is pathetic.

However, here, today, I see a production by Jean Louis Barrault about Columbus. Columbus is somewhere in the hold of a ship, chained up.[40] On stage are a huge sail and a storm.

Yes, yes the same storm that I rejected in the theatre, because the theatre is not the movies, and a sham storm is not a storm.

Nevertheless, here is a sham storm, and it is beautiful and terrible and similar to the truth, although theatrical.

Clearly it is some new device, a strong light, sharply different from the old projectors, it makes continuous lightning flashes, and the sail becomes bright white, transparent and then immediately black. And the sky behind it instantly lights up, painful to the eyes, and immediately fades away. And the wind and thunder are done not with a worthless manual machine, but with a sound recording of the highest quality. And all this together is so sonorous, so bright! Therefore, it is powerful. I see a *particular* white light and a *particular* sudden darkness that I never saw before. During this, three actors, [carefully] managing their bodies, heave up thick ropes and return to the stage so that the reality of what was happening could not be denied.

On stage, the fantastic world of a real storm is recreated.

Moreover, remembering a silly child's theatrical impressions, I thought: Here is a theatrical fairy tale in which adults sit quietly with the same beautiful expressions as those of a child. Moreover, while the subject is the life of Columbus, it is nevertheless tragic, and told with humor, although no less significant because of it...

What is Chekhov "About"?

When I read something, I read "what it is about" least of all. No, I certainly understand, for example, what Chekhov's *Ivanov* or *Uncle Vanya* is "about." But I like Chekhov not because he writes about this or about that. Nevertheless, because behind everything, whatever he wrote, someone good and familiar to me is hidden away.

Actually, he is not even hidden because how could an author be hidden? Even if he really wanted to? However, Chekhov, in my opinion, did not even want to.

He did not think about himself when he wrote, however, and this absence of concentration on himself characterizes him.

Chekhov was a cultured man, but what is this culture—knowledge, intelligence, erudition, a good "family tree"? I do not know about erudition, but he had no "family tree" to speak of. As the saying goes, the intellectual is only in the first generation. All the same, what an intellectual!

Because this word, as everyone knows, does not indicate that your grandmother was famous or that you know foreign languages perfectly. Something else is important here—either you have a subtle psychophysical organism or you do not.

Naturally, we are not born with identical psycho-physiques. Grandmother and knowledge of other languages probably count. However, the example of Chekhov's life proves that something else is at work here, and that someone special can develop from someone who is virtually undistinguishable from someone else.

They say that Tolstoy said Chekhov reminded him of a woman. Possibly some sort of special delicacy was found in his very male character. A man, because what woman could do what Chekhov did at Sakhalin, including the decision itself to go there?[41] No, perhaps a woman could also do the same thing, and there are examples, but a woman who has *courage.*

Isn't this the most beautiful combination in the world—feminine tenderness plus courage? Call this combination something else; however, call it anything you like, except not everyone has this *anything you like,* but Chekhov *had it!*

They say Ernest Hemingway was a hunter, a daredevil, wore heavy wool sweaters, was a success with women, was not afraid of war, was a *soldier,* wrote while standing up...

Chekhov was none of these. He was sickly, modest, withdrawn, and lonely.

How sad it is to look at this figure in his long old coat and his unfashionable hat. Those rimless eyeglasses on a string and that diffident gaze. It is both sad and somehow charming to see it.

In addition, his letters to his wife or to Maxim Gorky or Lydia Avilov.[42] So much modest humor there, tact, and reserve under a comic mask.

They say that strolling around Yalta he heard the young boys' taunt, "Antoshka the consumptive! Antoshka the consumptive!" Hearing this, he grinned and kept on walking by himself along the embankment. Moreover, maybe he imagined his story, "The Lady with the Lapdog."

However, is that how Hemingway, the courageous hunter who killed many lions, could all of a sudden write *The Sun Also Rises*? A hunter, a soldier, then suddenly *The Sun Also Rises?* Moreover, he ended his life so dramatically. It means there is not only strength there. Does it mean this *sacred combination* is there, too?

A Month in the Country

I read Inna Soloviova's interesting article about the production of *A Month in the Country* done at MAT in 1909.[43] In 1909! "Just think!" as Semyonov Pishchik would say.[44]

When I read what Stanislavsky did, I would like everything to be *different.* The thought that you would only repeat what has already been done somehow does not inspire you when you begin *your own work.* It is good to learn about the past and understand that what you devised is not the same as the past, and still has some sense. Anyway, that is what I thought while setting out to read the article about Stanislavsky's production.

On the other hand, I also simply wanted to corroborate the correctness of my own thoughts. Your invention should not be a fabrication. What value is there in a fabrication? If it is not a fabrication but a discovery, then in spite of all the difference in years and characters, something fundamental should correspond with the former and your discovery.

That is why I was delighted when I read that Stanislavsky regarded this play to a certain extent as a study of passion. Both clear and confusing passion.

There was some concern [on his part] that the play did not resonate [sufficiently] as a "grand dramatic enterprise." However "duty and passion," "honor and passion"—these themes are actually here.

Natalya Petrovna is a restless woman who has lost her self-control. Here on a divan, Stanislavsky believed, there should be a storm and an eruption.

Stanislavsky thought about the lively energy in this play, about its pace, about not making it unnecessarily dense, making its material transparent. Where is the lacework there? Their trivial stories have become hateful to Natalya Petrovna.

Olga Knipper-Chekhov was reproached for showing too little of Turgenev in her portrayal.[45] Natalya Petrovna, leaving after one scene, opened a door blindly, pushing it with her knee.

What the critics did not say, however, was that Stanislavsky wanted to produce the *play* and not to stage influential judgments about it.

Stanislavsky's analysis of Rakitin's lines did not contain any fragment of vaudevillian lightness. Nor any share of an indulgent attitude toward the character. The knightly faultlessness of Rakitin. Her husband is from the same knightly circle as Rakitin. And how wonderful it is to feel *the dignity of these events!* However, this underlying nobility can be a difficult issue. After all, directors as well as sculptors work in a certain material. I do not mean to say that nobility does not exist in modern actors, but when it does, it is expressed differently somehow.

Stanislavsky's Rakitin could not even raise his voice in anger. Stanislavsky said that it is not necessary to play "fire," but it is necessary to develop a basis for the feelings, and then he adds, however, that after developing them, it is necessary to conceal them with actorly adaptations. He continually used the term "corseted."

I understand what it means, "to develop a basis for feelings," and I even understand about being "corseted," but I am afraid this would be far less successful for us [today] than it was for Knipper, who was not considered true to Turgenev in this role anyway.

No, I am not concerned about the women, but the men in my company are far from being corseted [emotionally].

Although it is possible to tighten the corsets of those whom you want, wouldn't our men lose a share of their expressive technique then? There is already a big difference between a typical modern man and those typical men who were represented by Turgenev, Stanislavsky, and Rakitin.

In addition, is this corset still needed in modern productions of Turgenev?

All this, naturally, can only be shown in the work itself, in the rehearsal process.

And if there will be no corset, it is not because [today] we have become [more emotionally] stirred up, but because in contemporary living actors one has to search for something different to express the essence of an old play.

Soloviova writes in the same article that the paintings [of that time] frequently portrayed a traditional farewell inventory of the earthly world in the period of mourning for deceased nobility.

In the magazine *Old Years*, for example, stories about old estates seemed like inventories before a fire. Moreover, it often seemed that everyone knew that a fire was indispensable.

Seven years prior to Stanislavsky's production, Nemirovich-Danchenko conceived of *A Month in the Country* close to this in spirit.[46]

Stanislavsky had the added advantage, however, that he analyzed the play directly, as though he did not know anything except the text of the play. Therefore, no sense of [historical] style entered into his analysis.

All the same, the epoch that was closest to him imposed its own distinctive features on his super-lively and direct imagination.

With every passing year, on the other hand, it becomes more difficult to resurrect the past without falling into stylization or killing the living soul of the meaning by reviving a forgotten way of life.

Why did Natalya Petrovna fall in love with a student? Such a question is ridiculous, however, when speaking about love. And yet? Because he is ten years younger than she is? I could feel perhaps how the love of a mature man for a young woman could happen. As far as women are concerned, it always seemed to me that a young woman, and Natalya Petrovna is only twenty nine years old, most often reaches for a person more mature. However, alongside Natalya Petrovna are two men. Rakitin probably seems like a refined ditherer to her, however. (Although to play him like that would be extremely silly.) Moreover, her husband seems an unsociable person to her. (Although he does not have to be acted as an unsociable person. As a person he is worthy, honorable, and kind, only he does not live by the same laws that Natalya Petrovna wants to live by.)

However, why does Alexei Belyayev, the student, arouse her interest? Only because there is nobody else in that relative emptiness she lives in? Nobody except her well-known and completely repellent friends?

Moreover, suddenly there is a new face, young, lively, intelligent. Instead of the everlasting boredom of her husband talking about land management and the "gentlemanly" refined chatter of Rakitin, suddenly a young person who exudes freedom and independence...

In fact, probably by its own nature, love is not a completely homogeneous feeling. For one person it arises from passion. For another, almost from parental tenderness, pity, and thoughtfulness. For a third, it is the result of worship before the real or imaginary riches of the other person's internal gifts. And so forth...

For Natalya Petrovna, it seems to me, love has begun from jealousy, even from envy. Suddenly, completely unanticipated by her, it turns out that her vanity is stung. A new teacher has arrived. He is young, independent, and, according to her extraordinary nature, he is extremely indifferent to her. To this person, arriving somewhere from *outside*, she is of no interest. She is part of the household, like the twisting column or wooden table on the veranda. Thus it seems to her, at least. Moreover, this is not only offensive, it plunges her into sorrowful reflections about herself, her life, and her age.

Always polite indifference in his blank look. Belyayev came here to be of use, earn some money, and leave. Moreover, she is stung by his apparent superiority.

It is incredibly annoying, even painful, to feel herself outside this worthwhile person's field of interest. Because of this, she loses faith in herself, begins to feel her age, her enforced provinciality, etc. It begins with this, and in just a moment it seems that she is already madly in love, and that she does not have the strength to think of anything else. Everything in the house now submits to his presence and depends most of all on her imagined nuances of his behavior. A certain illness is beginning, so peculiar to people and well known to them. One of those psychological illnesses that is so interesting to examine and study. Is this any less interesting than a doctor's study of physical ailments?

We study the pain, of course, and not Natalya Petrovna. She is incapable of making a report to herself about it.

A doctor writes a dissertation about one of the many influenza viruses. In addition, a writer writes a play, studying the most fundamental variation of this ailment of love, lasting not three or four days, but a month, and inflicting such wounds on a person, which influenza isn't capable of, thank heaven. We think a lot about each psychological ailment of a person. We comprehend ourselves in everyone, our customs, habits, and our way of life.

Thus, Natalya Petrovna believes that she means no more to the student than the bookshelf in the nursery. However, he notices her ward, Vera. With Vera, he is on equal footing. There, obviously, is some affinity, some natural desire to stroll or sit together, to laugh, chatter, perhaps even to embrace.

As for Natalya Petrovna, she is a housewife, a mother, part of the house, where there is a husband, and Rakitin, and housemaids, and cooks. At first, she is not so much in love as she is hurt. Hurt from being cast aside, useless. In Belyayev's indifference to her is a kind of secret that she wants to comprehend.

One way or another, her nature is interested in him, but this nature must be understood. Imprecision or reticence here would be disastrous. What it is happening here must be understood in a particular, concrete situation. Is it passion, envy, interest in a *stranger*—what is it? There is no such thing as love *in general*. People say that the author has written *everything* down [in the play]. Maybe. However, any commentator or actor or director will inevitably work "from himself." Even though they will try to study everything, read the text a hundred times, etc. Nevertheless, eventually everything will be decided by the actor. Who is he, and what of himself will be found in the role? How is Belyayev different from those two other men?

It depends on Natalya Petrovna. What will the actress concretely play in her attitude to him? What is the seed of her fascination? Where does it begin?

In the Polish production, the student was an ordinary student—slender, lively, and that is all. He deftly jumped back, very much confused, when he saw Natalya Petrovna. Possibly, it was clear to her that she loved him, but *it was not clear to me*. She looked at him lovingly and nothing more.

She loved him only in keeping with the plot, and no more.

However, if it is not [merely] in keeping with the plot, then what is it actually? What is he like, and what is at the center of her attitude to him?

Avoid an abstract, tender view of Natalya Petrovna here... In this love, it is necessary to reveal a certain fury in order to express more distinctly the drama of impossibility, impracticality.

It would be interesting to produce it so that Natalya Petrovna's moods swing from stormy desire to sharing in a kind of game with Vera and the student. From their running around, enthusiasm, and other things (she actually does these too), to complete gloomy aloofness, when Natalya Petrovna, having become isolated, looks at everyone from the outside and almost with hatred.

Chekhov's Faith

I belatedly read an article about Chekhov by Alexander Kugel.[47] How he "undresses" Chekhov.

Allegedly, Chekhov collected ridiculous last names in his notebooks. He saw only the ridiculous in everything. He was cold, melancholy, and saw only melancholy around himself. In addition, because of this, he lived without faith and was at the same time fatally ill.

So Kugel writes, and he is very pleased with himself. He is plainly happy that he counted all the ridiculous last names and put them in a series, and he is convinced that this is what preoccupied Chekhov! However, coldness in what and melancholy about what? Maybe Kugel managed to notice only what was ridiculous and trivial in the notebooks of the great man. More accurately, not merely noticed the trivial, but perceived it only as trivial.

Other humorists use ridiculous last names too, but in Chekhov's case, the same stone tossed in the water created other circles around it.

Maybe it does not happen in science. However, in art, the same mark can have completely different meanings. In addition, a critic should understand this. Chekhov only began with humor, of which perhaps only the external signs remained. Moreover, behind the ridiculous pen name is a different landscape.

However, here comes a very clever critic, very arrogant; and exactly where it is necessary to feel and understand, he writes very cleverly, and he enjoys his cleverness very much.

Here we have a Rembrandt, for example, and over here, we have a Degas. In addition, standing before them is a clever critic who has understood Rembrandt for a long time. He disparages Degas because he does not see the power of his color or considers that his *themes* are not those of Rembrandt. He does not want to understand that there are *very many worlds*. In addition, each one not only needs to be *defined*, but also *felt*. In addition [as a critic], he needs to reveal this world, only not from the pose of the Great Man, who pretends to know virtually everything about faith, and despair, and illness. Chekhov often wrote about the *absence of belief*. Others often wrote that *they believed*. So what?

In *Three Sisters,* for example, Chekhov loves Irina, loves the Baron, but he does not manage to write about this openly. That is the kind of man he was. He does not love Solyony, but he is capable of understanding him. He pities Solyony. Chekhov has a whole army of such people he wants to speak about. In this case, Chekhov could be depressed for many reasons. In one go, he has shown this army [of characters], revealed it, and we have learned about it. Despite his melancholy and illness, he was convinced that such an army exists and we should learn about it. In this was his *faith*.

Essential Movements of the Soul

Today, a former student of mine, who has been knocking about in search of suitable work for some time, showed us his next "evening" work, that is, a small performance prepared outside his regular time. Actually, it was a play done in many of our children's theatres, a play about a young artist who died early, Nadia Rusheva.[48]

I did not know the participating actors, for some had only finished theatre school, and the others were in indeterminate situations at various theatres. The play lasted an hour, and only a quarter of it was interesting to me, but its participants, including the director, were sympathetic, and, if this is the right expression, had not *calmed down* until now, even though an entire half day had passed. First, they were outwardly charming people. It is no small thing when actors are *charming*. Hardly any of them had any money for personal things, but each one was dressed well.

They were dressed so that they could fall on the floor if the staging required it, but in the same clothes, they could appear among the spectators without worrying whether they looked all right. This style of dressing appeared not so long ago. In addition, how this clothing suits the young! I think these sweaters, pants, and skirts would make even ugly monsters attractive, but the young people I am writing about here were not monsters by any means. With great ease and plasticity, a young man climbed up somewhere near the ceiling, holding in his hands a stool, which at that moment represented a movie camera. Then he jumped down and sat on the floor with the same stool, and I thought that pantomime should become part of modern dramatic art, and that those who are overweight and unable to pantomime should not be actors.

How they moved, and how the young women danced. I will not try to describe them; I will only say that looking at them I was upset about my age. How well they know what clothing suits them best, how cleverly they make use of their old blue jeans. I involuntarily recollected Gogol, who tried to describe women, and then said that he could not do it because, after all, it was impossible.

The play is about the life of the young girl Nadia, whose life passed by in an instant. She died when she was only seventeen years old, but had time to sketch hundreds of perfect drawings that were as elusive and fleeting as her own personality.

However, how can you transfer this *moment*, these swift conversations with one person, with another, with a third? How can you embody the instantaneousness of her life, her fleeting happiness, and her fleeting loneliness?

After all, our [traditional] scenic resources are so crude and heavy in comparison with, for example, music or painting. Our "substantiality" and "corporality" often interfere with the expression of all these light but so essential movements of the soul. How can you make something in drama that would be like a Mozart melody or the strange and unearthly dissonances of Prokofiev? How can you transfer to the stage what could be done with the light brush of Renoir or with the same light but firm brush of Modigliani? In addition, would you believe, word of honor, that I caught a glimpse of these strange rhythms, these changeable colors, a hint of that *light touch* of the text, in the play of my student, who was still unemployed. No, three-quarters of it was done incorrectly, but a whole quarter of it was good. A whole quarter! I recall that at one time, many studio theatres were being created, and there they searched and tested and sometimes even found something from which something *new* was born. However, where are they lately, these tests? Why don't they exist? And in which direction will dramatic art move after us?

Othello

The process of Cassio getting drunk needs to be presented to the audience slowly, one piece at a time, from the moment he turns down a drink to the moment he wounds Montano.

However, this is not so easy, to present it piece by piece.

It is almost necessary to create a pantomime of the intense work of Iago's mind on the invention of the next move of his intrigue. Moreover, to finish this intense pantomime with a sudden relaxation...

He has figured it out!

Iago paints for Roderigo a picture of Desdemona and Cassio in love. He visualizes it so well that after he leaves, Roderigo remains under the spell of this vision. There is a sinister humor in all this.

Desdemona speaks to Othello all the time about the need to forgive Cassio. Stanislavsky noticed that she does this, confident that the Moor was raised in the traditions of humanism. Thus it was at the start of their relationship and so it has continued until now. Now the conditions have strongly changed, but Desdemona does not notice that she should no longer speak about Cassio.

I was very proud of many of my discoveries, but it appears all this was already revealed by Stanislavsky long ago.

In addition, how well he described all this; how *carefully* he described it, and how clearly!

Analysis of Moments

Passing by the wardrobe room, I noticed that our bellowing watchwoman had stopped and was listening to a chapter from Tolstoy's story *Resurrection* that was being read over the radio.[49] Putting on my coat and leaving, I listened along with her to that part when Nekludov and Katyusha kissed once, then again, then looked into each other's eyes as though questioning whether they should kiss a third time and, we assume, coming to that conclusion, they kissed a third time. This text stayed in my memory for a long time, and I thought: What an analysis of moments!

In *Othello*, Stanislavsky proceeded moment by moment, so that nothing remained *unclear*. However, we live in the twentieth century, with its tanks, airplanes, and completely different rhythms. In addition, under this pretext, we miss everything that happens between people exactly in the domain of those [momentary] nuances that are the breath of life. Without these nuances, an actor is only a *robot*. He can kiss once, twice, three times, but to look into her eyes and understand if the circumstances are right to kiss her a third time, a robot certainly cannot do this work.

Analysis, however, is a relatively slow thing. Moreover, in life, everything is instantaneous. On stage, ultimately, everything should be instantaneous, without superfluous delays, but only *after* analysis and *firmly established* upon it.

...When the internal pattern is accurate, when every psychological shift is clear, engraved in one's consciousness, then it is possible to play swiftly, since in nature itself, all reactions, all innuendos, all expressions of action—everything proceeds more rapidly than it is done by us on stage. Accurately find the tempo that resides in all the details!

In such scenes as Othello's eavesdropping scene, it is necessary to reach for daring theatrical methods, without being limited merely to everyday constructions.[50] A sharp formal and rhythmic pattern is needed here.

Time Is Passing

When rehearsals are canceled because of an actor's illness or for other reasons, I become ill as well, only mentally. I am bothered all day long with the thought that *time is passing,* and it seems as though I can feel its empty motion. Rest? I cannot do it. Get busy with other work? Yes, I try, but the work that was already planned torments me.

I can hardly wait for tomorrow.

Oh, how wonderful to be a painter and not have to depend on someone else. To wake up, pick up your brush, and paint by yourself!

It would be nice, of course, to find out what torments painters.

"Anatoly Vasilevich, actor 'X' has a toothache."[51]

"Anatoly Vasilevich, today we accidentally forgot to call actor 'Y'."

"Anatoly Vasilevich, actor 'Z' felt that he had heart palpitations."

All this is sincere, of course, and not deceitful, but when we miss a rehearsal, I think: Do they really expect that time will actually *stand still* and all of us *will have enough time?*

Othello

We have changed the opening moments of *Othello* many times. It would be better if Iago summons Roderigo with a barely noticeable nod, he approaches him, and they both move forward while the others remain sitting on the large bench.

Coming forward, Iago and Roderigo turn to those sitting on the bench and look at them for a long time. There, in the back of the stage, are the victims of Iago's future intrigue. Let the audience settle down with the feeling that something is about to happen here. Then, walking to the side and continuing to indicate those on the bench, Iago begins to say how he hates the Moor. It is necessary not to illustrate *life*, but the *theme*.

A surprising conversation takes place between Brabantio and the Doge.[52] In addition, the actors need to play it very seriously so that its meaning is clear. I once saw a Doge, however, who for some reason was portrayed as a foolish old man. The stage time for his role is small; it is necessary to plan the characteristics carefully—but here the actors made a mistake.

Between the foolish old man and the other, rather poor, actor playing Brabantio, there was nothing satisfactory.

Meanwhile, according to Shakespeare as I just said, a *wonderful* conversation is taking place between them.

After Brabantio's daughter [publicly] prefers the Moor, the Doge decides to console the father, and tells him that he should take his misfortune calmly. In reply, the Senator asks the Doge why he does not deal calmly with the idea that the Turks have captured Cyprus. In addition, with further sharp words, he lets us know that only someone else's grief can be perceived calmly. A powerful conversation with such characteristics should be clear to everyone.

However, how can we understand it if the actor does not understand it himself, and he plays anything he likes in this scene except a serious subject.

When it is a question of *general* visions or *general* interpretations, I am compelled to disagree even with Stanislavsky.

After all, creative work is *personal*, and I have *my own* interpretations. They are objectively inferior, probably, but unfortunately I do not have the power to feel and think like *him*. I have another life, and all my habits and knowledge are different. Moreover, everything around me is different. Very different from Stanislavsky's surroundings. Moreover, here lies the difference in our interpretations.

When the craftsmanship begins, however, when Stanislavsky makes his own analysis, then it is not to my liking!

Because there would be no lines left in the text to be developed. All the connections are found [already by Stanislavsky], each one compared with another, everything has the most precise design of internal life. Nothing is left for "acting." Because acting proceeds based on [one's own] precise analysis.

The same analysis that Stanislavsky did with Tolstoy and Chekhov, he did with Shakespeare. In addition, not the kind done by certain directors, that is, hurried, flashy, fussy, throwing sand in the eyes of the actors and the public.

In any passion, there is calmness, accuracy.

Even hysterics has an internal plan.

In life, everything is *life*. However, in art, it is analysis, analysis, construction, design, and then hysterics, if it is necessary, of course.

In Shakespeare only four *eruptions, outbursts* are necessary, and the rest is the silence of carefully developed meaning. There is more emotion in such silence than in *noise*.

Scenic Locale

To represent the [scenic] *locale* in literal fashion, it seems to me, is meaningless. For example, it is not necessary to represent Venice or Cyprus in *Othello*. It is not necessary to represent the hall where the Senate meets. It is not necessary to represent Desdemona's bedroom, etc. Not at all. In addition, not just because it requires ten scenic designs and ten scenery changes turning on a revolve, which is a nuisance and obsolete in itself.

It is possible to find other ways of changing the [scenic] form, but it is important to establish that even the best stage technology does not justify a literal representation of the locale. Even very good technology is already very elementary, even if it is done beautifully.

It is true that often certain locales are devised that can radically change our basis for representing events. For example, in *The Marriage of Figaro* at MAT, Stanislavsky changed the marriage scene to the *back yard* of the nobleman's castle.[53] This was not simply a locale where the action took place, but an *interpretation of the content*. Moreover, the interpretation was also artistic in the highest order, and there you already have a great principle.

Nevertheless, this principle exists, so to speak, in both timid and sharply expressive forms.

Let us leave in peace *Figaro* and all that is found in the theatre of the past. Not in the sense that the past no longer has any right to exist, but the past in terms of simple temporal understanding.

Let us not speak about *classical*, which for scrupulous people always seem to be fraught with a hint of disrespect for the best of the past.

Let us address the present.

In the present day, there is a very simple way to illustrate locale. Such illustrations can be beautiful or ugly, poetic or prosaic. In *Hamlet*, Elsinore can be represented "as it is," or in any case, as we generally visualize it to ourselves. In addition, Dvoretsky's play *The Outsider* can be devised using the general outline of a modern factory, a shop, the sketch of a factory foreman, and so forth.[54]

In a word, [a distilled realistic] *locale*.

In Ostrovsky's play *The Forest,* there can be a country estate as it was represented a hundred years ago, so familiar to us from books, but modified a little so as not to be repetitive.

In *Woe from Wit,* there will be the well-known manor hall with its columns, only perhaps with a certain unfamiliar twist, again in order to relieve the monotony of the usual representation.[55] Nevertheless, I repeat, [essentially] it will be an ordinary [realistic] locale.

Someone will say in self-defense, however, that this also is an *interpretation*. Yes, it will be an interpretation, but *only a little different from the ordinary*.

Other kinds of interpretations—strong, sharp, definite [i.e., absolutely non-realistic]—are found far less often.

However, here, naturally, there can be ugliness as well.

For example, we have a play in which life is expressed as a swamp, and so on stage is a "quagmire"—mold on the walls, etc. Such an interpretation is too banal, or in any case, too superficial. To illustrate a place so plainly is feeble. How can a personal *interpretation* be illustrated, especially if it still has to represent *the general quality of a locale.*

No, this is still not the point!

The point lies in something different, in finding the essence of the subject, the essence of the events. Nevertheless, at the same time, this essence needs to be expressed in the most *artful* way.

Therefore, I sit here, and I am puzzled about how to express in *Othello* that *intrigue is pernicious.* To place *the experience of intrigue* before the eyes of the audience, so that it would still be in Venice and in Desdemona's bedroom and in *the essence of all the events.* A certain collective *artful* image of our personal meaning in addition to the general story.

Oh, it would be good to be the critic! How he would reproach us then! After all, *everything* is usually obvious for a critic. He knows that the music here is *not that music,* the costumes are not *those costumes,* and we did not compose the correct *emphases.* I know all this; I read the same books. However, does he know how difficult it is actually to *create* something?!

Othello

How remarkably clear and with what perfect language Stanislavsky writes about the *past* of the characters. The way Cassio looked after the parlor maid to help with Desdemona's elopement. How Iago once saved Roderigo from some carousing drunks. How Emilia cleaned the General's bachelor apartment. All this is not empty fantasy, but a complete system of rebirth, as Stanislavsky writes it, the past *justifying the present.*

Clearly, Shakespeare himself did not always think with the same thoroughness. Realistic scrupulosity, which was characteristic of Stanislavsky, apparently did not interest him. He could even forget, for example, that in the first act Cassio does not know about Desdemona. However, in the third act, she talks about what a great help he was in her elopement. It is possible to find an amusing actor's line here, of course, as though in the beginning of the play Cassio hides from Iago what he knows about Desdemona. Could be, but Shakespeare was often negligent in such questions, frequently because in all his love for psychology, for true life and true details, he nevertheless thought in more general terms than the later Realists did. However, this does not mean that those who lived after Shakespeare were right, because many times Realists repeatedly change their practices. In addition, really, isn't the issue ultimately up to them, instead of the *content* of the art, [to decide] what is a lie or the truth?

Chekhov's method is different from that of Aeschylus, but we hardly need to decide which is better.

Stanislavsky draws a detailed portrait of a soldier named Iago. Iago sleeps in the same tent as Othello, he is a favorite of the other soldiers, for he can sing, drink, carouse when it is necessary. Besides, he is brave and honest (in the sense that he does not steal). He can put an enemy to death severely, but he could look after the child of Desdemona and Othello. Everything about him is known, for which they either fear him or love him. Nevertheless, there is a secret inside him that even his wife cannot comprehend. It is the secret of his malice and vindictiveness.

He is offended because he was not appointed the lieutenant. Now, having taken offense, he recollects the old gossip that Othello was intimate with his wife. He is also insulted that Desdemona's elopement was kept secret from him.

All this is a true portrait, not only of a soldier named Iago, but an entire class of people.

I read this discussion [of Stanislavsky's] and of course agree with every word, but today I want to comprehend certain more *general* things.

Everything certainly comes from the insult that he was not appointed the lieutenant. This is so. However, what if he *had been* promoted?

Perhaps he would find another starting point from which to rebel, humiliate, torment, and destroy!

In addition, all this because of contempt for another, for *someone different,* and even more so because that difference consists of a *higher soul.*

I once saw a certain man who went for a walk with his dog. A little old man emerged from a building, he appeared kindly enough, but then he noticed this little dog—and he changed into a monster.

What words he could not find to offend the other pedestrians! He sincerely did not understand how anyone could love a dog. To him they were spoiled, overindulgent people. Not only did he did not want to admire the dog—the dog was nasty to him and the owner, too. The habits, tastes, and moods of the old man were different. Moreover, a dog did not enter into the circle of his habits. He shouted so much that I thought he would kill the dog, or in any case strike the person who was walking the dog. He did not understand them, they were *different*, and therefore he *hated.*

Alternatively, along the street walks a stout woman. With a shopping basket. Toward her walks a [trim] woman in a beautiful blouse and a fashionable jacket. In addition, the first woman is filled with all sorts of dark rage. She lives another life, and this is enough reason for her hatred.

From such examples, we could move on to others. When you do not like black, you consider that black is *dirty.* Meanwhile, it could be crystal pure, gentle, poetic, but for the *other*, it is only *dirty.*

For Iago, of course, it is not racial prejudice by itself that is the basis of hatred. The basis is that Othello is other, different, and this is enough.

That is where the "blackness" comes in, and Desdemona, and the fact that I am a soldier and he is a general (although it could be the other way around), and that Cassio was promoted and not I, and everything else in the world.

Another, a stranger, incomprehensible to me, no, intelligible, but not like me, who thinks he can control me, but I will control all of them, everything will be the way I want it to be, and if not, I will smash, burst, destroy, strangle!

Everything is indifferent to me. It is good for me only when it is bad for them!

I remember once I saw a rather cultured Iago. Probably it is what compelled me to assume that Iago should be completely uncultured, coarse. So that our play would not be a melodramatic intrigue, but a deep dissimilarity of natures—Othello's loftiness and Iago's baseness. So that the hatred proceeded from the ruthless nature of Iago. In a word, I intended to give this characterization something brutal, gangsterish, and low.

In addition, in Othello's characterization, I thought, to start with, there will even be an element of refinement. There are certain people with innate external and internal grace. There are certain whites, there are certain blacks, and in them, this grace is sometimes especially captivating. However, Iago, with his criminal nature, must hate this grace in particular; it is radically alien to him.

Looking back, however, I see that Iago would be too one-sided with only this single feature. Yes, Iago is a gangster, of course, but maybe it is necessary for the whole play to be carried out with a soft smile, moreover not feigned. It is necessary to play the intrigue very modestly, not to expose more than necessary. We often expect trouble from a [conspicuous] villain, but sometimes the world is blown up by a meek person, who has hatred not in his fists or in clenched teeth, but somewhere in the lymph nodes. In addition, this hatred is so great that even the least manifestation is enough to destroy the world.

> —Though in the trade of war I have slain men
> Yet I do hold it very stuff o' the conscience
> To do no contriv'd murder. I lack iniquity
> Sometimes to do me service.[56]

I want to deliver these words positively deceitfully, for, after all, Iago is a liar. Othello trusts him, however, and other people trust him, because he seems to be a man of *peace*. Iago pretends that Desdemona's father is a villain because he offended the Moor. Brabantio is a villain whom Iago listens to painfully because Brabantio is insulting his General in the Senate. Moreover, all this, certainly, can be played hypocritically, that is, letting us know that Iago is different from how he represents himself to other people. However, complexity and living truth arises at the point when this lie becomes such a habit that it is, as they say, second nature, just as it is in spies, perhaps, who are only discovered after twenty years.

This will probably create magnitude, depth, novelty of interpretation. Because no interpretations can be considered new except those that add new *magnitude and complexity*. To achieve such a performance, perhaps, is possible only in our dreams. I do not blame the actors here as much as myself, for often substantial ideas like this crop up when it is already close to opening night.

The Cherry Orchard

What a good idea to produce Chekhov at Yuri Lyubimov's Taganka Theatre.[57] At a theatre where Chekhov would seem to be unthinkable. Where there are always naked brick walls, and where actors *show* their characters according to Brechtian principles.

Maybe it is right that truth must be sought only in contrasts. The comedy of Gogol must be presented tragically, and then it will be *ridiculous*. Brecht must be presented "like Chekhov," without the sardonic Brechtian tone. Incidentally, in his own time Brecht was presented at the Taganka *in Russian,* which may be why it began to be played here in this tone. Moreover, *The Cherry Orchard* should be produced at a theatre where the last thing they are familiar with is "Chekhovian tone."

Maybe the time is such that a well-worn path will not lead anywhere?

Alla Demidova as Ranevskaya, Vladimir Vysotsky as Lopakhin, theoretically this is already good. In addition, invite for the design, not David Borovsky, whose aesthetic is "Tagankan" through and through, but Valery Leventhal, yes, yes, operatic Leventhal from the Bolshoi Theatre, and let him devise something precisely *for the Taganka.*[58]

It will be interesting when Levanthal's cardboard models start to incorporate Lyubimov and Borovsky.

It will good when the expressive methods of the Taganka actors begin to work within this gentle [Chekhovian] fabric. Only this *gentle fabric* must be there, this *pain,* and then it will be a Tagankan Gaev and a Tagankan Carlotta. Maybe Chekhov will turn out to be a Chekhovian "psychological farce."

A dying tribe of eccentrics. A small, helpless, unfortunate flock. But at the Taganka, it will not be sentimental. In the center, on a patch of ground, is a garden, a stone cemetery marker, and even a chair—a complete still life of their past and present life. A strongbox of their life. They often sit there, all of them, as though waiting for an ambush.

Six thousand small white flowers will be made by MAT craftsmen for the cherry trees at the Taganka.

When Lopakhin pours out the glasses of champagne in the last act, he throws the bottle in there, in this patch of ground, as they throw something useless onto a rubbish heap. Only this rubbish should be beautiful. It should really be a *still life*. A "literal" rubbish heap would be banal in the theatre. Everyone makes a "rubbish heap" on stage these days. A Yugoslavian director once told a story about a theatre company from some country that came to a theatre in Belgrade, demanding to cut down ninety dead aspen trees for their production, and the floor to be covered with six tons of real earth. All this is a reaction to the theatre of the past and is understandable, but everything in the world ends. This idea is stated in *The Cherry Orchard,* by the way.

Only Borovsky, perhaps, has the right to make scenery for us from bare wooden boards. He created it and he should kill it himself.[59]

In the same theatre, two designers should work from opposite directions—then the work will move forward. In addition, two directors from different schools. I produced Gogol's play, *Marriage,* in opposition to Yuri Lyubimov. Were it not for him, I would still be directing the same as I did with Viktor Rozov's play *Good Luck!* at the Central Children's Theatre [in 1954]. What a pity that Oleg Yefremov [at MAT] does not direct something in opposition to me. Naturally, I am expressing myself more or less figuratively. It is impossible to think that you are alone in the world. The majority of theatres live in dreadful isolation. Their premieres seem to them the most important in the world. Meanwhile, it is necessary to live, so to speak, in a state of *comparison.* What can I oppose to Lyubimov on his stage? After all, he has such a powerful directorial means at his command. But what means are at my disposal? As with an army, it is necessary to re-arm oneself every few years. Naturally, remaining one's own self throughout.

Directors are rarely allowed to understand who they are and what means they use. They write mainly about one or another *performance.* Only when the director dies do we learn about his creative work as a whole. At that point, writing as such is no longer necessary for him. If there were no mirrors, people could at least look at themselves in the water, then they would be able to understand what their nose or ears looked like.

However, where can the director or actor or designer look if his reflection is so incomplete?

Do you re-arm yourself *beyond recognition*, or remain as you were in the last century? Both are bad.

Critics very seldom write articles using comparative analysis. They are afraid of offending someone. After all, there is no obligation to compare the very good with the very bad. It is possible, for example, to take something very bad and talk about how it might be done *differently*. The same could be done with something very good.

Only the most venerable are so lucky. In addition, their luck is only in terms of praise, and not in the sense of what we are talking about here.

I would like to read somewhere about who Georgii Tovstonogov is.[60] And what his *means* are. Nevertheless, I read very little.

After all, it is bad when *nothing is heard* about a play. Just as bad as if *nothing is heard* about a book or article that was published but no one was aware of.

I am not speaking about a specific book. I am speaking in general. I am speaking philosophically, like Tuzenbach or Trofimov, only now I happen to be working on Chekhov once more. This is simply the way I prepare my work.

Chekhov's Emotional Mathematics

There is emotional mathematics in Chekhov's plays. Everything is built on subtle feelings, but everything is structured with subtle skill.

Now, perhaps, is a period in art when this emotional mathematics cannot be transferred simply through the characters' way of life. It is necessary to convey it to the audience in some somewhat open, clear way. Picasso draws a bull with one stroke; all the motion is complete and accurate, grasping the entire pose. In addition, this is almost a symbol, an arbitrary symbol. It is also possible not to draw it like that, but three dimensionally, using hair and the color of leather. It is possible to have a living bull, and it is possible to have a sharply outlined image of some general idea.

It is the same in the theatre. It is possible to create the illusion of life, to create an atmosphere, living characters, etc. Moreover, it is possible within all this life in the play to find that unique stroke which will express a very important feeling and idea in the present day. The actual way of life represented remains only a reference point.

For example, Ranevskaya arrives, enters, and sits down to drink coffee beside Pishchik, who lapses into dreaming all the time. It is two or three o'clock in the morning and day begins to break. It will never be better than it was done at MAT, because there was a whole school just for this. Moreover, at that time this was a contemporary play. That was the reality it is necessary to revive, restore. However, that is not even the issue. The issue is that the school has gone, too. The rhythm and style of rehearsal became different because thinking has become different.[61]

I imagine the *core*. Ranevskaya enters; stands on a ramp as though in the doorway of her nursery, and all the others are crowded behind her. At this point, Firs enters with a cup of coffee. A big conversation arises, but I watch *only her*. Everyone lives only *for her,* understanding that this visit is *for her*.

In the small circle of people are Lopakhin, Gaev, Pishchik, Anna, and Varya. Everyone understands one thing: she has returned to say goodbye. She is finished with this life. However, some passions still boil, and there will be scandals and disputes, hopes, but somewhere it is understood that everything has already been decided. Here everyone stands, and we observe how she remains. The patient has returned from the doctor, having learned the awful diagnosis, and you go with her and chatter about the weather, the town, and shopping.

She talks about the room where she once slept, and how she went on the train, that she likes coffee, but everyone understands that the issue is really something else. Anna and Varya leave, unable to endure the tension.

The core, the point of internal tension, is important. In addition, for the sake of this, it is possible to forget the other details of daily life and existence. To slide past what is unnecessary, unimportant, and get to the core.

Not a clay model of life, but a courageous stroke of very important feeling and an important idea.

Danger and carelessness.

Defenselessness.

Rapidly changing life and "stupid people."

Inept resistance to approaching misfortune.

The past departs, and the future has not yet arrived.

Schiller and Romantic Declamation

Schiller and Romantic declamation. A type of equal sign has always been placed between these two concepts. Like between Shakespeare and passion. Or between Chekhov and lyricism. Nevertheless, today I saw Schiller's play *Mary Stuart* performed without Romantic declamation, without stilts. Before me, on the stage of the Hamburg Theatre, were absolutely living people, generally speaking even simple, but in any case very intelligible, and Schiller did not lose anything from this, no, on the contrary, the familiar court intrigue acquired in my eyes genuine significance and seriousness. I understood that the discussions dealt with very serious things, absolutely, completely unpretentious.

Who ever thought that it was necessary to play Schiller loudly, noisily, that Romantic stage settings were necessary, etc.? At one time, this was good, possibly, but then it degenerated. Just as it happens in some families when, for example, the grandfather was a great person and the father was already a much smaller person, for he always lived under the thumb of the famous grandfather and was not accustomed to independent thinking. What was good for the grandfather appears only as imitation in the father's case. In addition, the son, that is the grandson of the grandfather, turned out to be devoid of any birthright at all. Isn't it true that such families exist? The good influence of the grandfather was great; however, there is a limit to everything, even good influence, because each person should find *himself* by *himself* in his own life. That is how it probably is in art.

At this time, no one, thank heaven, demands that Shakespeare should be played just as he was at the Globe Theatre. In fact, Shakespeare scholars pretty well know how things were played there. Nonetheless, you conclude that, of all the scholars, the wisest in the world, the most liberal, are the Shakespeare scholars. They seldom say to others, "This is not Shakespeare." Maybe Shakespeare himself, with his broad point of view, accustomed them to develop a certain special open-mindedness Maybe there was simply so much of everything on this path that Shakespeare scholars *have grown accustomed to this way of thinking*.

However, I cannot say this about Schiller. Most likely, the experts would decide: in this performance, there is no Schillerian Romanticism. Perhaps I am witnessing the first such performance of a play by Schiller. Such simplicity and depth in its content. Such simple effects, such genuine seriousness.

Therefore, this is Schiller, I think. Schiller! In addition, personally speaking, I did not miss the Romanticism in this production. What strange habits some people have—seeing one thing, they miss another. They lose so much from this. Before their eyes are always the same picture, meanwhile there are very many excellent pictures.

The entire court is dishonest in this play. What fear there is in everyone's eyes, and what a web of intrigues. Somewhere outside, perhaps, there are other people, but this *court* is a world in itself, with its *own* laws and rules. Everyone is so sly, slippery. Adaptability to evil.

Here even heroic deeds are born from egoism, a certain personal impulse. How terrible this distortion is. Moreover, how instructive. Ah, if only those reading Schiller in the ensuing years could have learned to love goodness and hate evil! However, after Schiller all sorts of things happened in Germany. In addition, almost everything has already been written about it here in this play.

In the intermission between the acts of *Mary Stuart* at the German theatre, I heard a conversation in the lobby: "Is this really a queen?" says a stout lady to a young man, who apparently does not agree with her.

I move to the buffet, and on the way, I think to myself: Why is this not really a queen? Which actress was she speaking about: the one who played Mary Stuart or the one who played Elizabeth? For me personally, they were both suited to play royalty. In what way, I think, are they not queenly for that woman? Both of them act well, and here I am speaking as a professional. With great meaning, with passion. Could it be in the manner of their behavior, in their appearance? Could it be that Queen Elizabeth was not as small as the actress in this production was? Is Mary Stuart insufficiently stately, too plain?

It would be interesting to know how the woman, whose reply I heard in the aisle of the auditorium, would recognize a queen if she really happened to see one? Is she convinced that a "real queen" must be stately, with a "royal" bearing and "royal" speech? What about Goya's kings and their children? After all, he painted from nature, as they say. No, this woman would not recognize royal blood in Goya's figures unless she heard that Goya was considered a genius.

I am so angry at this woman because it seems to me this is the same person who sat behind me, as luck would have it, at my production of *The Cherry Orchard,* and at every entrance said with a malicious sneer: "These are aristocrats?!" Most of all, Alla Demidova, performing the role of Ranevskaya, did not satisfy her as sufficiently aristocratic.

During the whole act I did not dare to turn around and look at this woman, but I imagined her to be a certain elderly lady from "former times" [i.e., Stalinist times]. Imagine my surprise when I turned around at the end of the show and saw not an old and aristocratic woman, but someone, as they say, as ordinary as my neighbors do, or me; and this is the woman who did not find Ranevskaya "genuine." We were born much later, I thought, and so this woman does not speak from knowledge, but, on the contrary, from *ignorance*, prejudice. Just as one would imagine an academic as necessarily old, with a beard and moustache like the scientist Ivan Pavlov, or a [capitalist] millionaire as stout and with a large cigar in his mouth like Winston Churchill.

Oh, these experts on the affairs of the aristocracy! However, I must confess that the woman sitting behind me at *The Cherry Orchard* was not the same one who spoke up at *Mary Stuart*. They are probably two different women.

Othello

Twenty years ago or more, when a large number of directors and actors began to become interested in the so-called "Method of Physical Actions," I learned Stanislavsky's production plan for *Othello* very nearly by heart.[62] Well, maybe it is an exaggeration to say I *learned* it, but I really knew it backward and forward, from cover to cover.

Many years have passed since that time. In addition, when I planned my own production of *Othello*, of course, I did not look into that beautiful little book. I hope it should be clear why I did not do so. Because the past should not be experienced in words, but in one's own nature, it is necessary to study the past, but it is impossible to sing with someone else's voice.

Now, after almost ending our work on this play, I could quietly begin to read Stanislavsky's plan once again.

I confess, however, that I read it a little differently. Some things, of course, enchanted me as before, however now I allowed myself (Oh, horrors!) to disagree with some things.

It is very interesting, I admit, to read how this play would have appeared on the MAT stage. Roderigo and Iago are riding, for example, in a gondola. The gondola should move up and down as though it is on waves. It is written in detail how these waves should be done technically. How to achieve a genuine splash of water from the oars just as it is heard in *life*.

Then another gondola docks at the house where Desdemona is hiding.

Othello looks up at the window from time to time. It finally opens, and Desdemona is seen in it.

When Iago remains at the beginning of the scene in the Senate, Roderigo speaks with him through a latticed window. Because in *life* Roderigo would not be permitted to go into the Senate.

At this point, for example, I thought that the Senate probably is not a single room. Moreover, naturally, Roderigo would probably not go into the Senate. However, if he suddenly went into the neighboring hall, then perhaps he could meet Iago in there.

Shakespeare probably was indifferent to such "living truth." Later, however, after many hundreds of years, the gondola and the waves and Desdemona in the window and the lattice in the Senate seemed necessary because the vision of realism in art had changed over time. However, they invented another convention for the [scenic] image of reality. After all, waves in the theatre are also artificial. Nevertheless, at MAT they used large stones to form enormous wall in Cyprus, and of course, they were not in the mountains, but there, in the theatre, where [artificial] theatrical properties were constructed.

However, make-believe stones, these waves, and this small window would probably seem even more artificial on stage today.

It would be better if they only say that this is Cyprus, only say it.

As though everything had returned once again to those years when Shakespeare himself was alive. As though people had tried to *imitate* real life in art, succeeded satisfactorily, and then settled among themselves that, despite everything, any sign, let us say, of a flower, was far closer to a living flower than a detailed paper flower sprinkled with perfume. The sign and the paper flower, however, are the same type of convention. However, the conventions of Shakespeare's theatre seemed to Shakespeare, and maybe seem to us, closer to nature. Although in comparison with a wall, a window, or a stone on stage, it is much farther from actual life.

Indeed, for some people the mark of reality is actually its imitation. Who is correct here, and who will out-argue whom, I cannot judge. Or more accurately, I do not wish to. I simply know that Stanislavsky and [his scenic designer] Alexander Golovin were the high point of a particular point of view.[63] And Rembrandt is a high point, and Repin, and Picasso, and Gauguin. You can choose, or better yet, having studied everything, try to create and convince those who are coming to the theatre today that you are exactly right.

Having written all this, I immediately begin to have doubts about the correctness of my ideas. Is it possible that Golovin's [realistic] formulation has really become obsolete, and those pitiful attempts at another convention which we often see nowadays are really modern? Moreover, is it fair to compare the peak of one style with the "low point" of another? We shall assume that equally talented things are subject to comparison, and then the difference among the *principles* will become clearer.

Golovin, for example, portrayed the locales [realistically] in *Othello*. Venice, Cyprus, etc. Naturally, this palace and that mass of huge stones are seen with the eyes of an artist, but they are [realistic] *locales*.

Meanwhile, another view of things exists, when there is an attempt to express not only the place in which the action occurs, but also much of *the essence of the occurrence*. For example, designer David Borovsky's *Hamlet*.[64] Is this the castle of a king? No, of course not. Then is this perhaps the bedroom of Gertrude? This is certainly not shown either. There are neither walls nor windows nor doors nor even a genuine throne; there is a single [enormous] woven curtain, which sweeps everything away at the end of each episode, sweeps away the furniture, and often even the people. In front of it, there is an earthen hole and a skull on the edge of this hole. Finally, there is in the distance, on the back wall, a mere hint of how they built homes in earlier times, some sort of elementary symbol of buildings found in that far-away epoch. All this is done visibly and boldly—a white wall and dark, authentic wooden boards nailed across each other. In addition, the curtain is made with authentic coarse fur, knitted together coarsely, as though it were an ancient and rough country carpet. What is this? The locale? Yes, only *in general terms*. This is not Elsinore, but let us say, the fifteenth century. The real issue is not the century, however, it is simply eternal hardness and roughness, and that is what is presented here. In addition, this coarse carpet sweeping everyone away, and this earthen hole like a mark of some misfortune, such as carries everyone away, whether you are a king or a jester. Everything is so *temporary*, meanwhile so much tragedy, so much intrigue. This, if you will, is what *Hamlet* is about. Moreover, the scenic form communicates the essence of the choice.

It is simultaneously *place* and *essence*, but not in the literal sense. An extremely generalized image of *place* and *essence*. Moreover, expressed so realistically, so objectively, in a way they did not express realism in the historic theatre. In fact, the [prop] wall in Cyprus was manufactured from ordinary everyday rags, but here it is real.

Meanwhile, it appears somewhat realistic there, but it is symbolic here.

What is preferable? Nothing! It is simply time to know that on the tree there are many branches.

Scene. Something new appears. It seems as though everything has been found out already, and everything has been thought up, but then it goes up on stage and you see that everything thought up earlier looks awful, poverty-stricken. In addition, you begin to search again. Cassio's drunkenness, for example.

When the actors sat in the rehearsal room before going on stage, in the episode with Iago's songs everyone sang beautifully, both those who acted and those who watched—everyone worked together. Moreover, a good, strange scene of the soldiers carousing was developed while Othello was at home with Desdemona.

On stage, the idea remained the same, but the means needed to change.

The broad powerful songs and external carousing, so impressive in the small [rehearsal] room, lost their luster on stage and looked somewhat amateurish. It was better to hide the singers behind a screen, behind which quiet singing is heard, and after a minute only Cassio emerges, drunk and pale. He sits down, unbuttons his shirt, and breathes heavily. Then Iago appears, comes out to do his business, and leaves again to drink. All this should be built to *hold the tension*. Then it abruptly blows up with a sudden awful scandal. Moreover, to achieve the limits of openness here; a sharp degree of "street truth."

If the performance could be built around a few "giants," what would be the effect? Imagine that Brabantio's fall from official greatness would be wonderfully acted in the first half of the first act. Played with such force that it will be remembered just as the acting of Jean Gabin in *Les Miserables* is remembered.[65] Then Cassio's turn would come. In addition, in the course of approximately twenty minutes, this actor would show the art of high tragedy. Moreover, it would be remembered forever, let us say, like Smoktunovsky's performance in *The Idiot* directed by Tovstonogov.[66]

Thus, in two shocks, the first act would go by

Then Iago, Othello, and Desdemona would enter the game.

In all, the work of only five actors; is this enough? Distinct, clear, and everything has its own meaning and importance.

Each actor would absolutely own the auditorium, and his strength would be distributed with his mind. He would know where to approach something important, and where the moments of revelation are. So that he would step on stage with the deep sense of an objective. So that he would manage his passion and his voice; so that he would know when there is passion and when there is *calculation*.

I recollect here a certain children's poem about the following: if we collected all the crashes and booms, it would make thunder. Moreover, if we collected all the drops of water, it would make rain. In addition, if we collected all the talents and correctly arranged them, it would make a performance. A good children's song...

Something New to Say

I was introduced to some written remarks which said that a reader's definite opinion exists about [the character of] Hamlet, for example, or Dostoyevsky's Prince Mishkin. Moreover, this opinion has now become fixed over the years, materially speaking. In addition, for some reason or other, when creating a production, it is not possible to consider yourself an innovator and get away from this stereotype. To attempt to do this, it is said, is simple conceitedness.

Of course, there are many conceited people and charlatans in the various branches of creative work, not only in directing, and of course, it is not possible to consider every interpretation that does not agree with fixed opinion to be an innovation. Yet somehow all those "received instructions" are not to my liking. After all, art properly begins the moment when it seems you have exposed something that was not known in an earlier reading of, let us say, *Hamlet*.

Naturally, this assumption can be deceptive, but after all, we are dealing with a principle here.

Is it possible to start work as a director without the exciting feeling that you have managed to reveal something new?

Certainly, there is preliminary study, getting the feel of the material, thinking it through, and everything that accumulates around it. Nevertheless, you see, creative work only begins when something sharp and clear is born within yourself about the object being studied.

Specifically, at that point when you feel an element of something conventional in the material, when it already seems somewhat sufficiently *worn out,* and it seems to you that by your own new work you could add something to what is already known—then creativity begins.

That's why it is ridiculous to interrupt an artist with such words as, for example, don't be conceited, don't pretend to be an innovator, don't think that we, the spectators or readers, know less about Prince Mishkin than you do.

Isn't it even greater conceit to deprive an artist of the right to be "independent"?

After all, an artist is like a scientist, except he operates in a different environment and what would a scientist do if they said: "You have babbled enough about a certain particle consisting of this or that. There is real, established opinion, and we are no less knowledgeable than you, scientist, and we understand this particle." Well, then there would be no more scientists.

Pseudo-scientists exist, of course. Possibly that is why each new [scientific] discovery is subjected to verification before acknowledging it. All the same, a scientist is expected to make *discoveries*.

Moreover, in science as well, nothing runs smoothly all the time, and quite often, it takes years to acknowledge what later becomes an indisputable experience.

That is why in science as in art it is necessary to show less skepticism concerning experiments, and why it is necessary for you to confront an experiment you even rather liked without the self-satisfied confidence that you already knew enough about it and did not need to know any more.

For me, it is better to tinker with [the judgments of] a pseudo-scholar than to get into the habit of "not tinkering," to accidentally crush a small particle of a discovery because of [someone's] overconfidence.

That is why I am surprised at people who write about art in absolute terms. This is not so, this is untrue, it must be this and that!

Strangely enough, such confidence often produces the reverse feeling.

I am usually angry, not with the sharpest critics, but more often at the personality of the writer who sees how [everything is supposedly] revealed in the text: "This is not my Chekhov!" writes somebody. Well so what, he is not yours! Is it really my task to come in and give you your Chekhov? You reveal *yours* to me, if you can, but from me you will receive *mine*.

Peter Brook's *King Lear*

King Lear is probably known to almost everyone.[67] In addition, anyone you ask about it will say approximately the same thing. First, in the play there is an old king. To almost everyone, by the way, he is represented with a long gray beard, rather shaggy, and swept back, as though blown by the wind.

Such an image arises even for those who have never seen a performance of this play, however possibly there was an illustration in a book somewhere or something like that.

Rarely will someone give you his or her own original portrait of Lear. Most likely, almost everyone will remain to some extent a prisoner of habitual representations.

However, in Peter Brook's production, I have suddenly seen a different Lear. This was a person who was generally gray-haired, very strong, with short stiff hair and beard.

Even before the performance I have seen photographs and been amazed (and not only me) by how the habitual representation of Lear had been destroyed.

In addition, I must say that it was destroyed for the better, since even before these unexpected photographs, I had imagined this play not as an "old fairy tale," but as a thing completely alive, and it made me want to think about it anew.

However, all these issues are trifles, although they are so important in any art. If Paul Scofield had played Lear in the makeup of a traditional "Father Frost," maybe much of his new interpretation would have remained unnoticed.

...But now about the interpretation. Ask ten people once again, and nine will answer that Lear is a *king*, but a rather good old man, that among his daughters is one who is ideal and two who are bad. However, Lear does not believe the good daughter, since he believes *words*, and the good daughter is stingy with words. However, the two bad daughters are not stingy with flattery, and consequently from Lear they receive almost the entire kingdom. Only then, in misfortune, in unhappiness, Lear learns what goodness is and what is evil. While Lear is a king, he sees everything incorrectly, and he only learns the truth in poverty, but, unfortunately, too late.

All this is quite true, although to some degree it is also a *fairy tale*. Why is this fairy tale so seldom done in the theatre? Perhaps by virtue of its familiarity. Perhaps because recently no one has known how to mold from this fairy tale the fact that it is Shakespeare.

Different hairdos and beards, these after all are only details, but how to find the turning points of the entire story so that the audience watches once more with heartrending sadness, which they never do.

We presume that Brook has not read this play as I read it in school and afterward at the theatre institute. He saw in Lear the same evil as in those two awful daughters. Lear is hard, wild, his retinue is gangsters, and his daughters are all fiends. They are complex, like their father. In addition, as in him there are sharp mixtures of life's features in them. In addition, here before us is no longer the fairy tale with its familiar moral admonition. Not a simple old parable, but a complex thing, where evil and good are interwoven, and this interweaving has the texture of hard truth.

I should say that I was not one of those who went out of my mind with ecstasy about this *King Lear*. For me, the experience was something even stranger. A certain severity in the actors' adaptations prevented me from *feeling* what was happening. However, at the same time, an unprecedented charge of *interest* arose in me. I watched as if for the first time, as if I did not know this old *King Lear*. I wished to understand it anew, even to read the play again after the performance. I thought how uneasily life is constituted, that people have to grope for truth within such a complicated tangle.

For me, the production was a lesson, not of school, but of life.

Yet it is possible to find another solution for *King Lear*. Moreover, someone should find it, will find it. In addition, this will not be bad for the play, since a good play is like *life*: the knowledge in it is infinite.

On Being Understood

Maybe there are people who fall in love and immediately become loved themselves. Are there any happy couples who have not experienced the tortures of unrequited love? He saw a young woman once, he liked her, he explained to her that he was in love, and she explained that she loves him; they were married, and lived happily. No one denies, however, that there are contrary examples when not everything happens so smoothly. There are so many gradations of unpleasantness in love, from simple misunderstandings, which are not easily resolved, to tragedy, as when a person like Werther does not find a response to his love and takes his own life.[68]

It is the same in creative work. To be more precise, in the mutual relations of creative people and those who surround them. So few manage to attain recognition. So many people write plays, novels, stories, paint pictures, act on stage, direct productions, appear in films, while understanding that few people know them and fewer still like them. The drama of a person in love, however, is always proportional to the energy expended. When Werther killed himself, this extreme point of desperation was the consequence of the irresponsibility of his *infinite* feeling. *Everything* was concentrated in his love, all that he possessed, all that formed his "I." The absence of a response that was so necessary for him was tantamount to death. His gunshot was not an exaggeration, but a natural reaction to denial, to dislike for everything he is. When some good-for-nothing develops an enthusiasm for someone in passing and does not receive a response, then the extent of the desperation will be very little, for this desperation directly depends on the extent of the expenditure. A good-for-nothing does not shoot himself from unrequited love, and if he would suddenly shoot himself, it would either be a consequence of ridiculous exaggeration or else we simply would not understand this good-for-nothing and the infinite degree of feeling that was hidden so skillfully in him.

Sufferings are also relative in creative work. Obviously, an artist can be disturbed by the absence of appreciation for his work—depending on the richness of his personal nature, of course, and how much he of himself invests in his work.

Therefore, I think that people who suffer possess both self-criticism and intelligence, and they know that they invest themselves in their creative work without rest, and that their boundless giving of themselves is *not a myth.*

There are quite a lot of Werthers in art as there are in love, but not many, and forgive me for this ridiculous comparison, but I am excited by Van Gogh as much as Goethe was excited by Werther. This unfortunate sufferer in the field of creative work, this lover silently in love with art, did not receive in his lifetime that strong "love" which he could count on. Picasso and Chagall were happy; however, poor, poor Van Gogh! There is a legend, though it is certainly not groundless however, that an artist is happy simply because he *paints,* and if he does not receive any recognition, then he does not have anything to compare his modest unnoticed existence with. This might be so, perhaps, but all the same, Van Gogh certainly suffered. It is possible to do a performance or maybe a film where the opening shows what Gauguin thought about the day that unhappy Van Gogh wounded himself. Then to announce that the same situation will be shown again, not with Gauguin, but with Van Gogh. In addition, to repeat the same day, minute by minute, only as it was spent by Van Gogh—until he killed himself.

Then, over a solemn and very spirited march, to show a perfectly magnificent city, a beautiful museum, and a crowd. Students and old people, in the rain, under umbrellas, happy, noisy, standing in line to see the portrait of Van Gogh with his ear cut off. Nowadays this [event] takes the shape of a holiday, however when I went and saw this portrait I gasped, not from seeing it for the first time, but because there were so many people around it, and everyone was staring, and he, dying so awfully, was not aware of it.

Then [in this fictitious film] it is necessary to return to that earlier time to show how Van Gogh, taking food to eat with difficulty, learns whether Gauguin is living, how he is living, and if he's happy.

In addition, Gauguin, dying in his shack, devil knows where, learns about Van Gogh.

However, it happens that Chagall is probably happy, knowing that the world understood him, that he is loved.

Now Chagall has gotten used to praises, but how beautiful the day must have been when he recognized for the first time that his completely strange world was *understood*. Was this a happy day or not? Did he recognize that he was understood, or was he excited about something else and only recognized this later on? Bulgakov learned nothing of such a day for himself. He did not learn that some young boy from his grandson's generation would draw pictures from *The Master and Margarita* and hang them on the walls of his room.[69]

Othello

Othello stands embracing his wife. Iago is walking around. Othello suddenly turns to him as if he heard something, though it was impossible to hear what it was. Iago stands frozen in fear.

Everyone is tensely silent for a moment, as though something has suddenly been unveiled.

Othello looks at Iago, and it seems as though he recognizes the secret that lives inside him. Immediately. He looks around and watches, then unexpectedly and *sharply* orders Iago to carry his things.

However, another approach is also possible. Iago, looking at the Moor and Desdemona standing next to him, whispers sufficiently loudly that he wants them both dead. However, Othello, intoxicated with happiness from the meeting with his wife, passes his love on to Iago. Detaching himself from Desdemona for a moment, he *affectionately* asks his aide to carry the chests. Then once again, he kisses his wife. In this contrast of two conditions, there is meaning as well. It is necessary to test this variant and others.

Speaking Shakespeare

What careless speech actors have now. They speak almost inaudibly.

"What tidings can you tell me of my lord?" Desdemona asks Cassio.

"He is not yet arrived; nor know I aught / But that he's well and will be shortly here," Cassio replies to her.

To say this (or something else), it is necessary to possess a certain professional will. It is necessary to have the skill to express both this question and this reply. It is necessary to find in oneself a special energy *to ask* and *to respond* to this. Neither what is important or nor what is less important can be spoken incidentally. Moreover, the issue is not only in the speech. It is necessary to involve one's entire physiology. This question and this reply must be *accomplished*.

These lines (like all the rest, however) must be *found*, as they were found by Shakespeare himself or Boris Pasternak, when he searched for the words in his translation. Question or reply needs to be *cast* in both the physiology and the speech, as they cast an object in bronze.

> —What tidings can you tell me of my lord?
> —He is not yet arrived; nor know I aught
> But that he's well and will be shortly here.

This not only a matter of diction. It is in the meaning of the entire body. In the orientation of all the energy.

Othello

Othello must be made a "quiet" play, without the actors' anguish, without scenic effects. Nowadays they often mistake noise for modernity.

It is necessary to find a *normal* form for this, so to speak, extravagant "foreign" story. To derive simple and intelligible sense from it.

To deprive this play of its habitual scenic locale. They say that Shakespeare should have impressive settings. However, how many settings does this play need? It is necessary to concentrate its contents.

In addition, not to obscure its simple and intelligible subject with pseudo-tragic acting or with pseudo-theatrical intensity. It is necessary to withhold false passion and false fantasy so that they do not obscure the *clarity*.

That is it—it should be as obvious as the *back of your hand*

Recognizable and Very Intelligible

Today, after the evening rehearsal, I have come to watch a moment of one of the classical performances [at another theatre].

People were conversing on stage. Everything was happening in twilight. In addition, there was a riddle—what is all this for?

Then I thought there would be a place when and where everything becomes clear. However, why is it necessary to sit and wait so long for this clarity? What are we to look at in the meantime? A lot of it is hard to decipher, murky, unrecognizable. However, it is necessary to be light, both recognizable and very intelligible. So that at any moment you could walk into the auditorium and be caught unaware by the clarity. Even the secrets should be clear, and that, as they say, is the secret.

Moreover, the [scenic] form must not be banal. So that all the combinations would be exact. So that this actor, for example, expresses his love exactly in this place instead of that, so that it could not be both here and there, or anywhere you like. So that everything has been found, so that everything has been finished. Then, possibly, the meaning has a chance to succeed in the theatre. Otherwise, it is shameful and somewhat miserable. It is necessary for it to be art. In addition, not simply a craftsman-like hand-me-down thing. It is necessary to have the opportunity to be proud of your work and know that others also appreciate its uniqueness.

Moreover, it is necessary to be afraid to fall into that group of creators of shows that people come to watch accidentally, without hoping to see you, but simply because they had nothing to do on an empty evening.

We are always on the verge of this horror. So many of us work in this hole. Although there will always be those who boast about it. You should know yourself where this hole is and what it consists of. Oh, how many productions, films, and books are found in this hole! Many more than are found *outside of it!* The ability to discipline yourself and think everything through to the very end—this is the rescue from the hole. However, for many this hole is pleasant, since they do not know any other. Moreover, there they sit importantly with their craftsmanship.

Innovation and Craftsmanship

Last evening I was filming *Dear Liar* for television, and the next morning I looked at my own *Othello*.[70]

Involuntarily, comparisons occur. The first impression from the television filming consisted of the fact that the actors were reciting. To my surprise, it seemed like the MAT style had gradually turned into something like a style of Romanticism.

In the past, MAT struggled against the "recitation" style of the Maly Theatre. MAT brought theatre closer to the normal life of simple people. Nevertheless, many years have passed, and either life has become simpler or the actor is forgetting about life somewhat and slipping into a certain abstract tone.

In the initial filmings, I heard the pathos, but I could not always understand what the speeches were about.

Dear Liar was not my production, and I only wanted to film it successfully. However, for a long time I could not get used to the style of the acting. I went home and once more headed for the text. The text excited me, but the pathos of the actors defeated all the clarity and simplicity of familiar text. Mentally, I inevitably substituted our own actors [in the roles] and heard once more the power of living nuances. In addition, I thought what a shame it that I could not produce *Dear Liar* myself, to work with my own actors once again.

Therefore, my two works went on in parallel—*Othello* in the theatre and the filming of someone else's production at Ostankino television studio.

Sometime later, however, I began to become irritated when listening to the "simple" speech and seeing the "simple" acting of our own theatre's actors. It should be livelier than the "others" are, but why does it have to be so indistinct, so *trite*? Why is it so *weak willed?*

Anatoly Ktorov is in acting the film, and he is already seventy-eight![71] Today they informed me that while making up he said he felt poorly.

"That means there will be no filming today," I concluded.

"No, why of course there will. He simply said he was tired, and he didn't say anything about cancelling the filming."

All the same, I waited for his appearance in the studio with apprehension. Ktorov arrived a minute after ten in a snow-white shirt, wearing a beautifully fitting suit. He was collected and cheerful, though he had spent the whole day at the hospital where they had operated on his wife. No trace of complaining. So neat, sociable, at ease, and his day had been awful. Observing him, I secretly admired him. However, the issue was not only this, of course. It was that I too, perhaps, had grown accustomed to his "recitation." Moreover, I even felt a certain charm in his precise speech in contrast to our present-day careless speech.

In due course, I even began to distinguish its laws and its truth.

He read a monologue eight pages long about the death of Shaw's mother. All around him, as usual in a film, were many unnecessary people. Someone reading and rustling a newspaper. Young men playing dice with great feeling at the equipment nearby. Someone said something noisily, disrespecting Shaw, his mother, and Ktorov. In addition, all this was going on right beside the actor, who was preparing the monologue. This always happens in the cinema, unfortunately, but not every actor is capable of *rising above* these nauseating conditions and absolutely *getting ready*.

There is a [type of] dignified status, and an actor always remembers it, but often he has to struggle pitifully to maintain it.

However, Ktorov has this status—*naturally*.

He does not need to remember it, it *is*. He stands and laughs together with everyone or recounts something funny, and right there and then in the shot, with grief ringing in his voice, he raps out the words of the text, instinctively *dismissing* us and *towering* over us.

In the old school tradition, there is an inexplicable charm. Moreover, it is a pity that we have forgotten about it in our involuntary love for what is super-new.

I arrived at *Othello* and wanted our actor Nikolai Volkov to know a little of that skill how "to recite."[72] So that, like Ktorov, he would get hold of the text, analyze it, and *deliver* it to us. So that, like Ktorov, he would economize his *movements*.

No bustling about. Moreover, no waving of the hands if it is not necessary. Then, when watching him, I would become *concentrated*.

If only he would hold onto the plan for one hundred successive performances, not mumbling, retaining vivid actorly colors, intelligible, capable of reaching the last row.

Othello has certain lines that are addressed to Iago: "Order your wife to *follow* behind Desdemona."

The considerate Moor, then suddenly, *"...follow her!"* All the horror of transformation is present in that. However, I do not hear this word, although I ask him a hundred times to pronounce it with more clarity. "Worldly" [style] is turned into sloppiness. He stands, hands in his pockets, absent minded. Meanwhile, this actor is good, subtle, and fine. However, this "modern manner" simply spoiled him. I devised it myself, by the way, and insisted on it myself. However, everything has a limit!

Yes, it is necessary to feel modern, to think modern, and to be fully armed with modern means. However, to be *scarcely audible* also means to be unmodern.

There is a time for everything. When you begin and make your way toward something new, then you are still a sort of child. When you conquer something as an *adult*, then it must be done *masterfully*.

That is when your new searches bear fruit. However, it is as if we begin at age twenty-five and [continue to] trumpet schoolboy nihilism until old age.

Innovation and craftsmanship (novelty and skill) should live together in friendship.

Othello

There is logic in everything Iago says, but he does not attach much significance to it himself. The need to do something evil is a "matter of the heart." Moreover, logic is used for coordinating this experience with reason.

To him it is bad that he only plays a scanty role in this world, to him it is bad that his wife could prefer someone else; to him it is bad that Desdemona belongs to Othello; that he is not the lieutenant, but Cassio is...

When he considers something, it should be not simply interesting, but *deeply intelligible*. Moreover, even, in a sense, (Oh, horrors!) we should empathize with him. Empathy, of course, is not the same as consent. However, if there is no empathy, then disagreement becomes limited.

Isn't the disagreement really the general point here? It is so obvious with a single look at Iago. The real point is knowledge; it is desirable to be *shocked from the knowledge* of such a phenomenon as Iago.

Internalized Truths

Almost from childhood, we internalize a great number of truths. For example, Shakespeare is a genius. Even if you do not enjoy reading any of his plays, you blame yourself, your upbringing, and not Shakespeare, since they have told you for a long time that he is a genius.

Incidentally, not everyone holds this opinion of Shakespeare. To say nothing of his contemporaries. There were many who believed someone else may have written wrote his plays, not Shakespeare. And later on, even Tolstoy was among the opponents of Shakespeare. However, Tolstoy probably had his own reasons. His religious faith, his system of opinions.

I am saying all this only because people who have read something, seen, heard something, usually have their own attachments, their own truths, their own idols. They have their own laws. We take it for granted, for example, that *internal action* is important in psychological acting. Isn't this really a perfect truth? There are a number of actors and directors, however, who know this truth and even believe in it, but do not do it *in practice*, even on into old age.

Something in our nature prevents us from internalizing *in our own life* those truths that even seem correct to us. Teachers tell their students in theatre school that it is necessary to know how to work with actors. However, often they are unable to work with actors themselves, they only know that it is *necessary* to be able to do so. Moreover, their students leave with the same *inabilities.*

In each truth there should be not only an intellectual but also, probably, a biological predisposition. I do not know what science would say in this situation. However, whatever it would say, I think a biological predisposition exists. It may be of little importance in itself, but the rest [of the work] the person does in a conscious or at least semiconscious process.

Maybe it seemed that Anton Chekhov's siblings were more talented than he was. In any case, one of them had big hopes. However, what a difference there was between *them* and Chekhov *himself.* Really, didn't the truths that Chekhov wrote about to his two siblings soar above them both? The personality of one [sibling] internalized these truths, changing himself because of them, while the nature of the other [sibling] rejected these truths just as well known to her. What is it? Biological or conscious? Or is it semiconscious? Of course, your own consciousness will concentrate precisely on *those* truths that are dear to you, and the *refinement* of your nature goes on under their influence. Yes, refinement, daily refinement. Chekhov squeezed the slave out of himself one drop at a time, just as someone should squeeze the dilettante out of himself, the ignoramus, the pedant, and finally the entire slave, one drop at a time.

However, each person, and especially a director, has so many external difficulties [to deal with] that he has no time to think about the internal ones. It is possible to think, but not to concentrate. In addition, where there is no concentration, there is no refinement to speak of. Therefore, the actor and director live for themselves, possibly knowing that 2x2=4, but not really knowing how to count. They know that there is such a thing as artistic ethics, but meanwhile they often live and work like very coarse people. They know that it is unacceptable to *pretend* and that it is necessary to "live through" the life of the character on stage, but on into old age they [continue to] *pretend.* That is why it is one matter to know something, and another to make it [part of] your nature.

Othello

My son is the designer for our production of *Othello.*[73] We make a model in white, then in black, we do less, we discard, we do more, and so on endlessly. When you work, let us say, with Bolshoi designer Valery Leventhal, you do not see the process. You come once a week to his workshop, you talk for half an hour, but you do not know what is created in between. However, here at home you work around the clock.

We know that there should be bench for the characters to sit on. Nevertheless, it is not easy to find *what sort of* bench. We thumb through a set of books to start from *life*, then to compose it.

Now we have finally found it! A cardboard model stands quietly on the table until morning, and in the morning at dawn, we smash it all up. It must consist of *harsh military conditions,* without any of that nonsense you usually see with *Othello*. Even Othello's bed should be "semi-soldierly."

Arriving in Cyprus, they are so tired that Desdemona immediately goes to bed, and Othello noiselessly settles in beside her. They fall asleep without getting undressed. Moreover, not far away, Iago gets the officers drunk. Let us see both of these [events] *together.*

Magnificent arches and magnificent curtains were even used by Laurence Olivier.[74] However, what for? The *scenic style of Hamlet* has been known for a long time. However, what is *Othello's* scenic style? True, *Hamlet's* "castle-ness" has also been a nuisance for a long time. That is why Yuri Lyubimov with David Borovsky came up with their woven curtain.[75] I remember one time at a lecture on Shakespeare, Mikhail Morozov maintained that Shakespeare is "woolen."[76] And for twenty years afterward, Shakespeare has been designed *from wool.*

However, what does *Othello's* [scenic] style consist of? A certain military campaign, a soldierly way of life? Or something different? Venice, Cyprus... Cyprus is not the issue, for Cyprus is whatever we want it to be. The real issue is *military conditions.* Many people marching around, war, danger, and nerves. In addition, here, for some reason, the General has fallen in love, married secretly, and married the daughter of a Senator. Already at the outset, there is drama, contradiction. Not in harmony with the time, not in harmony with the circumstances. Not in harmony with tenderness...

At night, it was necessary to talk about love in the Senate, but all the time sailors are entering and reporting about the Turks. The Senators only half-listen about the love question because the other thing is more important to them. Then in Cyprus, the beginning of the trouble with Cassio, and next morning the impact of the awful news about his wife. Moreover, Othello will not find out properly because of his position, and the people around him, and somewhere in his consciousness is the idea that he is unworthy of the good himself.

Black! And old! A military campaigner, the fleeting nature of happiness, the normalcy of people like Iago, and your "abnormality."

> —Farewell the plumed troops and the big wars
> That make ambition virtue. O, farewell!
> Farewell the neighing steed and the shrill trump
> The spirit-stirring drum, th' ear-piercing fife,
> The royal banner, and all quality,
> Pride, pomp, and circumstance of glorious war!
> Farewell! Othello's occupation's gone!

When a director worries about something constantly, then this something changes, alternates, and is never established conclusively in any way.

It seems like everything has already been *thought out,* everything is clear. Then two weeks go by, and you feel it is finished at last. However, far from it. In ten days, once more you encounter a completely new idea.

In the beginning, you started from a simple idea that came into your head. Next, you understood, studied, but suddenly you notice that this simple idea has gone. Yet that idea was really what was most valuable. The idea was to set forth, very graphically and simply, the mechanics of an intrigue against a person like Othello. To say very simply "how it is done." To try not to lapse into habitual "Shakespeare-ness." After all, we have very rarely produced intimate, familiar Shakespearean performances, plainly understood and plainly felt. Everything always becomes a little elevated, as I have already said more than once, like a passionate fairy tale, which is already too naive for a modern person. The cumbersome, theatrically fantastic Shakespearean productions of earlier times, however, have almost vanished.

When you recollect some of these earlier productions, they definitely seem insufficiently serious from a present-day point of view, not only because of the archaic form but also from the general concept.

I have heard the recording of *Othello* by the well-known actor Alexander Ostuzhev many times, of course, and was impressed by his acting.[77] In addition, I have also seen the performance of the great Georgian actor Akaky Khorova three times, and I saw other good performances.[78] Such tragic actors do not exist any longer. However, there is probably a time for everything. No more tragedies, but other plays have arisen to take their place, plays in which *thematic structure* is perhaps more important than tragic emotions.

It is not easy, however, to pack all the formidability of a Shakespearean play into a small, compact, present-day performance so that nothing is missed; moreover, to handle all this [apparent] incoherence, this chaos, behind which any serious philosophy is seldom detected.

To preserve all this excitement, but at the same time to present everything quietly and clearly, so that nobody has any doubts about what it is and why.

Naturally, you want to make the actors play with spirit from the very beginning, and to interweave the action in a Shakespearean manner.

In addition, *a very clear idea,* not clouded by anything.

Here they sit, all these characters. Everyone has his own life, troubles, and joys, but, in general, one aspiration unites everyone toward a peaceful life, love, happiness, etc. And a person and his friend separate themselves from these characters, and they look at all the other people, and especially the one in the center, with the malice and envy of oppressed mediocrities. It is understood, however, that they are not aware of their own inferiority. Their self-defense even has certain "principles." To them it seems they have completely valid reasons not to love Othello. These valid reasons are formulated by them. Then the intrigue begins. In addition, we see all the threads of this intrigue, and we see who falls into it.

Of course, Shakespeare is spirited, but if a spirited actor does not have enough stillness and deep content, perhaps it is still not Shakespeare.

To obtain the General's pardon through Desdemona for yesterday's drinking, Iago instructed Cassio to seek help from her.

Now Iago catches sight of Cassio departing from Desdemona, and he starts to operate.

He characterizes the event this way: his General is a trusting and good person, a Christian. To be the genuine helper of such a superior means that Iago must develop vigilance, suspicion, a wholesome mistrust of everyone. Iago seems to dictate [the nature of] the relations between Othello and himself. You supposedly have important affairs, and I am only your bodyguard. You can be carefree in your personal manner, but my duty is precisely to protect your personal safety. I will not conceal, or conceal from you, certain suspicions if they concern your safety.

Moreover, here, not concealing anything, but speaking fairly, directly, and sharply, Iago immediately starts to speak to Othello about his uneasiness regarding this sudden appearance of Cassio.

All the time, however, Iago insists that maybe he is too distrustful; he even stops himself, as though he knows that his own excessive suspiciousness is behind this.

Othello hardly understands what the issue is. Possibly, he thinks that Iago is worried that Cassio went to Desdemona to ask for help about yesterday's drunkenness. Othello is even pleased about this visit. It means his lieutenant has a guilty conscience, that he cannot live without a pardon. In addition, Othello, of course, will pardon him.

However, it seems that Iago is not concerned about this, but something else. Othello does not have time to be instructed in detail. He becomes angry and asks Iago to express himself more clearly. Some kind of [political] conspiracy perhaps? The General is worried about his wife least of all. Today is the first morning after their marriage! He waits while Iago says something about the Turks, about the island, about the guards. Moreover, suddenly Iago says that it is necessary to beware of jealousy.

Othello is not the kind of person to allow his aide to worm his way into his soul.

A [political] conspiracy would be a different matter. However, to get into the relations between a husband and his wife—this is too much. It is impossible to allow this. At the same time, Iago [secretly] thinks Othello must be some kind of savage indeed, if he can be jealous of Cassio. This must be the last time, says Othello. I am not that kind of [jealous] person, and I will not allow a stranger to discuss such affairs!

Angered, Othello leaves. Iago remains alone. He waits a minute, and after Othello leaves, he says that if that is true, if Othello is not the kind of person to be afraid of his wife's fidelity, then Iago will allow himself to be more open.

Now, unafraid to offend or upset, Iago only seems to be concerned with the matter at hand, that is, the safety of the General. Therefore, Iago will disclose the truth: Desdemona is *cunning*, and she is having an *affair* with Cassio!

Let the General be angry with Iago, let him even chase Iago away, but the truth must be told.

Iago serves up precisely this "truth" to Othello, now let the General himself decide what to do.

For a time, it is not clear whether Othello hears this.

Then the General enters very quietly, goes to his aide and looks him in the eyes for a long time. So long, that everything freezes...

Moreover, to our horror, it suddenly becomes clear that *he believes!*

More accurately, he gives Iago the right *to get involved in this*! Furthermore, Othello recognizes that for his aide to become involved, he has *admitted* it to himself!

Othello recognizes this because he is *black*. Because he is a stranger among them. He recognizes it not only now but also *for some time* before, when he believed he was unworthy of Desdemona. In fact, this idea was probably hammered into his head since childhood.

Oh, these terrible early prejudices!

Work Relations

During a filming, a certain cameraman mistreated his assistant. Mocked, abused, and humiliated him. Some people have this habit, no respect for their subordinates. I do not know why, whether it is from nervousness, a bad temper, or bad manners. This particular assistant was tall and stout, not so young. Moreover, very polite. This politeness and thoughtfulness also exasperated the cameraman. Once, when the work was especially tense and the cameraman could not manage to slip out to the buffet, the assistant left for a minute and returned shortly afterward with a slice of bread and two boiled eggs on a plate. Cautiously, he put the plate down near the cameraman so that he could have a little refreshment. The cameraman was dissatisfied with something in his work, he could not achieve some effect, he was especially irritated, and this kindness of the assistant for some reason only enraged him. Continuing to work on something, he casually glanced at the plate and just as casually threw one of the eggs behind him and the other at the wall.

All of us were stunned, and, to my shame, I was also stunned—I was young then and frightened of the cameraman myself. The assistant stood still for a minute, and then went behind the scenery and stayed there a long time. Everyone was stunned for some time, and then the work carried on.

I recall all this in connection with the way Cassio speaks. He says there are souls that can be saved and souls that cannot be saved. I simply want to say, however, that there are people with whom it is pleasant to work. Then there are those with whom it is not pleasant. To be amiable at work is a great skill indeed. What can be written about those who do not have this skill? The majority of sales clerks do not have it. A young woman stands there just waiting, and she is unpleasant. She does not see you, does not hear you, but this is not so serious for you. You wait for a minute and then walk out. However, what if you had to work for seven hours straight with this co-worker at your side? His look is absent, he is proud, lazy, despotic, and so forth.

In an equipment room on television, where certain stages of work proceed on tape, a young woman, a sound operator, or so it seems she is called, sat all day reading a book, never pulling herself away from it, and looking neither at the tape recorder nor at the television screen where the scenes of our video were rolling. She simply put her hand to the button and pressed it when she was ordered. When she left the room for five minutes, I quickly looked at her book: it was a trifle, insignificant. Meanwhile, the music she was cuing was beautiful, and our scenes had some meaning. However, to this young woman we had all become as annoying, probably, as every one of the shoppers to the previously mentioned salesgirl. She wanted to fence herself off from all of us, to hide in her own world and concentrate on herself. One can understand her, but it would not be pleasant to work with her, for after all, this work continues the entire day. Next day, another young woman arrived, almost the same as the first, equally young and pretty, but she worked in an entirely different way. She quickly brushed aside those who had no direct connection with her work, and began to live actively within the framework of her specialty, actively cooperating with us. By contrast, with the previous day, I could not help but admire the dexterity and elegance of her work. It was remarkable, and I was afraid that tomorrow the first young woman would return.

I observed the same thing while working in radio. The young woman who adjusted the controls never sat with us the entire time, but in the corridor. She smoked, visited the lunchroom, or simply looked on indifferently. We did not interest her, however, since she was not interesting to us. We soon understood how to work around her since the others knew her job pretty well, although they had their own responsibilities. But how these others worked! They loved those reels of tape, and they loaded the machine with such skill. Thus, they really *heard* the broadcast, understood it, and participated in its creation. Working quickly, they always managed to joke, they had their own manner of verbal communication, their own jargon, but it was pleasant to listen to all this. During the entire period of work, I never heard anything that would spoil the atmosphere. For us, everything was cheerful, and the work *moved along*. I have many things to do during the day. After rehearsal, I have to hurry off somewhere, to another theatre, radio, or television. Rehearsal at the theatre is always very important to me, but during these "radio days," I caught myself thinking that I would rather be there. And when this work was finished, I was sorry to leave.

Generally, a certain type of effort probably is necessary for that sort of *communication* to happen. Working without genuine relationships is like a human being without air. And for me, there is nothing better than *work relations* are. The rest is good too, but it is not the same thing.

When you see how beautifully and easily a person works, perhaps nothing can be compared with it. Once, in Prague, I saw a waiter who handled his trays and plates so skillfully that we wanted to applaud. He did not do this, however, for the applause. He found pleasure in it for himself. Both in the way he carried the tray, and in how he associated with us.

However, sometimes it seems that the waiter hates you. Moreover, in response, you hate him, too.

Consistency

I recently read a review about two Moscow performances. In the beginning, the critic pointed out the merits of one work, and then he noted the deficiencies. He did the same with the second performance. Merits and deficiencies. In addition, when the time came to sum up, the critic wrote that each theatre chose a different method, but both methods were entirely justified. However, at that juncture he unexpectedly concluded that it is necessary to be consistent! I read the article again and thought that his appeal to consistency does not follow logically from his preceding [review]. He would have had the same success arguing that the women in these performances should learn to act better than the men, or vice versa. Until the end of the review, there was nothing about inconsistency, even in an implied sense. It was simply an analysis of what was *good* and what was *bad*. Not even an analysis, but a statement of merits and deficiencies. Perhaps by consistency he meant that it was necessary to act well from all the way through. In that case, it was fine advice.

Apparently, it is not so easy to be consistent even in a brief review, that is, to follow one line [of argument] from beginning to end. After all, it is possible to read this article in four minutes. In addition, it is easier to connect a brief review end to end than to do so with a huge performance.

The critic, of course, would say that his review was spoiled by the editor, that the ending was originally different, that he wrote three times more about one actor than what was left, that the original title was much better, that in certain paragraphs one had to read not the words but the sense hidden behind the text. The critic wanted everything to be intelligible, as though he depended on your co-authorship while you read his article.

All the same, why did he write so carelessly, why such trite phrases, why is there no consistent viewpoint, and everything so incomplete, incomplete, incomplete? Because it is *difficult*. Because it is almost as difficult to write even a good brief article, perhaps, as to make a good performance. *Almost...*

A Light Approach to the Classics

A long time ago, Peter Brook's production of *Hamlet* was performed at MAT.[79] I remember the mixed reactions. According to public opinion, this production was in some ways fine, of course, but also perhaps too dry, peculiar. We have gotten used to acting and producing Shakespeare another way. More loudly, brightly, tragically. And lengthier. First, his production was not long, and second, it was somehow without unnecessary noise, without noisy tragic flights and noisy tragic descents. In our [Russian] Shakespearean productions, we had excellent stars, even though alongside them were some awful actors in the supporting roles. However, here, in Brook's, there was none of those difficulties, because of the general tone of restraint, or maybe because there was more consistency. Hamlet was not played by just anybody, of course, but by Paul Scofield, yet it cannot be said that this production was built around him. His role was one fine part of a very good whole. It was very studied and business-like. Moreover, *light*, and this lightness in connection with Shakespeare was, for me anyway, new. Nothing was cluttered up; nothing obscured the simple flow of the sense. The sense, it seems to me, was that it was not just any old story, but absolutely new; furthermore, it was relevant to us, which is no small accomplishment. When the first posters and photographs in the windows along Gorky Street indicated the arrival of the English company, the passers-by scrutinized the face of this Hamlet for a long time. Actually, the appeal consisted of the fact that he was a modern actor and not made up *as someone else*. There was no traditional Hamlet wig on his head, and his costume seemed without any sort of pretension. If truth were told, sometimes even modern productions manage to appear old-fashioned. They obtain the wigs and makeup from one trunk. From another trunk, they "extract" some style or other to photograph or be photographed. However, the "calling card" of *this* Hamlet was simple: a young man who is entirely connected to the modern world will arrive. A performance will arrive that was not pulled out of a trunk, but which exists now, composed now. Apart from this utterly undemonstrative, quiet, and completely modern manner, however, nothing else in it carried me away. It could be that I was too young and did not understand something at the time. We were not captivated by any sort of special concept in this *Hamlet* except the intelligible simplicity of its scenic style. In addition, the easy scene changes and rapid development of the action. All this was important to an extraordinary degree. All this was unfamiliar and beguiling, though the feeling of a certain deficiency left that mixed impression that I began this story with. Nevertheless, (and I was working at the Central Children's Theatre at the time) I arrived at my next rehearsal utterly confident that it was necessary to master the experience I had learned the previous night.

Pushkin's *Boris Godunov* [which I was directing at the time] has never really been successful in the theatre.[80] Mainly because of all this superfluous stuff, from being pulled "out of the trunk" largely. If only I could develop it lightly and actively, without any superfluous accessories.

Hamlet is easier to produce than *Boris Godunov is*. The history of *Boris Godunov* does not have as many successful interpretations as Shakespeare's plays have. Consequently, there is no historical experience it would be helpful to draw from. Moreover, this play is less active and theatrical than *Hamlet*. Yet, to produce Shakespeare right after Brook would be ridiculous. However, *Boris Godunov*, perhaps, would be suited for such an experiment.

Master a new lightness for an old and very complex play. Make a simple plot, a simple story intelligible; reject this dull old "boyar" play.[81] Make the performance modern, with rapid scene changes, so that the logic is not lost during any long changeovers. All this, strangely enough, was quite new. Moreover, it did not come easily; it involved a number of professional conflicts. Although the remarkable experience of MAT's *Tsar Fyodor Ivanovich* already belonged to history, everyone still spoke slowly and solemnly in such historical plays, read rather than acted, moved little, either sparing their energies or not knowing that a very different style exists in the world now.[82] It was not so easy to get those boyars to move quickly from one end of the stage to the other or to express a certain meaning, despite the verse, in rapid clear speech. To cope with all those old mannerisms, and what is more with a young director, was difficult enough.

I said there was no particular meaning to be drawn from Brook's *Hamlet*. However, there were new means. In my *Boris Godunov*, there was no new meaning at all, and the new means appeared only slightly, though the strong old means remained. Children still watched this complex play with difficulty, but all the same with less difficulty than in the past.

Fifteen years later, I directed *Boris Godunov* once again, only on television.

Now I was more mature and had some experience behind me directing classical plays. I had not worked in television before, however, and even looked at it rather ironically. Television had now become *the thing,* whereas before this actors only worked there to earn a little extra money; that is all. Some time ago, I also decided to work there on the side once, but cursed the entire experience and did not do it any more. However, *Boris Godunov* not only offered earnings but much artistic interest! I went into the darkened studio and started to dream. First, I rejected the idea of big scenery, palaces, churches, onion domes, and so forth. In fact, the idea of a *simple* performance could really be improved here. *A flow of clear meaning* instead of a heavy trunk-load of pseudo-historical junk.

This meaning, however, needed to be understood better. Although it is quite simple, this meaning. Boris has ordered the murder of the young [heir to the throne] Dmitri, so that nothing will prevent him from ascending the throne himself. In addition, at this point, pretending that he is reluctant to rule, Boris all the same ascends the throne.

Everyone knows, however, that he is a murderer.

Moreover, he knows that everyone knows.

Earlier, he thought that he would get over this. He is not the first to murder, nor is he the last.

However, something *special* happened to him.

They did not forgive him for the murder, and he was tormented by this murder of Dmitri himself. Sensing the weakness of the government, now *another* contender [Gregory] appears who opposes the murderer of young Dmitri. In addition, since the idea of a struggle with a murderer is suitably appealing, this other person had [public] support. Gregory was already close to victory, only one step remained, it was only necessary to kill Godunov's heirs. Therefore, he ordered them killed, and they were killed! Wait a minute; this person is also a *tyrant*? And this person is a murderer, too? And this person is covered with blood, too? Here is where the [theme of] confusion appears. This is the fairy tale about the [historical] "Time of Troubles" that Pushkin wrote about [in this play].[83] This is the *parable* about the imperial throne and blood. And about national confusion.

It is possible to do all this like an opera. We are so accustomed to the musical genre that we listen to someone's beautiful singing, and we look at how beautifully someone has designed the scenery, but we do not remember anything about the meaning, apparently.

The issue of *habit* is a complicated one in art. It both gladdens the soul and hampers the possibility of opening that same soul and apprehending something with genuine new force.

Something needed to be *condensed* in *Boris Godunov*, something needed to be done more modestly, so that the *meaning* ceased being modest and virtually buried beneath the overall grandiosity of the style. Instead of false imagination, it only needed the mind.

It seems that imagination is a sign of talent. *Often*, but not always.

Pushkin's "Tales of Belkin," for example, are short and allegedly dry.[84] Everything, however, depends on imagination there. Each word and each color is precious, as though made from pure gold. In addition, *Boris Godunov* is written according to this same principle, but we take this gold and treat it as if it were iron. We bend it and twist any way we want. Moreover, add more flourishes around it. In addition, the voices vibrate, the cheeks shine, the gestures are effective, and the costumes are made from brocade. But the meaning? The heck with that, with the simple meaning. It will be a show. Moreover, this is not only true in opera, but, as you see, even in drama.

This beautiful little jewel box [play] insisted that we put away the fantasy and calm down the over-heated imagination. It was good that there was no money for building the usual Kremlin palaces or the majestic steps of a cathedral.

It was good that it was limited by the budget to only three or four extras in the roles of Boyars, Poles, Germans, and Russian soldiers. It was good that there were such limited possibilities!

In Pushkin's third act, apparently, three peasants say that people are clinging to the domes of the churches [to catch sight of the Tsar], and in the movie they hurry to show us these onion domes. However, Pushkin has only *three peasants* who merely speak about that event. And what verses they speak!

Perhaps a movie could show all this satisfactorily. After all, Eisenstein made a movie about *Ivan the Terrible*.[85] However, I was not impressed with it, not impressed... I do not know why. For me, it is necessary to be a hundred times simpler in such cases, and subtler, and more accurate.

Othello

A car races across rugged cross-country terrain with unbelievable speed. The driver handles the car well and enjoys driving fast. All the turns on the way, the holes, and the bumps entertain him. Beside him sits the passenger, trying to appear as though he enjoyed it, too. But in his behavior, there is a hidden meaning. He got into the car to tell the person behind the wheel some unpleasant news. It was necessary for his friend the driver to figure out for himself, however, what the news was about. Therefore, the passenger conducted the conversation in broad terms, yet close to the *subject.* The driver, enthusiastic about driving, listens but does not hear. The words of his passenger were just a *general* conversation that could continue only insofar as it did not disturb his driving. The driver even gets angry when the chatter is not about the road but about something else. However, the one who has the secret purpose continues to carry out his own line, since he knows that eventually the driver will hear the *secret meaning.* Finally, the driver hears it. He has ceased to be interested in his driving, quieted down, gradually reduced his speed, and at last come to a stop. After a long silence, the driver said to his neighbor, "Ah, so that is what you are getting at." Then they drove on in silence.

This is almost the same design as Othello's conversation with Iago, when the latter decides to slander Desdemona.

Going from the text, however, it is possible to find a different solution. A classical text is roomy enough. There is much here that can vary from the general interpretation.

An interpretation can be *fabricated,* of course, but it is also possible to *extract it from the play.* Obviously, a subjective factor remains all the same. However, it will be strongly mixed with the material itself. This mixture should be explosive. Logic alone will produce nothing here.

Very much is prompted by intuition. It is possible, however, to analyze everything when it is necessary to do so, and with the aid of the mind. Only not by cold logic. After all, the mind is different [from ordinary common sense].

Othello is intrigued by Iago's innuendoes and demands a precise explanation. This type of beginning, however, is purely *literary.*

Othello is well known enough from a literary point of view. Why retell it, even with different scenery; why retell everything that is already familiar to every cultured person? Theatre should be built on something different. It is necessary to read not what is written in the text, but what is revealed behind the text. In addition, taking into account the need for sharp action. Not merely conversation, even very interesting conversation, but sharp action, which is not only interesting at the moment it occurs, but also contains the possibility of *sharp development.*

Furthermore, using more than the simple plot introduced in the play itself.

Therefore, at this moment Othello should be unprepared for what Iago tells him. His behavior should contradict a direct perception of the news. Of course, Othello is not sitting in an automobile like the driver of the car. He is deeply engrossed in something, however, for he even asks Desdemona to withdraw.

Let us say you are preparing for a complex rehearsal. Before you lay the text of the play, and you are considering something.

Othello has his own internal problems to deal with, whether he sits poring over the papers or simply paces back and forth across the stage without any papers. Desdemona's arrival has already distracted him from his work. Now Iago begins a conversation about his own worries.

All this interferes with Othello's concentration, and he actively rejects Iago's attempts to talk to him. This *rejection* in itself can carry a different feeling. That is, it is possible for Othello to agree and dispute with Iago, and to do each actively, but to concentrate his attention on something else.

Then the opportunity arises for a more interactive direction from Iago.

> IAGO. Ha! I like not that.
> OTHELLO. What dost thou say?
> IAGO. Nothing, my lord; or if — I know not what.
> OTHELLO. Was that not Cassio parted from my wife?
> IAGO. Cassio, my lord! No, sure, I cannot think it,
>   That he would steal away so guilty-like,
>   Seeing your coming.
> OTHELLO. I do believe 'twas he.

Even though, as I already said, the thought of future trouble sits deep in Othello's soul, at this particular moment nothing portends misfortune.

The fact that Cassio hurried by somewhere in the vicinity seems natural to Othello.

After all, a dismissed lieutenant certainly must ask for a pardon. Cassio, apparently, came to apologize.

Iago suggests a different motive for Cassio's appearance. In his opinion, if Cassio came to apologize, then he should have done so openly, fairly. The way he did it, through Desdemona, was not polite.

Iago *openly* expresses his attitude to this sort of appearance by Cassio. Iago plays off the fact that he always expresses his ideas openly, directly. However, here he cleverly subjects his own suspicions to doubt: Cassio probably would not have come here as a petty thief. Iago does not introduce this reservation casually, but frankly as well.

After all, he is watching over Othello's interests. The bad behavior of the former lieutenant is disagreeable to him; however, maybe it was somebody else, not Cassio.

Othello is undisturbed by this. He is busy with something else. Cassio does not arouse his anger any more. Othello is ready to forgive him. Cassio's visit to Desdemona for mediation, possibly, even pleases him.

> IAGO. My noble lord, –
> OTHELLO. What dost thou say, Iago?
> IAGO. Did Michael Cassio, when you woo'd my lady
>   Know of your love?

Iago continues to develop his plan to reveal some of his suspicions to Othello. As yet, however, there is not enough material. He must clarify many things that happened earlier, compare facts, etc.

Moreover, Iago must seem to act openly. He says candidly that he wishes to learn something that he needs to compare with something else.

Othello must not swallow the bait of his aide too quickly.

Iago conducts the conversation in hopes of arousing Othello's interest, but now he is not so much interested as he is angry that Iago speaks in such a roundabout manner.

Iago's secret thoughts have still not become clear to him. He does not want to understand it. He wants Iago not to distract him when he is busy.

However, Othello can become angry, as it were, cheerfully, since his affairs are going well for now. Possibly Iago's questions about Cassio even give him pleasure. He remembers the time when Cassio helped him.

> OTHELLO. [Is there] some monster in your thought
>   Too hideous to be shown. – Thou dost mean something.
>   I heard thee say even now, thou lik'st not that,
>   And when I told thee he was of my counsel
>   In my whole course of wooing, though criedst, "Indeed!"
>   And didst contract and purse thy brow together,
>   As if thou had shut up in thy brain
>   Some horrible conceit. If thou dost love me,
>   Show me thy thought.

It is not necessary to be led to *challenge* Iago. That would be petty. He does not challenge, he merely *objects to any sort of confused speeches*. Moreover, this is not a suitable moment for conducting such a conversation. Possibly, Othello even sneers ironically at his aide's pseudo-vigilance or is simply annoyed about it.

Therefore, Othello is not curious, but, on the contrary, he protests and ridicules Iago. It is necessary to calculate the development of this protest or ridicule so that the [actorly] colors are distributed well. True, Othello is busy with his own thoughts, but even if he only listened a little, the path of Iago's thinking would be unpleasant to him. He should not care for Iago's extreme diligence in protecting him. He does not like such comprehensive suspiciousness. That is why Othello *is not interested and rejects him.* Iago utilizes this experience as an even greater opportunity to speak frankly. Othello is not concerned with any thoughts about jealousy, which is why Iago can speak *completely openly.*

Now the moment arrives when Othello discovers the hidden meaning behind the ideas he has heard. Suddenly he understands what Iago wanted to explain. The issue is not jealousy. It is simply that in one second that tragic sensation revived in Othello's soul, that sensation of unavoidable misfortune. After all, the happiness that had come to him was not expected. It was difficult to believe in it. In his soul, in his consciousness, it always hung by a thread.

However, you cannot live every second with such thoughts. Life distracts. Now this thought returns *anew* with greater force.

> ...Yet 'tis the plague of great ones;
> Prerogativ'd are they less than the base.
> 'Tis destiny unshunnable, like death.

If no one ever challenged the suspicion rooted deep in Othello's consciousness, then there would be no need for revenge. However, Desdemona challenged it. Othello believed her. However, he was deceived. In addition, because of this, the idea of revenge appears.

He does not shout, but speaks very slowly and quietly:

> ...Blood, blood, blood...

How many times he seems to ask Desdemona to tell him the truth.

In one scene, he tells Iago that it is better for him not knowing the truth, but this is a temporary unconscious defense.

He waits for an acknowledgement [of the truth] from Desdemona. Moreover, it seems that if she tells him she had an affair with Cassio, he might even forgive her. However, her deception is intolerable. Duplicity. She stands right beside him, looks into his eyes, and lies. Death is the punishment for this.

The particular misfortune here is that Desdemona actually tells the truth. She does not know any other truth.

Shakespeare's Desdemona actually understands that Othello is jealous very early on. She *understands*, but does not want to believe it. In addition, Emilia *understands*. Both of them discuss it. However, we have allowed ourselves to delete that part of the text where it says she believes that Othello is jealous. We have decided that Desdemona does not know. Right up to the end. She does not know what is happening to her husband. Does not know why he is angry with her, why he slaps her across the face, why he is not himself.

There is greater drama in *ignorance*. She learns about everything only half a moment before her death. She laughs, for it would be possible to dispel everything so simply now. However, the next moment Othello kills her.

New Paths for Old

I like Shostakovich's music very much. I could talk for a long time about the feelings it produces in me. I cannot listen to Shostakovich's harmonies calmly. I am not only excited by the general arrangement of his symphonies, but also by each combination of sounds. These sounds have a special effect on me, often arousing unconscious dramatic feelings. Having said this, reason prompts me to understand why it is true. However, I only wish to speak about one moment here. For me his music is also treasured because I sense no banality in any transitions, as when you can predict the transitions from one end of one musical phrase to the beginning of another. Listen to regular ordinary music. You will hear hundreds of the same transitions and endings that have already been repeatedly heard, yesterday and today, in one work, and another, and a third. Such a composer, not realizing it himself, arrives at the usual well-worn path, and following him, you reach as far as the well-known fence and return. Consequently, envisaging only one or two paths for yourself every day.

Good music is another matter. You actually travel somewhere new because of it; it may seem that you will bump into this well-known fence—but not on your life! By subtle harmonies, you are guided to a new and unfamiliar place, and you eagerly look from side to side.

Audience Contact

Not everyone takes a great interest in art, especially a serious interest. There are many reasons for this. One is an unconscious *distrust* of art. It starts at an early age, maybe when children are conducted single file into the theatre. They are excited by a cultural excursion: no teachers will be there, there will be no examinations, and the parents will be far away. Moreover, this feeling of emancipation inhibits the concentration of teenagers during a play. Sometimes they would like to separate themselves [from their friends] and become more involved in what is being said on stage, but they are afraid of seeming sentimental. A general easygoing indifference prevails.

Bear in mind that at a so-called "group-rate" performance, where the audience is, let us say, from a single organization, the reactions are often confused. The atmosphere created by a "group-rate" audience is not often conducive to intelligent perception. It is much better when the hall is filled with a variety of people, strangers. Then there is a more sensible unanimity [of reactions]. This is true even with adults.

Moreover, the atmosphere of the theatres themselves is not always conducive to quiet and concentration, from the interior furnishings to the operational staff.

Adults, perhaps, will know how to set aside such extraneous, secondary impressions, but children, at least unconsciously, become part of the generally inartistic atmosphere. However, the physical facilities can be poor. That is not the point. However, they must be "intended for art." The air itself should feel as though it were filled by art. Such an atmosphere does not happen by itself. Enormous work is required. Unfortunately, not everyone engaged in creative work can do this.

In addition, here the three greatest enemies of genuine art are united as one. First, the teenager's absolute lack of aesthetic preparation. Second, (is this really so necessary?) the "cultural excursion" itself. Last but not least, the inartistic atmosphere of the theatres.

Furthermore, the most important and greatest enemy of art is art *itself*, when the performance or film is filled with large or small mistakes. In addition, mistakes, as a rule, are abundant.

Therefore, here is the result: at the "serious" places of the play or film, the audience displays annoyingly inappropriate levity.

Despite its unexpectedness, this reaction is always unpleasant for us, even though *we prepared the play for a long time.*

Each one of our built-in weaknesses, whether they concern school or parental upbringing or the absence of artistic atmosphere at the theatre, requires a separate discussion. It would be meaningless to talk about everything at once. I will only say a few words about what concerns our profession directly. How often our productions do not provide an opportunity for teenagers to take a great interest in the art of the theatre.

One time we performed our Malaya Bronnaya Theatre production of *Romeo and Juliet* at MAT. During the last act, I stood in the doorway to the auditorium, observing two youngsters in the audience. They were giggling. This disturbed me so much that I left the auditorium and went outside to think over what had happened. I thought that we had probably distributed the dramatic moments of the performance incorrectly. That we pushed the tension too much in the first two acts, and some [in the audience] were already getting tired, that some sort of limit of dramatic perception had been reached. I thought it should be played lighter and swifter in the beginning, so that the tragic moments would approach more suddenly, more unexpectedly.

Some will say that these students, perhaps, were simply distracted, they dropped their coat-check ticket or something like that, and there is no need to reexamine my entire aesthetic viewpoint because of this. However, if you are the director and you are standing in the auditorium, then the nature of any distraction of even one spectator should be intelligible to you. Moreover, at this time, the grounds for their laughter were found in my excesses, in my *extravagance*. However, it is impossible to enumerate all the possible mistakes we make that demand our continuous analysis, even when someone in the audience may have obviously reacted the wrong way. Even more so with a young audience.

There should be a special measurement, a special instinct for the truth, so that [audience] contact takes place. I have cited a subtle error as an example, but very many flagrant errors exist as well.

[Fairy tales like] Grandfather Frost and the Snow Maiden are good for the youngest children, while more mature children react ironically to this [sort of] simplicity. However, just imagine, very often we have the nerve to produce plays for teenagers and older students in the [identical] manner of Grandfather Frost. How many of such Grandfather Frosts I have seen in performances the plays of Ostrovsky, Gorky, and even Chekhov. Especially in children's performances. The content is often "Snow Maiden-like," [i.e., like a poorly conceived production of a children's fairy tale] and the execution is the same. You sit there and grow angry from wasting your time on nonsense. Maybe a child does not think about wasting his time, but it is simply uninteresting for him, for he understands that not all this is "reality," not the truth.

In order to take pleasure from the form of the performance, this form should also be extremely fascinating in itself.

To find serious contact with the public, to find the kind of artistic approach that will make each boy or girl or father in the audience feel an intimate involvement with the events on stage, is very difficult, of course.

[Dramatic] interest also arises from our deep understanding of the nature of theatre, or flags from our incomprehension of it, beginning with the fact that we frequently do not know how to make a performance effective instead of merely conversational. Effective not only in the external sense, but also in psychological terms.

Adults sometimes excuse lack of action, simply by listening to a good text, figuring out from the text itself what lies beneath the surface. For me, however, it is uninteresting only to listen to the text in the theatre. I want to understand what happens, what those special processes I should watch are.

In the theatre, however, a scene is often developed and designed exclusively for listening, and then it is even boring for adults, not just children. Then to obtain even a minimal impression they force the speech, and the result is nonsense. However, this is only one side of the question of theatrical appeal. On the other side are a thousand other examples that we handle so poorly.

In the cinema there is montage, continuous changing of shots, there is simply the movement of the film, and finally there is the reality of execution—apartments, buses, streets. If there is meaning as well, the attention of a child is captured. However, what does genuine theatrical theatre consist of? Not counterfeit, not coarse, but the kind that makes us want to watch a performance really?

Give a child one bad toy, and one that is wonderful. Doesn't he understand the difference between the two? Moreover, he understands this in the theatre too, when there is only scenery. He understands not in his consciousness, but in the elementary sense that this is "rubbish." Furthermore, it often is "rubbish," beginning with the poses and faces of the actors and ending with their intonations.

That is why the main thing is to develop in ourselves a taste that does tolerate "rubbish," no matter how it manifests itself. Children laugh (I learned this from a director at one of the provincial theatres) during the death of the heroes in *West Side Story* and during the Gestapo interrogation in *The Young Guard*.[86] What does this mean? Does the fear of appearing sentimental reach extend this much?

However, what would happen if these children were not shown a play, but a documentary film of an awful interrogation or an account of a man murdered on the street? I am confident that no one in the auditorium would laugh. Maybe, in theatrical performances or during the viewing of artistic films, children simply do not feel enough truth.

I assume that somewhere in the back row, however, children are giggling even at the documentary film. However, it does not necessarily follow that they are cruel. It is probably a protective reaction from an unexpected degree of truth, which is unusual to them in art. Furthermore, there is the role played by the "social context," even in an authentic account. In the skill of showing it right now, today, and precisely to this group of people. There is a whole science in this, or if you will, an art.

Show a teenager or even an older student (someone in whom the psychology of a teenager remains for a long time) a love scene, let us say. For all its "truth," he will laugh, which can also be a protection from an overflow of adolescent reaction: it is too honest for him.

Part of our task is to incorporate displays of love between two people so that it is not necessary to be ashamed of all the beautiful or not-so-beautiful manifestations. Make up your mind to let them laugh, but behind their laughter, they will feel the truth all the same. However, you must be certain of this truth. It is difficult in art, but it is necessary to feel around for it. So that you will not be mistaken, whether children laugh because of too much truth or because there is not enough of it.

Children laugh! Moreover, maybe for them as well as for adults, it is necessary to write and produce good audacious comedies in which seriousness is woven closely together with humor. At one time, Viktor Rozov's plays, *Good Luck!* and *In Search of Happiness,* were precisely such plays.[87] They were dramas in the form of comedies. The audience at the Central Children's Theatre watched them cheerfully, in a lively way, coming into close [psychological] contact with the actors, and when the dramatic moments arrived, I do not remember a single case where someone laughed inappropriately. In addition, in the cheerful places, there was no hidden giggling, contradicting the content of the play or the performance of the actors, but open, loud laughter. It was not extended one second longer than necessary.

The laughter of teenagers needs to be expressed externally. Give them the opportunity to laugh loudly in accord with their wishes, and then with a skillful turn, switch their attention to something serious.

Didn't Shakespeare do this himself, even though he did not write for children? It should be said, however, that this combination of comic and tragic is a hard thing to do. To grasp this [special type of] laughter today, even in the plays of Shakespeare, is not easy. His laughter is not found in the language of today's humor. Fearing not to correspond with today's sense of humor, many directors throw it out and remain only with the [serious parts of the] drama, which complicates the required contact with the audience.

It is possible to appeal for a general improvement of culture, for more education, which would be correct. Moreover, there is some merit in these appeals.

However, within the limits of every profession, it is also necessary to fulfill these appeals to the utmost in ourselves. No one will bring a different sort of children to us in the auditorium tomorrow. We should compel them to concentrate on our creativity and on its own terms. Even at those moments when they do not want to.

A Month in the Country

One of the secrets of *A Month in the Country* is found in the middle of the first act when Rakitin's asks, "What's the matter with you?" and Natalya Petrovna replies that if something was the matter with her, it was the fact that everything had already happened to her.

What was it and why had it already happened? In the beginning, she behaved extremely nervously. Although Turgenev wrote that Natalya Petrovna "embroiders her needlework," her internal state does not quite correspond to what she is doing.

She behaves very confused. She asks Rakitin to read *The Count of Monte Cristo* to her, then she interrupts before he has even read two lines. When he doubts that it is necessary to continue—reading, apparently, does not interest her—she persistently demands that he continue; however, here once more she interrupts him.

She asks Rakitin if he knows where her husband is at this moment. Rakitin answers that her husband is explaining something to the workmen at the weir they are currently repairing.

She wonders if Rakitin had considered that her husband gives himself over with exaggerated enthusiasm to all sorts of matters. Rakitin agrees with her and Natalya Petrovna remarks sharply that it is very boring when he agrees so quickly. There is no doubt that her husband and Rakitin cause her considerable irritation today. One is boring in his agreements, the other in his enthusiasm for economic matters.

The only one who evokes her sympathy today is the new teacher, a certain student they hired to tutor her son for the summer.

Speaking about the tutor, Natalya Petrovna treats Rakitin so impudently that even he is lost, "Natalya Petrovna, you are treating me terribly today."

Once more, she asks him to read, and once more, she interrupts him on the first line.

In her behavior, there is a certain arrhythmia, if we can express it in medical terms.

Now she asks Rakitin about Vera, but she does not wait for a reply; and, demanding that he stop reading altogether, she asks him to talk about something unimportant.

Rakitin had not noticed such confused behavior in Natalya Petrovna before. What is it? He talks to her about the neighbors, the Krinitsyns, and how boring they are. Here Natalya Petrovna deflects his sharp irony, however. "You are angry with me about something today," Rakitin concludes, frustrated with her sarcasm. She notices, however, that he is completely impenetrable.

He guesses what the matter is, what has happened to her, but he cannot understand it. He does not comprehend her look today. He sees some kind of change in her. However, what is it?

When her son runs in and his teacher enters, they distract Natalya Petrovna, and Rakitin reflects. Natalya Petrovna asked him to explain to her what, in his opinion, had changed in her.

After they are alone again, Rakitin wants to return to their earlier subject; however, it seems that Natalya Petrovna does not even remember their conversation.

Doctor Shpigelsky arrives; Natalya Petrovna is pleased to see him. Or pretends to be. The Doctor has a wicked tongue, so let him talk about something it is possible to laugh at.

The Doctor starts to speak about a familiar maiden who had two fiancés and could not choose which one to love.

He finishes the long tale, convinced that it is a funny story, but Natalya Petrovna remains pensive.

Then she finally says that perhaps the maiden loves both men and this is completely realistic.

They apparently terminate this awkward moment.

The Doctor has a plan to marry Vera off to the neighboring landowner. The doctor stands to benefit from this affair, but Natalya Petrovna laughs, for Vera is absolutely a child, and the idea of marriage for this young girl seems ridiculous to her.

At this point Vera enters, and Natalya Petrovna begins to act somewhat mysteriously toward her. Affectionate, but with a certain latent sarcasm.

When Rakitin comes back, he finds a *different* Natalya Petrovna. She is peaceful, quiet, with no sign of the irritation that she showed at first. She seems open again, gentle, and as simple as before.

Rakitin is happy that everything has calmed down. All the same, what was it?

Natalya Petrovna does not wish to see her husband; she runs into the house, but comes out again to meet the student. She speaks with the student for a long time, speaks to him like a housewife, but with a certain special desire for conversation. She speaks independently, proudly, but overly persistent, greedily. And, of course, we understand her interest in him. However, what does this break in her mood signify?

Has the Doctor's plan for Vera's marriage really changed her? Well of course, she is not simply in love, she is jealous, she is not herself from the idea that Vera has run off somewhere all day with the teacher, and that they consider her an old woman.

Suddenly she has found a treacherous way out: Vera needs to marry the neighbor! Now Natalya Petrovna comes back to her senses. This act reveals her growing spitefulness toward Vera. Then her nervousness and her uneasiness cease, and she boldly goes up to the student and begins to chatter freely with him.

Natalya Petrovna is fascinating. Moreover, she is in love. At the core of this love, however, is an element of planned villainy. The combination of this villainy with the fascination and charm of her female nature is the special feature that has arisen here in the play. That is the secret, the dramatic knot, which holds the first act together, at any rate.

The second act of *A Month in the Country*.

After a long scene between Vera and Belyayev, which probably needs to be analyzed separately, Rakitin and Natalya Petrovna appear. She enters after him. He went ahead to prepare a place where she could settle down more comfortably. She comes in very slowly and looks gloomy. She walks around for a long time, not looking at anyone, withdrawn, and languidly takes a seat. Then, not raising her head, she impassively asks Rakitin whether it was Vera and Belyayev that just left. After hearing that indeed it was they, Natalya Petrovna observes after a silence that Vera and Belyayev left quickly upon their arrival, as if escaping from them.

Rakitin answers correctly and tersely, understanding that Natalya Petrovna is in a bad mood again. The path of her ideas is not intelligible to him, but to us, of course, it is already obvious.

After a silence, Natalya Petrovna asks whether the Doctor has left, and when Rakitin answers that he has, she discontentedly remarks that he should have stayed awhile because she needed to speak with him.

When Rakitin inquires what she wished to speak to the doctor about, Natalya Petrovna says sharply that it is none of his business.

She is so gloomy, so immersed in her own world, so laconic, that it is difficult for Rakitin to talk to her. It is hard for him to endure her incomprehensible, unfounded unfriendliness toward him.

He cautiously tries to suggest this to her. He says that he is worried about the change he notices in her.

"Sometimes you sigh so deeply," he says, "the way a tired, a very tired person sighs, someone who doesn't get enough rest."

She is grateful for his concern; however, she asks him to change the subject.

Rakitin agrees and suggests they should walk somewhere today. The weather is good. However, Natalya Petrovna says that she is too lazy and declines the stroll.

Once again, a long burdensome silence arises. For Natalya Petrovna, it is as though Rakitin were not even beside her. Suddenly she begins to ask about the neighbor, whom the Doctor spoke about in the morning. About the neighbor who could marry Vera. Rakitin is surprised that she is interested in such a silly and insignificant person.

Then Natalya Petrovna falls silent again.

Rakitin speaks about how beautiful the trees are and how bright the sun is. Then, unexpectedly, she bursts into a long tirade against Rakitin, so swift, so cutting, and so sudden that he has a hard time dealing with it.

Then, in an instant, leaving him completely bewildered, she departs, letting him know that she would like to walk alone.

Such behavior from Natalya Petrovna is insulting to Rakitin, offensive, and in any case, incomprehensible. Can she really be interested in the student she has talked so casually about so many times?

Under the impression of this improbable supposition, Rakitin starts a conversation with the arriving student.

Two very different people talk together. One, burdened with the weight of gloomy ideas, has gotten used to a certain strict, traditional way of life; and the other, uninhibited, even thoughtless in some things, *not complex*. He creates a feeling of bewilderment in Rakitin: is it possible for this young man to have any sort of internal connection with Natalya Petrovna?

Now she unexpectedly appears again, already changed from the languid mood she was in recently and now cheerful and young.

Not hesitating in Rakitin's presence, but even, on the contrary, seeming to enjoy his presence, she breaks into a ridiculously warm conversation with the student.

A few minutes pass, and Natalya Petrovna becomes involved in a game, in which only her son Kolya, Vera, and the student should be participating.

Meanwhile, Natalya Petrovna had only recently been saying that she felt herself growing old and tired. And this was true. She was old and tired because she felt unneeded by those she wanted to need her.

And right now, as though overcoming her feeling of uselessness, overcoming it with a huge effort of will, she returns again to some years ago, to her youth, which she lived not the way she wanted, not how she would have lived according to her present understanding of life.

Her charming nature and the dramatic idea are bound up in this sudden cheerfulness, and it is intelligible to us and to Rakitin.

The arrival of the Doctor with the neighbor who is Vera's assumed fiancé only increases the gaiety, giving it an ominous, nervous nuance.

This note of sharp reanimation concludes the second act, which, according to our present custom, should be joined to the first, making a single one, which examines an entire major cycle of this story.

Now I am worried, however, of my unequivocal confidence about the interpretation of the play. I attempt to treat yesterday's confidence skeptically. After a test of such confidence, it either completely disappears or becomes stronger, or in any case more voluminous. In the middle of the first act of *A Month in the Country*, Rakitin says that Natalya Petrovna is as soft and quiet as an evening after a thunderstorm.

"Was there really a thunder storm?" she asks.

"Gathering," replies Rakitin.

What is behind this thunderstorm and why has it passed? The change in Natalya Petrovna's mood is connected with Vera. When Vera or the teacher is not nearby, Natalya Petrovna feels worried. A little later, the teacher will appear with Kolya but without Vera. The teacher is modest, obedient. Natalya Petrovna's mood seemed to improve. A few minutes pass, however, and she is disturbed again.

The Doctor's tale of the love story about the young neighbor with two fiancés translates to Natalya Petrovna as her own situation concerning her husband and Rakitin. Then she learns from Vera that she spent all morning with the teacher. Moreover, Vera is like "an absolute child."

Natalya Petrovna's former anxiety seems ridiculous, childish, and even indecent. She is ashamed of her earlier state of mind, of her former nervousness.

She searches in Rakitin for a possible defense against any recurrence of her own ridiculous excitements. She rests after her recent nervous apprehension. Rakitin is surprised at her emphatic request [for him] to be resolute with her. Rakitin has not known such nervousness or tenderness in her until this very day.

In Natalya Petrovna's fluctuation of moods lies the secret that holds our attention for the entire act. However, we shall leave this "business" side, that is, the question of continuously preserving the audience's attention. The main thing in this secret of hers, this variability, is a certain charm in her character.

Meanwhile, Natalya Petrovna has a conversation with Belyayev. At first, she is extremely reserved, and then she is intolerably frank. Behind all these different moods and behaviors is not only passion, but also complex interest in a stranger from an unknown world. It is as though Belyayev were a foreigner. This stranger attracts Natalya Petrovna. It is dangerous to allow a simplified interpretation of her attitude to Belyayev. It would be thoughtless to show only one primitive action in the performance. All these mood changes stem from *complex feelings and a complex character*. The highest thoughts take priority in Natalya Petrovna, then the lowest, but even the lowest are complex, not direct.

For just about the entire act, she probably does not attach much importance to the Doctor's suggestion about Vera's marriage. In any case, there is no intended and direct "villainy" as I wrote earlier. She immediately ridicules the idea brought up by the Doctor about the possible marriage of Vera. By the end of the act, however, and once more against her will, this idea comes back to her again. Although at this point Natalya Petrovna is completely aware of the impropriety even of allowing herself this thought.

It is good to create a complex psychological portrait in which the solution of the behavior does not lie on the surface.

Naturally, all the motives should be emphasized and explained.

However, the motives themselves are also complex and their fluctuations are complex.

On Being Able to Notice

It is strange that people often classify one or another great artist as a malicious person. They are irritated if he does not agree with their artistic viewpoints. Meanwhile, this difference is like a small glass fragment in a large stained glass window. Moreover, when they succeed in knocking it out, the hole remains for a long time.

Time passes and it is understood that they will recognize a genuine artist and pay honor to him. However, this fact does not teach them to look at other artists with the same trust. It would seem that a person would be glad that next to him, let us say, someone is painting a picture. Often people are pleased. However, sometimes they are only indignant, since they think of art differently. Knowledge for them means nothing, but their convictions are everything.

Indeed, there were people who lived at the time of Meyerhold, but did not go to his theatre. Moreover, did not pay attention to anything that stormed in and around there. They *overslept* Meyerhold.

How beautifully the critic Pavel Markov—who was a contemporary of the original MAT—had the time to notice one thing, and another, and a third. It is a pleasure to read his books. However, the others, if they were not asleep, vilified, let things slip by, or in any case failed to notice for themselves. A critic, it seems to me, is not someone who is able to condemn, but someone who is able to notice.

The critic is someone who has special binoculars and looks through them to make things closer, not farther away.

Stanislavsky said that a director is a midwife. However, if the critic is not a midwife as well, then the artist has a hard time of it. It is easy to write about Van Gogh now. But wonderful is he who noticed him *then*.

Othello

The third, fourth, and fifth acts of *Othello*. Desdemona's first entrance.

She insists that Othello return Cassio to the rank of lieutenant. A comic scene, but with serious content. Comic because Desdemona is apparently angry that Othello does not give in to her request as quickly as she would like. She behaves like a *spoiled child,* but of course, this is only a charming game for the General. A clever game. Othello laughs, his wife behaves charmingly. Meanwhile, Desdemona achieves a serious result. Othello is a little stubborn, but agrees to forgive Cassio.

When Desdemona leaves, Othello remains under the spell of her charm. He thinks that if he ever stops loving her, chaos will come.

Desdemona's second entrance. Somewhere in other quarters, people are gathered to celebrate the victory over the Turks. Desdemona finds her husband in an inexplicable, painful condition. She does not know that shortly before this Iago awakened a terrible idea in Othello. Desdemona takes Othello's word that he is suddenly ill. Hearing that Othello is feeling badly, she promptly acts, trying to help him in some way. Othello looks long and steadily in her eyes. She behaves so naturally, and she is a deceiver, thinks Othello, as only a very perverted person can be.

Desdemona's third entrance. She comes running in to learn if her husband is feeling better. This time, however, Othello has had an additional conversation with Iago, the contents of which she does not know about. Othello has already vowed that he will kill Desdemona and Cassio.

After believing the slander, Othello searches for all the refutations, and unhappily concludes about Iago's correctness again.

He rushes to Desdemona, hoping to either dispel the evil thoughts or conclude that Iago was right again. Othello asks Desdemona to show him her hand. He asks why her hand is so moist and if Desdemona knows that this is a sign of promiscuity.

Up to this day, Othello never allowed himself to speak to his wife this way. She never knew him like this. Perhaps this is a general characteristic of men, to become different after marriage. In any case, Desdemona tries to restore their earlier relationship. The petty tyranny of a husband, if it is not from bad health, is simply petty tyranny, but for her this is unthinkable.

Desdemona would not want to submit to a husband's whims, such as that a handkerchief given by him should be unfailingly kept on her person.

Othello's short replies, with demands to show him the handkerchief, are only a husband's tortured requests to show him the necessary proof of her innocence.

For her the question about Cassio is now a question of double importance. It is not only a question about her former good friend, but also whether there will be equality in the family life of Othello and Desdemona or whether the husband's arrogance will triumph. This, unfortunately, is how she perceives this strange and incomprehensible behavior of her husband.

At this point, they carry on a brief and intense dialogue:

HE. The handkerchief!...!
SHE. Cassio...!
HE. The handkerchief...!
SHE. Cassio...!

This terrible, terrible, evasively wicked woman, Othello concludes once again.

It is not just the deaths of Othello or Cassio that are important to Iago, but also *the process of their moral enslavement.*

Desdemona, being completely innocent, does not suspect that the terrible things happening to Othello are because of her.

She imagines something else; that maybe he is mentally ill.

This uncertainty about the reason for the suffering of the man she loves, this *secret,* and this *ignorance* constitutes the dramatic core of her role.

What happens to *her personally* does not concern her. She is disturbed by what happens to Othello. She cannot find the solution to his torment. This is far more terrible than her personal misfortune.

Iago could triumph, for he has tormented first-rate people, people whose consciences are aggravated, aggravated by a feeling of closeness to a beloved person.

He would celebrate, if that monstrous game in which he implicated others did not trouble his already corroded soul.

Therefore, perhaps this terrible activity does not even bring pleasure to the executioner himself. Driven to madness by torturing other people, he loses any sort of normalcy. His hatred is not only the tragedy of others, but also his own tragedy.

Mathematics of Rehearsal

Just as in other professions, probably, in directing there is arithmetic and there is higher mathematics.[88] Both concepts are closely interconnected. Go to rehearsal, simply go and look at who is sitting in this corner today and who is sitting in that one. What is this—arithmetic or higher mathematics? Both, possibly. Some directors go to rehearsal and pretend to be amiable, they like everyone there, and they come bearing kindness. Others pretend to be angry so the actors will fear them. These practices are not even arithmetic. Arithmetic begins when you come to rehearsal without any sort of pose, either the first or the second kind, and with your cares left in the coatroom, you really try to understand the mood of your colleagues. Then, irrespective of your own mood, you quietly arrange it so that everyone suddenly has a desire *to work.*

Perhaps this is not exactly arithmetic.

Do you think it is easy to do all this with people who are pampered, capricious, and often famous; who sometimes place their own mood above that of the group?

However, let us pass on to the work for which this atmosphere is actually created. First, let us not discuss the working method itself, but simply the style of the work. A little conversation not about the content of rehearsal, but how it should proceed. Whether you are investigating *Othello* or any other play is not important now.

Once, many years ago, when I was still working at the Central Children's Theatre, I accidentally encountered the idea of the so-called open rehearsal. Here is how it happened.

At some inconvenient time during the evening, the young actors and myself, students from the acting studio, were rehearsing some unscheduled play. I think it was *Romeo and Juliet.* We were all young, cheerful, and very much in love with the profession. Moreover, the method of rehearsal itself was very lively, which was also pleasant for us.[89]

Sometimes actors who were not involved in our work heard about this rehearsal method. Or simply friends, not actors, but playwrights or even a few acquaintances from outside of theatre. We let them in to observe.

Ever since then, curious people have always sat in at our rehearsals. It even happens in a small room: three or four actors are sitting and working, and ten others are from God knows where—Tallinn, Sverdlovsk, other directing courses in Moscow, etc.

Our actors generally got used to it and no longer were bothered by it. Naturally, a few grumbled sometimes, but not for long.

However, sometimes, unexpectedly, no one came except our actors, and then rehearsals were not as good. When the visitors were there, everyone was always sharper; there was less assorted nonsense, and so forth. Moreover, in these situations I particularly remembered one of the laws described by Stanislavsky. I remembered about the "circle of attention." How wonderful it is to know how to use this law. Other people surround you, you feel them, and they excite you, while at the same time you "switch them off" and live only within the scene. This mixture of excitement and *disconnection* probably forms the whole charm of our creative work.

The actors absolutely feel this relationship at a performance. Let them start to get used to it from the first rehearsals; less will be lost, and the whole rehearsal process will become even more interesting.

I observed how our actors became weaned from the almost professional habit of putting on airs before strangers. How, in open rehearsals, they learned modesty, concentration, efficiency, and responsibility. To be sure, it is not harmful for you to check up on your own *taste* as well. Indeed, it is nauseating to see how our brother directors often behave so self-importantly before the strangers in the auditorium.

Back to the "circle of attention," however, and quickly!

How interesting and cheerful it is to rehearse and feel a type of double check—that is, what you see in relation to the stage, and what happens in the audience—this gives you a certain new hidden push.

Now it is time to start speaking about *method* [i.e., "higher mathematics" above], since without an effective method all this public attention is not worth two kopeks. God knows what it can degenerate into. After all, it is not hard to find five people to sit in at rehearsals, all kinds of unusual people. However, *who* will they be, and *what* will they come look at?

A genuine rehearsal method is built from the subtlest professionalism, but also filled with authentic living content. After such lofty and obscure verbiage, it is probably necessary to provide an explanation.

The subtlest professionalism always involves a very special type of rehearsal expertise. A professional craftsman always holds his file like this, but an amateur like *that*. Moreover, a professional knows exactly which file is needed, while an amateur grabs the first one at hand.

Our type of rehearsal expertise does not consist of going round and round a subject, not knowing how to begin. There is so much "wasted motion" analyzing even a simple scene this way. For us, true expertise consists of immediately working out the *structure, skeleton, and texture*.

A good mechanic must have taste and knowledge of metalwork in general. In addition, knowledge of what type of screws and wrenches are being made *in the present day*. In addition, *how* they are currently made and *for what purpose*. Let us find a mechanic like this one.

It is the same with us. Some people can immediately find the outline of a scene for you, but it is only a primitive outline. The essence of our type of rehearsal expertise, however, consists of not only finding this simple outline, but also filling it with deep meaning.

Our Dependent Way of Life

All day, for completely unknown reasons, I have been in a nervous state, simply always some kind of groundless anxiety. However, I arrive at the theatre and calmness comes over me. Not indifference, but more specifically a certain relaxation. Rest from the knowledge of everything that will be here today, was here yesterday, and will be here even tomorrow. The familiar ticket collectors and wardrobe attendants. By the way, at our theatre, they are extremely kind, or at any rate, it seems so to me. On duty are two women who always behave with remarkable understanding to requests allowing someone in without a ticket. When it is awkward for them to stand in the doorway because of the people scalping tickets outside the entrance. In addition, how nice it is when there are no tickets left, but it is possible to kindly let in a visitor from Riga [Latvia] or Tyumen [Siberia].

Then you ascend to the foyer and walk among the photographs of our actors. Moreover, behold, no one [from the staff] warns you to stay away from the pictures.

Once I made a recording for radio. In addition, I told my assistants that I needed to invite a particular actor. As it happens, this actor was rarely involved in my plays, and when they called him, he did not believe them. He pretended he was his roommate, and then he called someone to find out for himself if we were really asking for him. Finding it was true, of course, he came.

I was upset when I learned about this because I thought: The life of an actor is very complex because it is so dependent. Moreover, it is necessary to know about this and be tactful. This does not mean, of course, that it is necessary to give someone a job that does not merit it. Everyone should understand, however, which plans he is needed for, and there are no *arbitrary* favorites.

...Then you go to the theatre manager's office. There sits the same secretary. For ten years, we have had the best [casting] secretary!

If you were going to write a comedy, she would not be suitable for it because she is too normal, natural. Yet she has a good knowledge of people and she is fast, she can determine who is right [for a role] with only one glance.

I like Bulgakov very much, but I could not write his story *A Theatrical Novel,* not only because I have not the talent, but also because I do not have an ironic attitude toward theatre.[90]

A Month in the Country

Possibly Natalya's Petrovna's greatest desire is to be seen with Belyayev. However, in the first act, aside from brief meetings *before everyone*, they speak together only once, and that is almost at the end of the act.

It is possible to imagine how hateful everything around her is when Belyayev is not there. She talks with Rakitin, but she is *absent* from this conversation. Either she does not hear what the discussion is about, or what she hears suddenly shocks her, and then Natalya Petrovna marks this or that moment of the conversation somewhat caustically. She does not so much converse as she tries to get through a conversation imposed on her, get through it without losing the main idea, the main interest that exists secretly in her.

This special feature of her nature will help to provide many preliminary scenes with lightness, transparency, and an aspiration toward that moment when the conversation with Belyayev finally comes.

This [essence] is very important, for otherwise it will merely be ordinary, cleverly written dialogue.

However, charm is charm, and essence is essence, which consists of the fact that no one is necessary for Natalya Petrovna now except Belyayev. It is not hard to remember how a person who is in love and worried about this love dismisses all the rest and tries to pass swiftly through anything else to reach more what is important more quickly.

However, throughout all this Natalya Petrovna needs to maintain the appearance of propriety. She maintains this appearance in the dialogue. Nevertheless, all this only increases the dramatic nature of her desire to be free from everything and see only *him*.

It would be easier for her if she did not need to be concerned about anything else, but Natalya Petrovna is compelled *to be concerned*.

The internal message, the internal motion, the flights of her feelings and thoughts are not diminished, however, from this requirement to keep herself in check.

Therefore, the movement of the action is toward the scene with Belyayev.

By the way, this movement, this absence of excessive interpreting in the preliminary dialogues, this free driving energy—*continued* to the next, more essential scene—not only provides ease of access into the performance, but also allows the preservation of the secret that exists inside Natalya Petrovna. In fact, if we assume that we are reading this play for the first time, then everything that relates to the student is like an elusive premonition of some kind of important future relations. In order to hold onto this state of elusive premonition one should not, naturally, "pad" the first dialogues just because they are so charmingly written by *Turgenev*.

Even the half-minute scene when Belyayev appears for the first time should not be overemphasized. On the contrary, Natalya Petrovna, hastily and somewhat unfriendly, carefully says only two words to him, and that is all.

And later, when she enters into a long conversation with him, she does this rapidly too, without any implied meaning, and only in the process of the conversation itself does the truth start to become clear to us.

Othello

Two famous actors from the Leningrad Children's Theatre visited our rehearsal. One said that the rehearsal produced a strange impression on him. They rehearse in a completely way at that theatre.[91]

It seemed to him that our actors would not remember anything for the next rehearsal. From his point of view, possibly, something was left disorganized. We did not try to "secure" any moment. We were rehearsing the scene in the fourth act of *Othello* when Iago talks with Cassio and Othello eavesdrops. By the way, during the rehearsal I told our actors that Iago has arranged a theatre scene for Othello, even a pantomime theatre scene, since Othello probably does not hear what they are talking about. Bearing this in mind, Iago wants Cassio to be expressive enough for Othello to understand. He behaves expressively himself, and poses vivid questions so that Cassio's responses would be equally vivid. Precisely because of these vivid responses, Othello begins to assume that their conversation is cynical, and certainly about Desdemona. This is why I said that Iago arranges a theatre scene for Othello. The actor from Leningrad understood this perfectly, only he did not understand why we failed to *develop* this theatre scene. After all, the solution was so perceptible and concrete. For some reason, the actors and myself did not linger on this *theatre scene* very much, and once more we began to do something that was so casual it seemed [to the visiting actor] that it would be forgotten as well. I explained to him what we had done today, and how this was not really so strange and would not be forgotten at all because we would remember precisely those things we analyzed for ourselves today [by means of Active Analysis].

As far as theatre technique is concerned, of course, it would be possible to secure the solution, however it would be so immediately clear to any spectator that the *secret*, which should always be present in each scene, would have vanished. The spectator must see something more worldly wise than the fact that Iago arranges a theatre scene for Othello. The spectator should watch this scene anxiously, and then suddenly the conclusion will flash: Iago has arranged a theatre scene. However, it will be his own conclusion and not what we presented to him ready made. However, his conclusion could be something else, or a third or fourth, we should not "masticate" the construction for him. We should not even put some very direct solution into our heads, because life is complex, and it is interesting to comprehend this complexity precisely [by retaining an improvisational approach].

In the beginning of the fourth act, Iago has selected a certain course of action. He pretends that he does not comprehend Othello's extremism. Can't a woman really kiss another man or even lie with him in bed and still be considered virtuous? Can't a wife really give her handkerchief to someone else even if her husband gave it to her? Finally, why attach so much meaning to off-color conversations? After all, awful people conduct these conversations, and so it is probably necessary to learn to protect you from this filth. Iago [seemingly] calms Othello down, but naturally it is not difficult to understand the real significance of this calming down here. Seeming to calm down Othello, Iago only finds new means of *reminding* him about the misfortune.

Othello has already ordered Cassio to be killed. He has also decided to end Desdemona's life. Only four acts have elapsed, however, and there will be a *fifth*? Why a fifth act if the decision is already made?

Because even though Othello loves his wife and accepts the decision—it means nothing yet.

After all, it is one thing to *say* something, and another to kill someone, and Othello is exhausted by [so many] ideas, and is primed to hide from any new shocks. Now, tired and tormented, in order for him to return to his purpose, what is needed is not a straight line, but a special path. Only unexpected questions can take him out of his semi-conscious state. In addition, Iago takes advantage exactly of this super-unexpected method. With the energy inherent in him, he suggests that Othello should protect himself from the charge of jealousy.

Isn't it really jealousy, he asks Othello, to forbid your wife to give your handkerchief to someone else?

Iago knows that Othello, with his [morally] upright nature, feels the need for protection [from worldly deceitfulness]. Thus, a new conversation will take place. However, Iago does not need Othello's defensiveness. He simply needs a conversation in which repeatedly he tells the tired Moor everything needed to prime him to lose his mind. It is not important for Othello that Iago disagrees with him. He simply hears over and over the words that will make him ill, like being jabbed with a lance until he is completely covered with wounds. He mechanically gives in to the necessity of denying Iago's "defense" of Desdemona. *Not mechanically,* but with his entire body and soul, he feels these painful reminders again: the handkerchief given to Cassio, she has lain with Cassio, etc.

For these reminders, Iago carries on his casuistic conversation seemingly directed toward the defense of Desdemona. And he achieves his purpose. Every touch of the *lance* increases the pain, clouding Othello's mind. It is increasingly difficult for him to protect himself from these jabs, and Othello finally falls into a faint. He feels the approach of this faint a minute or so earlier, his hands beg Iago to spare him, almost inaudibly, he warns that he will faint at any moment, and he *faints*.

Iago wipes away his perspiration; this work is not easy for him. Indeed, in this game he rushes into the sort of chasms where there is no place left for pretense.

Destroying Othello, he incinerates himself. Eventually there will be no winner in this duel.

When Cassio comes in during this fainting scene, Iago behaves the way a servant would behave if he were exhausted by the assault of his master. He is tired, worried to death, bitter. In addition, the paradox is that he really is exhausted and bitter, in spite of the fact that Othello's fainting was the result of his hands, the result of his desires.

Knowing that Othello will not come to himself immediately after awakening, Iago dares to speak something roughly and almost frankly derisive directly in Othello's face. It is pleasant for him to feel in such a high position, if only for a moment.

The Moor comes to himself and pulls Iago toward him with some ingenuous questions. However, Iago must again become involved the duel, hotly playing a protest against the weak will of his master, so weak that he even fainted.

Meanwhile, at the same time, Iago needs to devise what to do next. After all, Othello is still alive, which means the game is not finished yet.

Iago takes Othello, who is not thinking clearly after fainting, and hides him behind some sort of corner, promising to tell him new and even more terrible impressions. At this point, the *theatre scene* we spoke about earlier begins.

Possibly, Iago does not completely realize what will happen in the following minute. He rushes into an unknown game, but he does not know how it will turn out. Cassio unexpectedly appears before him and seems to arrange himself so that he could be seen by Othello hiding around the corner, just as Iago would wish. After all, you do not think all this up in a second. Moreover, will Cassio behave just as Iago wishes?!

Good-naturedly punching Cassio in the stomach, foretelling a good joke, Iago suggests Cassio should imagine how soon he would become Othello's lieutenant again if it depended on Cassio's mistress, Bianca. Moreover, Cassio, of course, reacts with corresponding sharpness. Because it really is amusing to imagine how Bianca would handle this. Othello does not hear the words, but he sees the reaction, and understanding it in his own way, he groans from the impact.

This is a *theatre scene,* of course, but the approaches to it are complex. More accurately, this is not theatre, but *life.*

Iago notices Othello's reaction and again he swiftly provides a sharp new question followed by Cassio's super-sharp reply. He ascertains that Bianca is enamored of Cassio, but this idea should be coarsely introduced by Iago with such detailed precision that Cassio cannot contain himself and reveals it equally coarsely. In fact, not Cassio's short reply, but its sharp form capable of wounding at a distance is what is important. The new impact involves Othello, who is hiding around the corner over there, and who will be caught by *surprise* again.

Oh, this is a unique, prolonged execution, a whipping, in which even the executioner is exhausted to the limit!

Unsteadily, Othello leaves his hiding place. He lethargically agrees to Iago's proposal to strangle Desdemona. Lethargic not only because he is already exhausted, but also because when Cassio's perversity became clearly visible to him, he suddenly had a special pity for Desdemona. After all, she, who must now be killed, was at one time so gentle and kind...

Iago does not have the strength for any new arguments. It is time for him to rest after this battle. Almost worn out, however, he should be indignant that Othello shows softness again [toward Desdemona]. At last, Othello agrees to strangle Desdemona, and for a moment, Iago can lag behind and once more wipe away his perspiration.

A Perfect Work Of Art

It art it is necessary either to produce experiments that are very bold and explicit or quiet performances that will be attractive in their aesthetic completeness and perfection. Nothing is worse than when a thing is insufficiently new in its essence or form, but it is also imperfectly produced. Imperfection is pardonable only for a very sharp experience, for a very sharp test of something new. However, it is inexcusable if an extremely timid experiment is imperfectly produced. It is most remarkable, of course, when there is complete novelty of meaning and means of expression. Moreover, when all this is also aesthetically perfect. However, perhaps it is only possible to dream of this.

A Month in the Country

I have already devoted, apparently, more than twenty rehearsals to *A Month in the Country*, but I cannot grasp anything I am thinking about in concrete terms. Probably, after directing works by Chekhov and Shakespeare, I am approaching a new writer with my previous directorial-methodological standards. Everything seems clear before rehearsal, but rehearsal ends and nothing was accomplished. That is, very much has been accomplished, but somehow it was not accurate in relation to Turgenev. Alternatively, in any case, in relation to how it was perceived at the earlier readings.

First, Natalya Petrovna is audacious and daring in her psychological behavior. However, it is necessary to know how to *portray* this impudence. Without careful *portrayal*, this impudence will not come across. Everything turns out almost but not quite in the manner in which the play was written, that is, if it is read unbiased and very attentively. The impudence, the willfulness of her behavior needs to be converted into the design of the role, and furthermore, not external in design, but internal.

First, this involves her mutual relations with Rakitin. Overall, their dialogs are clear, but there is also some secret in them which somehow does not yield a solution.

It is as though Natalya Petrovna strives for conflict with Rakitin. He irritates her after she learns about Belyayev. Her irritation here, however, is not direct; it is *rarely direct*. It is hidden in some sort of complex scheme. It is only part of a complex scheme with many other parts. She suddenly sees that he is blind, deaf in his attitude to her. That he does not *feel* her. It seems to her that he is not clever, but slow-witted, even with all his refinement.

However, he is the only one close to her with whom she would like to be frank. Yet frankness is impossible.

All this complexity demands a *design*. All this demands a certain connection. Here we cannot get off with any sort of general understanding, any sort of general, subtle feeling, even if it is [factually] correct.

Here it is necessary to subdivide feeling into complex layers. Subdivide it, become accustomed to how it is subdivided, and then forget about the subdivisions.

Restlessness. Impudence. An emotionally impetuous nature. Striving for freedom.

1. It begins when she makes him read a book, not concealing the fact that this book is completely uninteresting to her.

Understanding this places him in a foolish position, nevertheless, she insists, and he reads. Then she ceases to listen and sharply changes to another subject.

2. This subject concerns her husband.

Naturally, it is serious to discuss her husband with Rakitin; it is foolish, and still... However, Rakitin is not capable of discussing this subject seriously, even to some extent. Thus it seems to her. Then it is necessary to ask him to *read* again. Apparently, this is the only thing he can do. He says, "I obey," and turns back to the book.

3. Suddenly, her mother asks where Kolya is. Natalya Petrovna replies that he went for a walk with the teacher. Moreover, involuntarily Natalya Petrovna becomes involved in a conversation with Rakitin about the teacher.

She behaves the way people do when they suddenly remember they have still not spoken about the most important thing.

With apparent naturalness, she rushes to a statement of the news that they have evidently hired a new teacher, moreover he is young, moreover he is handsome, and it would be a good idea if he studied with Rakitin.

In this natural, excited account of the news, however, a small portion of humor about Rakitin is interspersed: maybe Rakitin does not like the young man since he is not very clever, and Rakitin likes only very clever people.

Nevertheless, neither the reckless story about the news nor these moments of teasing are to the purpose.

The purpose, which has been well hidden, is that Natalya Petrovna somewhat secretly lets Rakitin know what she lives by, what excites her. However, perhaps he could guess this for himself!

Seeing his inability to do so, however, she again proposes that it is better to return to the book, to that ill-starred single phrase which he continually repeats, interrupted by her.

4. Again, she interrupts him, now deciding to ask whether he has seen Vera. This question did not occur to her at this moment, of course; she has been occupied with this question since this morning, as well as the subject of whether Rakitin thinks her husband is ridiculous. She is filled with these questions, but they "pop out" unexpectedly, confusing Rakitin, of course. After all, he only begins to read this sentence about the Count of Monte Cristo, which says, "...he jumped up, breathing irregularly."

Seeing his confusion, she feels sorry for Rakitin and magnanimously permits him to put the book down at last. At this point, silence is completely established.

5. Walking a little and seeming to switch off Rakitin from her field of attention, she suddenly and sharply turns to him again with a request not to read now, but to talk about something. He tries to collect himself in order to begin to talk about something.

She sits near him so, and begins to listen so, as if his conversation really interested her. However, he does not interest her, of course, and she tries to extract something from his story that would be interesting for her in her present state. She changes *his* conversation to a subject that interests *her*, wishing that he understood her state of mind.

However, he is in no condition to understand her, and then the conversation loses any interest at all for her. She again seems to forget about him.

6. Now, he should go directly up to her and ask what the matter with her is.

She asks him to guess what it is. And using the pretext that others have entered and begun to talk to her about something, he [moves to the side and] begins to guess

7. Meanwhile, among the *others* was Belyayev. In addition, when everyone leaves, only Rakitin remains, thoughtfully seated, and Natalya Petrovna begins to ask him how he likes Belyayev. Maybe this was interesting to her. After all, he was the cause of her excitement. However, apparently Rakitin did not even notice his appearance. He was sitting and thinking: "What is the matter with Natalya Petrovna?"

She understands once again that it is pointless to talk to him.

8. Therefore, not learning what the matter is, Rakitin again starts to ask what is wrong with her. However, she only brushes aside his questions half-jokingly. Moreover, the conversation gradually comes to a halt.

Only at one moment, she stops joking. Rakitin observes that the student would have been flattered if he knew that Natalya Petrovna had remembered him. Then she responds bitterly that, unfortunately, it is not true. For she really believes that the student considers her an expensive inanimate object, no more.

However, it was pointless to explain this role to Rakitin, and she is delighted at the appearance of a new person to talk to—Doctor Shpigelsky. Now she does not need to talk to Rakitin any more.

Belyayev cannot be played simply by any nice young actor. What is needed here is a person who can deeply understand the role, because if he does not succeed, it is necessary to challenge Natalya Petrovna's entire impulse. At one theatre (I saw this performance on television) Islayev, Natalya Petrovna's husband, was fat and ridiculous, Rakitin was sickly, and the student was played by a tall, handsome young man with a dashing hairstyle and a lovely small beard. If I were in Natalya Petrovna's place, I would not be in the least interested in this tall but completely commonplace young man. Yes, he is taller, stronger than Islayev, and healthier than Rakitin, but the resulting idea would be painfully trivial. It is would somehow be uncomfortable to watch several hours of such a story. Because she would be reduced to an extremely simple scheme with absolutely no relation to this play.

No, the issue is not that Belyayev is younger than those two men are. The point is that he belongs to an attractive, unknown world that can be explained by one simple word: *freedom*. It is very easy, however, to be caught by this simple bait. Just as Petya Trofimov's ideas [in *The Cherry Orchard*] cannot be simply *declaimed*, so also it is impossible to play Belyayev simply as a "the free-and-easy student." What is he? (By the way, the text is very similar to what is said by

Petya Trofimov in *The Cherry Orchard* and by another Chekhov character, Ivan Dmitrievich, in the story "Ward No. Six.")

What sounds like liberation to Natalya Petrovna, is real life to Belyayev, and this life has its own limits, chains, restraints. He is poor, badly dressed, and somehow he translated a French novel for fifty rubles, not even knowing French but only that he needed money. His lack of education torments and embarrasses him. He has his own complexities—a poor man who does not know how to speak to women, etc. In a word, he is not so ideal, but an ordinary young man, who finds no freedom in his own life, but in the life of Natalya Petrovna, for example. Their aspiration toward each other is a striving for "not me," for the unattainable, the unrealizable. This, however, is only one the possible interpretations.

...I am rehearsing in a room while the actors are sitting and reading their roles from the script.

I am looking forward to that period of work when, for me sitting at rehearsal, it will become terrible for Natalya Petrovna because she will begin to come apart. When not one drop of the lady remains in the role, resulting from the whim of falling in love with the student and tormenting Vera.

When I will understand, when I will justify her impulse and my soul becomes disturbed for her, then the real rehearsals will begin. Moreover, when I will also become disturbed for Belyayev, so cheerful, but so deficient in what he should be capable of.

Perhaps I am mistaken, but to me it is boring simply to play the plot, even if it is [Turgenev's elegant] lacework. I want to see *everything there is* in the plot instead of only *lacework*. I would like to see Ranevskaya and Petya in there from *The Cherry Orchard* and Treplev from *The Seagull*. However, some will say this is ridiculous, why such senseless expansion? Won't this destroy the lacework? I do not think it will destroy it. It still must be verified, however.

What Natalya Petrovna thinks about and what she feels seem clear. Now we need to find out how this feeling is shown and through what it is shown. She does not simply walk around filled with something, does not simply talk, she thinks about herself. Her feelings are shown in her unusual and impudent behavior. In addition, the entire unusual design of the display of her feelings must be grasped, constructed in itself, and rendered habitable. Natalya Petrovna's displays of sharp feeling are not quite expressed directly. Her behavior is often paradoxical. Despite all the complexity of her behavior, however, we should always understand what the issue is. Her character is not static, not closed. It is necessary to find open, sharp paths behind which her deep feelings are hidden and through which they are shown.

And more. Natalya Petrovna's behavior should be very diverse because she is restless. It is necessary to find lively, active behavior.

As far as her love for Belyayev is concerned, she was attracted to that life which will happen sometime after this "comfortable nest" [of gentry] no longer exists, or nearly so. That life seems tempting to her. She does not know, cannot know, apparently, that Ranevskaya from *The Cherry Orchard* will think the same and want the same thing. However, if Natalya Petrovna knew, if only she could know, how Ranevskaya will end!

"...Mama lives on the fifth floor, I visited her, she has some kind of Frenchmen and ladies, an old priest with a book, and it is smoky and uncomfortable. To me Mama suddenly became awful, so awful, I embraced her, took her hands, and I could not let go. Mama then played up to everyone, and she cried." (Anya. *The Cherry Orchard*.)

Each scene needs to be interpreted very concretely and at the same time *expansively*.

Rakitin talks with Belyayev. He wants to learn how this young man could attract Natalya Petrovna. There is more here, however, than *general* interest in a person from another environment, another generation. When an actor is capable of connecting the concrete and the general, when he regards the concrete as a prism for the general, then it turns out larger, more substantial. Not every actor can do this, however.

As with any play, there are major and minor issues. The major issue is the gradual disclosure of the secret that is contained in Natalya Petrovna's strange impulse. Where is this impulse directed? Where and how is it revealed? Where is it revealed openly and with force? In what sense does all this grow gradually? What is Belyayev? Where is that secret in him that attracts Natalya Petrovna? What place do Doctor Shpigelsky and the neighbor Bolshintsov occupy in this story? Do we understand the relationship among all the parts of the play; do we feel the transitions from one to another? In a word, are we capable of laying a path subtly and lightly before the eyes of others so that certain essential contents are revealed?

Out first act consists of the first two of Turgenev's acts, it lasts about one hour. This hour should be weightless to highlight only those moments needed for explanation of the contents, moreover in a form that is carefully planned by us.

Turgenev's third, fourth, and fifth acts (our second act) must be qualitatively distinct from the first. There is reserve, restraint, while here are open incidents, very stormy, passionate. Here is the unique story of Natalya Petrovna's crime. She does a number of the most impudent things, not guided by reason, but impulsive. At the same time, her conscience tells her to behave exactly opposite to how she behaves.

For me, it is reminiscent of Chekhov's story "The Black Monk."

Natalya Petrovna strives toward a certain abyss against her will. This abyss disturbs her, excites her, and torments her. She seems bewitched by something unknown to her and which is necessary for her to learn.

I would like to use the most widely known Mozart motif, which will sometimes call her somewhere loudly or softly. She should almost go mad from it. Indeed, this is written in the text. She says that she will possibly go mad, that her head aches terribly, that it seems as if they are following her, etc.

They are following her to keep her from breaking out of this vicious circle. However, she will try to break out. She will touch another sort of life. Then, like Kovrin in "The Black Monk," she will be cured of this madness and become what she actually is and what she should be. "All you beautiful people," Natalya Petrovna says to the truly beautiful people who try to stop her, wishing to help her. And yet...

Then, having said this, according to Turgenev she kicks the door open and leaves.

I read somewhere that there are butterflies that live for only one day. In the morning, they emerge into the light from their cocoons, and in the evening, they die, after giving birth to larvae. After a year, these larvae once again emerge as butterflies, and again only for a day. I cannot vouch for the accuracy, but I read something like it.

I thought that this butterfly has no awareness of its own misfortune, just as there is no awareness in us that we will not live as along as eagles, for example. We do not measure our life with the life of a tree that lives five hundred years, or the life of a snake or a crocodile. We think about our life within the limits of human nature, so to speak, and in our own way we measure whether our life is long or short.

But imagine a butterfly whose consciousness has not only awakened (who knows, maybe it does have consciousness), but a *comparative* consciousness has also been awakened about the scantiness of the lifetime allotted to it, the same consciousness there is in a human being, though not so tortured by it.

Now this butterfly starts to suffer. It has learned that other butterflies live two or three days, and some even a whole summer, and that there are eagles and mountains and many other things besides. In addition, it wants to live life as another butterfly or even an eagle. How this ended, it is easy to imagine. It does not live for even one day.

What Happens at My Rehearsals?

Whenever I explain something about a play, I get the feeling that my reasoning almost never concerns something that is precisely of the specific nature of the theatre. I am always afraid that my reasoning is too general. Meanwhile, the process of rehearsal is so specific and concrete that only someone who sees a rehearsal can understand with complete accuracy the general reasoning of this or that moment of the play or performance.[92]

However, it is possible to speak with some measure of success about various professional matters, especially rehearsal matters, but sometimes this also seems wrong. So many people in the theatre try to write in a *professional* style, but it is easy to lapse into primitiveness when discussing how to conduct rehearsal. After all, how can you describe what is, in many respects, the intuitive improvisational rehearsal process that occupies us at rehearsals? I have read many transcripts of one or another of our rehearsals, and personally, they tell me nothing. It would be even stranger to somebody else that it is to me.

Today, for example, after we engaged in long discussions about every scene and endless attempts at first one and then another dialogue, we finally tried to assemble one entire large act combining two of Turgenev's acts. Many people sat in on the rehearsal, but I think nine tenths of them hardly understood what happened. We had only one concern, perhaps, and it is hard to explain to the uninitiated. We wanted to break through the completely huge quantity of text to something that forms the very essence of these actions and not linger on any particulars, no matter how remarkable. After all, there are many of these particulars, and every one of them is a temptation.

Take the moments when Rakitin reads *The Count of Monte Cristo* to Natalya Petrovna. Each time she interrupts him, he begins all over again with the same sentence. In this one trifle, there are many possibilities for acting. However, is acting necessary here? Usually it is not. Moreover, I am speaking not only about this concrete example, but *in general.* Frequently, even in a huge dialogue, there is no place, or to be more precise, there should not be any place for unnecessary stopping. At this point, you should only be occupied with, so to speak, hurrying up. You ask [the actors] to play more dynamically, more rapidly, or if you will, more goal-oriented, and the actor begins to ask: But when do I [get a chance to] live through this place or another place? Moreover, you have to answer that it is necessary to live through it instantaneously, like life itself. It often happens that one person has just opened his mouth to say some lines and the other has already lived through the answer to it, not spoken yet but foreseen in the line. Moreover, there is a huge quantity of such moments, and if they are correctly played, their *unexpectedness* holds our attention as strongly as it could if they were all played as the main thing.

Everyone knows it, but they are unable to do it. They act everything in small pieces, with no feeling of motion toward something, [no feeling] that there is an overall meaning. Moreover, everyone seems to understand the meaning in his own way. In addition, although sometimes an actor will not be stuck on trifles, nevertheless the goal he is striving for is worthless. Just try to prove, however, that the goal you selected for a given scene or an entire play is better than the goal selected by someone else. In art, everything is to some extent subjective.

However, subjectivity is subjectivity. Even so, there should be integrity, completeness in the course of action that you chose for yourself.

Frequently, we not only choose an indistinct goal but we approach it with such uncertain and confused steps that it remains clear only to us and no one else. In some cases, however, this is not so bad: let a poor goal be poorly understood. However, when you are confident that your goal is interesting and significant, then it is a pity if the actor does not reach this goal, i.e., he falls, having stumbled over any trifle that he can turn to his advantage, but actually only caries him away from his goal.

In *The Cherry Orchard*, there was an extraordinarily memorable goal for me. It was the prolonged cry of Ranevskaya, saying goodbye to her childhood, to her own past, to her life. To me, it seemed important to move toward this cry swiftly, without unnecessary naturalism, without the traditional pauses, etc. However, to do this, the entire "orchestra" needs to feel a certain general mood, a spirit, and a certain general striving.

In a real orchestra, not counting the musical notes that every musician follows, there is still a conductor controlling this harmony of interests, this movement. The playing here cannot fail because there are always the notes and the conductor.

There is certainly a design in drama, of course, but just try to correct it during the action itself.

They say that Yuri Lyubimov stands in the back of the auditorium with a flashlight and, flashing it on and off, dictates to the actors the necessary rhythm, which shortly can be lost or found again.

However, what can you do if your art is built on subtle psychological adjustments? A flashlight cannot restore a lost design, but even more important, it would distract the actors from the truth.

In an art such as this, the actor *should* be left to himself, but what is also necessary in this case is teamwork, solidarity, accuracy of each other's sensations, and absolutely clarity of purpose.

And this is what we do at my rehearsals.

The Essence Behind the Form

We know that a child walking past an overweight person will often laugh. However, an adult will see a person with a health problem. The privilege of the adult is that he comprehends a certain essence behind the form.

Sometimes the audience is like a child. It sees, let us say, that the external form is ironic, but does not wish to understand this is not a sneer, but a drama. Meanwhile, that is precisely the point.

There are artists for whom deep content is expressed in a very simple form. Moreover, there are artists for whom the content is considerable and the form is complex as well. From many, many examples, which we know, however, this is in no way necessarily bad.

In addition, if someone who sees complex expressiveness assumes that someone is trying to fool him, in my opinion this only signifies that the person does not possess enough insight, or, in any case, is deprived of a lively curiosity about art.

Othello

If you follow the usual laws of logic, it can seem as though not enough time is given to strengthening Othello's belief in his wife's betrayal. Actually, he has only just learned about the betrayal, and then already it is "Blood, blood, blood!"

If he is simply a savage, of course, then everything is clear, but in fact, the play is not written about a savage.

As I already said, a certain internal nervous readiness for imminent and inevitable misfortunes is included in the whole play and in Othello's character. The issue is not even his trustfulness, perhaps, but *his predisposition to the idea that happiness is impossible for him.*

If the first two acts are not played with this in mind, and all of a sudden, he believes in the betrayal of his wife, then the image of savagery plainly appears.

Jealousy and trustfulness, certainly, but also a certain deep belief in the prospect of inevitable misfortune—here, perhaps, is the reason that his alarm, which arises the first time the slanderous phrase is heard, develops so quickly into full-scale desperation.

Clearly, ten different interpretations are possible, however it seems to me that, like some people, Othello has already gone though *everything* in his mind, and consequently it is only enough to begin something, then his imagination anticipates the reality so much that Iago's activity is facilitated.

Perhaps neither of them attaches great value to the words. Othello did not listen to every sentence of Iago, and Iago did not select any particular words for proofs. Although they speak a lot and apparently very fluently. Iago only touches on the subjects necessary to him, while Othello's imagination has outstripped all the words, and he has already seen the outcome many, many times.

The rapid development incorporated in the text should not be stretched out, delayed like a so-called "psychological game," but should be emphasized even more by the swiftness with which its psychological truth is accomplished, arising not from familiar old concepts, but from extremely concrete circumstances and characters.

So-called psychology in such cases must not be a stone that pulls a play down to the bottom, and in this case even more.

Set fire to a wood chip and it will smolder for a long time, but light a match (which is the same as a wood chip) with a piece of sulfur on the tip, and the match will flare up and immediately burn out. However, the sulfur was prepared in advance, just as Othello was prepared in advance, for what had happened.

The sensation that he is a person from another world makes Othello not only trusting when it is a question of troubles threatening him, but even a *hypochondriac* vulnerable to morbidity.

Meanwhile, despite the swiftness in the development of Othello's madness, it is necessary to distribute the stages of this madness ahead of time so as not to play what should lie ahead. In addition, not to destroy the development of Shakespeare's extant analysis.

At first, having reflected on his wife's betrayal, mentally he does not attack *her*, but immediately seems to find the reason for her betrayal in himself. This is improbable, but at the same time from his point of view, it is *natural* to some extent. In the sensation of this naturalness is his special vulnerability. Othello has become gloomy and silent.

It is even hard for him to exchange two words with the entering Desdemona. Can it really be true that she has deceived him because he is as he is?

After a short absence, Othello returns in a very different mood. Now he furiously protests against his new *knowledge*.

He asserts that it would have been much better if he knew nothing. Let there be deceit, as long as *he does not know about it!*

Then, just as stormily, he changes to a demand for *proofs*, without which he supposedly will not believe in Desdemona's betrayal. He even warns Iago that the proofs must be special, he will not believe in simple ones.

He accuses Iago of slander, he is aggressive, but this aggressiveness only testifies to the fact that he already *believes*. Because of this, Iago's proofs immediately seem *special* to him, as indeed they must be.

Desdemona did not love him, he was not sophisticated, and he was black, middle-aged. She did not love him—this stranger in Venice. He does not even try to consider the obvious: what she gave up for her marriage with Othello, that she lost her home, broke with her father, and went off to war. Moreover, all this to carry on a romance with Cassio? His wound prevents him from considering this reasonably. Blood clouds his mind, and at this point, he wants only *blood*. Then he almost calms down. No longer violent, and now seemingly in his right mind, he recalls an old and terrible thought—he is black, middle-aged, far from worldly. Happiness is not for him...! Why was he deceived, however?

When Desdemona appears, he conducts the dialogue, according to her words, rapidly and wildly. In his present condition, it is necessary to *discharge* everything immediately. He rushes to her in order to resolve everything. To say everything immediately, ask about everything, insult, learn about the handkerchief, but also hear something that could quickly dispel the entire horror of his suspicions.

However, he cannot pack all this into any logical conversation. He begins tactlessly, with crude hints. He has never spoken to Desdemona in such a tone before. To think and speak in such a tone is more characteristic of Iago, and Desdemona is stupefied.

She tries to get away from this tone, which is completely unfamiliar to her coming from Othello, but she does not know that she has touched on the most terrible subject for him—Cassio.

At this point, Othello has no need to deviate from his determined path. He demands that she return the gift to him, which, according to Iago, Cassio already has. He demands that she give it to him immediately—either everything must be confirmed now or it will turn out to be insane nonsense. However, unfortunately, Desdemona does not have the handkerchief, and Othello throws this fact in her face with terrible sharpness.

Further ideas should develop now, but they do not come. Othello is in a sort of fog. He would like to forget and have a have a break from the stress, but he [needs] to receive a new shake-up from Iago to operate further.

Moreover, in order not to [reveal everything] directly, now Iago takes up Desdemona's defense, protecting her right to give Othello's scarf to anybody she wishes.

Othello waves him away, reluctantly argues, does not want to listen, he is tired, but again he demands something *greater* from Iago, even tries to *discover* this greater [proof]. His interest here is already nervous, sick. He wants to know everything about his wife, every thing; he wants to drink this cup completely.

Having received everything he demanded from Iago, however, Othello loses consciousness.

Regaining consciousness, he has difficulty coming to his senses, hesitating from what just happened. With no time to think, he appears in the hiding place where Iago puts him out of sight to spy. Moreover, he overhears the conversation with Cassio, but because of his confusion, he does not understand that it has nothing to do with Desdemona.

Cassio's flashes the handkerchief slipped to him by Iago, and Othello leaves his hiding place, already completely prepared for the idea that Iago will now prompt in him: Desdemona must be suffocated in her own bed.

Othello's experiences, fallen on him so immediately and intensely, have worked on him with such force that before our eyes he, a strong person, became an instrument in the hands of another. As it often happens, perhaps, with people who cannot endure very heavy sufferings.

Othello loses all control over himself. In the presence of strangers and even officials from Venice, he cannot find the strength to pretend or restrain himself. He tortures himself and torments Desdemona.

His incomparable grief pours out in the form of self-torture.

Lodovico asks Iago if Othello is always this coarse. However, it is not coarseness, more likely it is nervous shock.

Before killing Desdemona, Othello meets her once more. He is longing to come here, he wants to speak, even to weep, he wants to tell her what she has done to him. Although he behaves abusively, it hardly needs to be perceived literally. It is the *means* he uses to pour out his sufferings.

Before the last scene, Emilia notices that Othello apparently became kinder. This is because he has made his final decision. He made this decision and became calmer. As people probably become calmer when they are resolved on suicide. More likely, it is not calmness but concentration. Maximum narrowly focused concentration.

More often, they try to play this scene passionately. Passion only flares up, however, when Desdemona suddenly screams after learning about the death of Cassio. It is seemingly forced on Othello. How dare she cry out about her lover to her husband!

Then the last terrible finale begins. Desdemona resists, for she understands that everything is a mistake, and she only needs *a delay to explain everything.*

He kills her, both of them roughly resisting.

Again the same lullaby that was heard at the end of the first act, only now transformed into a funeral march.

Maybe the murder, contrary to all tradition, is very, very quiet...

Desdemona does not resist completely. After all, if Othello does not love her, then her life is not worth anything. Othello lies beside her, and turns down the light as if they were going to sleep. When the lights come up vividly once more, Othello quickly rises and disappears for a few long seconds. Desdemona lies without moving. Emilia knocks and asks to be allowed in. Othello slowly enters, trying not to look aside at the bed, and after admitting Emilia, he sits on a chair with his back to Desdemona.

Objectivity and the Classics

When you produce a well-known classical work, then you [may decide to] intentionally avoid doing it by the book. However, this "deliberate deviation" automatically incites some people to compare your work with the [original] book and point out that yours is *not the way it should be.* They think that you do not know this. That you have intentionally made what they perceive as an unsuccessful attempt to reconstruct a classical work *the way it should be*. It seems to them that they know the "objective truth" better than you do. On the other hand, you would very much like them to examine *your* idea. It is very self-confident, of course, to believe that your idea could interest someone when there is a *fundamental principal* at stake.

Really produce [something according to] this fundamental principle and you will verge upon genuine *high quality*. However, *your new ideas* should exist only to the extent that you have a deep, all around comprehension of this fundamental principal. That is all! I really do not deny such a possibility.

MAT, for example, produced Gorky's play *The Lower Depths*.[93] What if MAT did not have its *own* Moskvin, who played the character of Luka? Nonetheless, he played Gorky's character three-dimensionally, *objectively* [i.e., "by the book"]. Now imagine a new interpretation of *The Lower Depths* in which Luka would somehow be "modified" in favor of a "new idea." It is possible to assume that this would arouse the resentment of those who knew Moskvin, of course, and were amazed by his acting at the time.

All the same, Moskvin's Luka is also an *example* in another sense.

Gorky himself may have considered Luka's character much more disapprovingly. True, it is only speculative. In his own statements, however, he was more severe toward people of Luka's type than he concretely expressed in the play.

It depended on the actor even more. It would have been possible for Moskvin to play another way, and the little old man, Luka, would have become not so likable to us. Indeed, Luka is a stubborn sort of caregiver in any case!

Moskvin had every opportunity for *this* approach. However, in my opinion, he chose another way.

Whether intuitively or planned, I do not know, but he chose something different. It could be that Luka's kindness, which is often said of his character, is actually harmful [in the context of the story], but Moskvin recognized that his Luka knew the meaning of grief. While the other residents of the lodging house were hard and indifferent. Anna, it seems, asked Luka why he was so compassionate. In addition, he replied that he had been abused a lot. And Luka sympathized with all those who were *abused*. It is not such a big thing, of course—to help the dying Anna to reach from the door to the bed and induce her to believe that the next world is better than this one. What else, however, would be best to do for Anna? Let her to die without being afraid there will be torment beyond the grave. Besides, to help such a person, when even her husband will not do it, is not such a small thing...

Moskvin had the greatest ability to act such roles not sweetly, not cloyingly. It is hard to imagine another actor who could play Luka in that way. The genuine, distinctive, suffering of old age was unique to him. It was his individuality even as a young man and maybe he interpreted Luka instinctively this way precisely because of this individuality.

Naturally, in his Luka, there was the usual guile and cunning, and maybe ten other features, but the interpretation was nevertheless specific. Moskvin did not *debunk* Luka. Although he could have done so if he wished. He apparently obeyed the voice of his individuality. Stanislavsky agreed with this acting because he was sufficiently powerful himself, after all, and if he wanted something different, he would have made it so.

Here you have an *interpretation* even in what would seem to be a classical situation. What about roles that lay many years away from actors and directors? Sometimes even centuries.

If the "subjectivity" of your interpretation is absurd, of course, then it is misguided to compare it with centuries of settled objective wisdom. However, after all, not everyone's so-called biased reading is absurd.

How many interpretations have there been of *Hamlet*, for example? Some were ridiculous, of course, but many were serious, of some stature, and *completely different,* expressing not only Shakespeare, but also a new epoch and its new artistic representatives. Meanwhile, many directors, probably, sincerely believed that they honestly revealed only Shakespeare. Others, by contrast, consciously supplied new accents.

In both cases, they were frequently *wonderful,* although not very "objective." Besides, what is an "objective" *Hamlet*? It is probably possible to devise a formula. However, each important researcher is important precisely because he reveals at least a particle of something new in *Hamlet*. Alternatively, let us say, he tells an old truth in a certain *new style*. Otherwise, no talented person would have performed Shakespeare any more.

In fact, thousands of books have been written about *Hamlet*.

Sunsets or sunrises are also [naturally] "objective," but should it be necessary to stop painting them because of this? Should we should stop painting sunsets? Yet it is possible to fill the entire country of Belgium, for example, with paintings of sunsets. A new artist is born if and only if he sees scores of unused possibilities in this "objectivity." It seems to him that they still do not know *his kind* of sunrise, as it *really is*.

Then for some reason he begins to paint, let us say, with fine points. While earlier, they painted with broad strokes. Moreover, immediately many people begin to scream that this is not a sunset at all. However, the years pass, and [eventually] we agree with *this* sunset. Moreover, today even this sunset will be used to intimidate the young, who do not paint like this any longer.

It is complicated to discuss all these themes, but interpretation itself, *genuine* reputable interpretation, is sufficiently *objective*. And demands independent analysis [on its own terms].

Moreover, this analysis should not just be compared with the [original] source. For in a sense a genuine interpretation is also a source.

All this "philosophy" probably comes from a wish to justify or defend what you do yourself.

...Some have said to us, Molière's Don Juan cannot be so indolent, awkward, and plain [as we have portrayed him].[94] Boris Godunov should not be so weak. After all, this is [the famous] Boris Godunov! They bring up the powerful figure of [the opera star] Fyodor Shalyapin, whom virtually none of us have seen, of course, and who can only be heard [on recordings].[95] Nevertheless, it is possible to read something about his acting, to look at pictures, and there you already have a ["definitive"] representation of Boris Godunov.

It is also possible that nothing was even heard or seen or read, that [only] a legend exists, which almost everyone knows about, and which all Boris Godunovs are compared to.

It is quite probable, however, that Godunov himself, the real Godunov, was a strong man, with a powerful will, who conducted affairs ruthlessly, was goal-oriented, knew what he wanted, and unwaveringly achieved his intended goals.

Boris Godunov, however, was wonderfully performed by Shalyapin in opera for a long time. It is not likely that Shalyapin simply wanted to show a powerful Godunov. This would not have been in line with Pushkin or Mussorgsky, or Shalyapin. Everyone knows that behind all this [alleged] power and coarseness was Shalyapin's interpretation of the panic of a man unable to forget that he is a criminal, and because of this, he is unable to concentrate on his [official] duties.

Was this true in reality? Maybe it was, who knows, but according to Pushkin, *it was.*

Godunov did not have power over the souls of his people because in each of them he saw a potential accuser.

This feeling of guilt consumed him. It is not the same Godunov who was historically strong. He is falling apart as an individual because he was—*a murderer*. Consequently, the entire government, built on a guilty conscience, also began to fall apart, and the "Impostor" appeared who began with a protest against the murderer of the Tsar and concluded with another murder. In addition, the people were stunned by this turn [of events].

Probably the historical Godunov did not question this issue, did not question this issue in isolation. Possibly what was [historically] there was only a hint of some other insight. However, this hint was extremely important to Pushkin.

Moreover, Shalyapin, of course, acted with an understanding of what Pushkin had written. However, in the eyes and minds of those who saw Shalyapin, if they do not dig deeply into some books, there remains only his general appearance, his powerful appearance.

Meanwhile, the years pass, and general memories become stereotypes. Now you take up a *Boris Godunov* that is not performed anywhere except in the opera house precisely because of these stereotypes, but in your own work you would like to resurrect at least a particle of some truth.

Without disagreement, however, without a strong turnaround, you will not be able to escape from the stereotype.

If it *succeeds*, everyone will understand and forgive. If it *does not succeed*, you had better beware...

Othello

In *Othello,* there is a scene where Iago persuades the Moor that he should not be so emotional about Desdemona's betrayal. Because betrayals like this are natural parts of life. "Millions lie," says Iago, "in improper beds." Moreover, the only way out is to remove the rose-colored glasses and ruthlessly begin to protect yourself. In addition, after hearing this, Othello approaches Iago and says that he is completely right and that he is clever. So says Othello, who is the opposite of Iago. However, what is he to do if Iago's arguments are convincing? Othello accepts his way of thinking, believes in his truth. He obeys him. This is a play about the weakness of goodness, about the inability of goodness to resist evil. Iago molded what he wanted from Othello. Under the pretense of love for him, under the pretense of struggling to rescue him, Iago has changed Othello's mentality, has begun to twist him around his little finger.

This is one of the most terrible fundamental dangers.

There are certain basic parables. About Christ and Judas, for example. One of those parables is the story of Othello and Iago.

In the end, when Othello learns that he was not deceived by Desdemona, but by Iago, he looks at Iago and says that he does not see his *hooves*. However, what if, striking with his knife, he does not manage to kill Iago? *Then* it will be clear that Iago is the *devil*. After being stabbed with a knife, Iago is still alive. He proudly stands up and pronounces that he is alive, although he is bleeding profusely. That he is the devil, of course, is only a metaphor.

But that he managed to "possess" Othello's soul, this is accurate.

Othello stands before this man-devil. He turns sharply away from Iago after pronouncing that he will not kill him but will leave him to be tortured. Then Othello apparently forgets about him. This oblivion, however, this curse will remain to mark Iago for centuries. And in a minute, when Othello kills himself and falls, perhaps Iago will lower his head since he feels that henceforth the name "Iago" will be a symbol of something disgusting.

The people who lift up the fallen Othello, on the other hand, stand up straight, even upright, sharply raising his head to the sky.

And this group, with the dead Othello in their hands and standing opposite the twisted form of Iago, will remain motionless a long time, substituting this for the customary bows, and when the lights go up in the auditorium, God willing, the audience's applause will be heard.

If the applause is good, however, then it will be no sin to take a bow.

Beyond the Obvious

Yesterday I read a beautiful, though not new, play by Tennessee Williams, *Summer and Smoke*.[96] In it, he describes an unfortunate woman and discusses why she is unfortunate. However, many of those around her do not feel pity for her. They only see that this woman is ridiculous, even unattractive in some way. Williams sees all this, however, but he is different from her simple neighbors because he is an *artist*. He sees what everyone else can see, but he also feels what is hidden from their eyes, he knows.

Someone's dog once barked at a hunchback. His master wanted to run away from shame. How could he explain to the dog that this person's misfortune is regrettable, and it is wrong to bark?

However, it is a dog. Yet people often act the same way. Try to force someone to understand, for example, that this is a portrait even though it is only so many broken lines. No, you will not be able to. They see what is *obvious*, but they do not want to feel what lies *beyond the obvious*. Possibly, it interferes with some prejudices. There are a great many in art. However, they say that I am only grumbling, they say they do not always understand art, and similar nonsense...

A Month in the Country

Meanwhile (as it usually happens at rehearsals), the second half of the play turns out worse because it is hard to grasp what distinguishes it from the first half. You are angry with the actors, of course, but then you go home and realize that you explained quite badly to them what is *new* in the second half. The third, fourth, and fifth acts begin here, but meanwhile, owing to your bad explanation, the car is running on empty. Overall, the play is [adequately] developed because the plot is still there, but there is not enough *internal novelty, internal development,* and so there is monotony.

In the third act, meanwhile, a *sharp change* develops. We will return once more to what is in it.

After hearing Rakitin's next reproach that she is hiding something from him, concealing something, Natalya Petrovna stretches out her hand to him and unexpectedly says that he is mistaken. That since yesterday a profound change has taken place in her, that today she has reconsidered many things, etc. In a word, she says that today she wants something to change. Today she is filled with a new conscious determination. The point is that today she has decided to be candid! Evidently, it is too hard to carry her secret inside herself. Now she has decided to describe literally and directly what has happened inside her. Isn't this in itself new? Isn't this different in itself from her former mysterious, secretive, and strange behavior? In addition, doesn't this demand, perhaps, a certain completely new human direction, a new adaptation?

Natalya Petrovna does not realize, however, that the real meaning of the earlier event was already clear to Rakitin.

"What, you noticed it? For how long?" asks Natalya Petrovna. What fear, what unexpectedness, what a question suddenly explodes from her in reply to his statement that her openness is not news for him.

Already this event in itself is unusual compared to what happened before. After all, in the previous two acts she accused Rakitin of lacking intuition. She laughed about his impenetrability. Now, convinced that he has not guessed anything about it, she has resolved to be candid, and suddenly she hears, "I already knew about it!"

—What, you noticed it? For how long?
—Since yesterday.
—What!

You can imagine how much is in this "What!" It means it was noticed! It means that it was *her* impenetrability and not *his*! What news this is to her, and what an embarrassment. It means that he is not in a ridiculous position from his apparent blindness, but she is, with her conviction that no one sees or knows anything. Rakitin not only informs her that he suspected everything, he also pitilessly sketches out for her yesterday's foolish behavior, her sharpness, which, as he considers, only humiliated her. He speaks to her sharply about this. So that she will be ashamed of her wish to give the impression of a little girl, when she no longer is.

Having said all this, Rakitin even turns away from her. He despises her. Moreover, here *another new requirement* comes into play for Natalya Petrovna. To explain her frankness. To clarify, explain, prove. After all, she had not counted on *this* interpretation of her confession. She assumed that Rakitin would understand the *implied* sense of her passion. Besides, she never even dreamed about a real romance with Belyayev. At this point, she feels a terrifying melancholy from her unspent youth. Moreover, Rakitin, the best friend she has known her entire life, apparently *could* understand this. However, this needs to be interpreted subtly. Only as an unbecoming passion for a young man. Natalya Petrovna should now come to some extended interpretation of her frankness. She says that this feeling went to her head, like wine. That she has no intention of a *romance*, she asks him to understand her and not turn away from her. She says that this is her *misfortune*, but not her *fault*. In addition, that she came to him in hopes of hearing some sort of advice, etc. She speaks about all this sincerely, with pain, crying about it, *praying for help*.

However, Rakitin was offended and left.

"And this one!" says Natalya Petrovna, remaining alone. "He! Why, even he wouldn't understand!" Then an idea occurs to her. It is time to stop all this! "Yes... It is time!" Natalya Petrovna repeats.

At this point Vera enters, and although it seems the decision has already been made, the wind seems to blow Natalya Petrovna in another direction, away from reason, away from the dictates of reason. In one jolt, so to speak, she informs Vera that Bolshintsov has asked for her hand in marriage. She does this swiftly and almost unconsciously so that the restraints of reason have no time to work. Then Vera's laughter sobers her up. Then both of them, playing the fools, bury the imaginary Bolshintsov, that man who only a moment ago was to have been Vera's husband. Vera's laughter at Natalya Petrovna's offer is more eloquent than the bitterest tears.

For a minute, they simply *rest* after the severe shock. One from the impetuous, half-consciousness of a conniving deed, and the other from a stormy reaction to that deed.

In a moment, however, Natalya Petrovna is once more overcome with the overwhelming desire to *continue*. What is Vera hiding behind her refusal to marry Bolshintsov? Is it simply hostility to an older man, natural at her age, or something else? Once more Natalya Petrovna *rushes ahead,* leaving reason behind, to understand Vera's secret.

This is often the way people want to learn the truth, even the most tragic truth, to learn it, instead of living in *ignorance*. Reason, on the other hand, suggests to them that it would be better not to know, but almost unconsciously, they strive for the truth, for the truth that pushes them toward the abyss, and then they learn what they wanted, even if they collapse afterward. This moment of collapsing, or more accurately, almost collapsing, this moment when the entire force of the will is required not to collapse, needs to be played psychologically and strongly, accurately, for this also is *news*, it is *new: Natalya Petrovna has learned about the mutual love of these two young people.*

When Vera leaves, Natalya Petrovna has a big monologue. It can be read as one long sigh, of course, in the same *mood* as the previous scene. And this is probably how it needs to be done. All the same, it has its own logic, its own development, which cannot be neglected.

In the beginning, after Natalya Petrovna regains controls of herself, she sensibly, reasonably, precisely defines what has just happened. What has happened, in fact, is not only that she has learned about Vera and Belyayev's love for each other. More important, what has happened is that she has *apprehended* this love precisely this way. That she conducted the scene with Vera precisely *this way.* That despite her wish, her motive was *devious*. That she almost collapsed when Vera acknowledged it. What does it all mean? Has Natalya Petrovna really fallen in love? Natalya Petrovna?! Has she really fallen in love to such a degree? She frankly and severely sets before herself everything that has happened to her up to now.

"Well, so that's the terrible feeling!" she concludes.

However, maybe it is not true, and Vera and Belyayev do not love each other? This is her only hope. It is necessary to find out about this! Then the nightmare is either *confirmed or dispelled.*

Rakitin's arrival only disturbs her; she does not need him. She continues to whisper something to herself; she does not hear Rakitin.

She offended him, not wishing to do so. She runs to apologize. Then she runs off when her husband arrives and comes running in again. Neither her husband nor Rakitin disturb her in themselves, but only the fact that someone may prevent her from getting through to Belyayev. It disturbs her that someone may get ahead of her and presume something that is not true.

She is so tense in her attempt to be free from Rakitin's watchful eye, she is so tense in her desire to grope for a particular way to have a conversation with Belyayev, that she frightens Rakitin with *her strange smile and her pallor.* Now she is beside herself, she does not hear anything, does not see, she wants only to find out whether Belyayev loves Vera. Further, she must learn this for herself!

Natalya Petrovna remains alone for a moment while they call for Belyayev. What is she thinking about? That Rakitin is *correct,* although he is disgusting to her now. Belyayev must *leave.* She only needs to find out whether he loves Vera. However, he must leave. "I will only learn if he loves her or not!"

The tension is such that her head aches, it even seems to her that everyone is watching her. Yet she is resolved: "I will learn right now if he loves her or not."

When Belyayev enters, she sits tensely for a second, as if preparing for a leap. She is certain that she needs *to find out,* but she does not know how to get down to business. Meantime, it is too late to think anymore. Belyayev is already standing and waiting to learn why they called for him.

And once more, like the previous situation with Vera, Natalya Petrovna leaves reason behind and rushes into a conversation with only one feeling, with only one passion: to find out. This is not easy to act, for on the way *to this goal* are two tons of text. However, she has to get through it to this goal. And she finds out: Belyayev does not love Vera. Now he wishes to leave, he leaves, he says goodbye; however, it is necessary to detain him. All these are swift, lightning transitions, but they are there, and they must be noticed. Now she needs to detain him, and he agrees to remain.

Then a new suspicion appears that he has deceived her and wants to remain *for Vera's sake.* It is better to leave things as they are for a while and think things over.

She remains alone. Belyayev leaves. At this point, she begins to come back to herself. Reason tells her that Belyayev does not love Vera. Is she *calm*? However, at this point a new feeling comes over her, a feeling of *guilt.* It suddenly becomes clear to her what she has done. Once more, she has been *treacherous. She fears it, she feels ashamed, and she would like to hide from herself.*

That is the third act. The *novelty* of it lies in Natalya Petrovna's behavior. The comprehension of this novelty and all its zigzags is the *motion of the play.* The *development.* However, this is not simply the motion of the plot. Indeed, that will develop even when the play is performed badly. The real issue is the development of an internal life.

The fourth act, like the third, begins with Doctor Shpigelsky. In addition, everything connected with him. These scenes are humorous, provide highlighting for the *canvas*, and give it dimension. This direction is necessary not only for light and shade, however, not only for laughter following the serious places, as in Shakespeare. In this direction, there is also destiny, and *character.* Yet the *charm* apparent here depends on *balance*, a feeling of space and time. It is necessary to calculate things so that the main plot is not forgotten. In addition, in this calculation, there must be a special charm.

It is just like in rehearsal, when a good joke, a sudden distraction, and someone's amusing story, someone's unexpected arrival is very necessary. This arrival has highlighted something essential, possibly even puts it in its place. However, it is bad when the digression is prolonged, when the storyteller forgets about time limits, when the new arrival breaks up the meaning of the rehearsal. Usually you watch over rehearsal closely so that it will not become boring, however the work should not suffer from a good, necessary, and even very useful joke.

And the plot returns. After a rest, it is always a little difficult to get back to work. Without a special skill, it could be bad.

New *impulses* are necessary for development of the internal life. It is necessary to know about them. They need to be controlled.

The first such impulse in the fourth act is in the performance Belyayev's role. Specifically, he begins what is new in this act. More than that, his role prior to this is only that of a selfish youth. *Corruption* has not touched him yet. The plot has not touched him yet. The *plot* has not passed *through him yet.* All this begins only in the fourth act. Just think, only in the fourth act! And it is necessary to play it knowing that your serious moment, your "contribution," will only appear in the fourth act. In the beginning of the fourth act, Shpigelsky will become important. At this point, the moment of Belyayev's *initiative* will arrive. However [here it is important] not to put a blanket over yourself, as the actors say, but to underscore the *matter*, the *essence.* It is necessary to let everyone know that something new is beginning now. It is necessary to reveal this novelty. What is it? It is that Belyayev suddenly *feels* a certain secret. He is almost a detective.

Belyayev feels a secret, feels it, but for the moment, he cannot understand the secret. Now, before our eyes, he tries to guess. This is the moment when the last scene with Shpigelsky, if it was done well, should suddenly be set aside in favor of *the further development of the meaning.*

If, in the third act, almost everything depends on the development of the thoughts and feelings of Natalya Petrovna, then here all of us are under the influence of how Belyayev will begin the fourth act. Now, after a minute, Vera appears.

Her role actually begins around this point too. Even the last scene with Natalya Petrovna is *nothing* compared to this act. For everything up to that point was limited to her life as a child, but now the plot proceeds *through Vera.* In addition, the lightning speed of *the new course of things* amazes her. How interesting it probably is to play this boundary. Not to waste time with trifles in the lines, but *to engage in the event* at hand completely. Belyayev's attempts to calm her are ridiculous to her, it is so clear to her that this is the end. He either has not understood yet, or hides it.

Anyhow, there is a *chasm* between them now.

In addition, a chasm between her and Natalya Petrovna. That is why for the first time she is disrespectful. The issue here is not in Vera's tears or cries, but in her contempt for the fact Natalya Petrovna wants, as before, to seem like her guardian. Meanwhile, the lie is obvious, and it is necessary only to reject this lie. This is a certain free and natural impulse to repudiate a lie.

This is the *first time* for Vera, however, and the fact that it is the *first time* is revealed to Natalya Petrovna suddenly, she is not used to this, she is lost, confused. After all, Belyayev is standing beside them. Moreover, in his presence Vera says that she is deceitful, false, that she has fallen in love with him, etc. This is the sort of disgrace that must be hidden, either by a new lie, or by a new, even greater deceit, or by a sharp stop, a sharp turn, a sharp line.

It is probably like a moment when, in the folly of running away somewhere, you suddenly come to your senses and return home so there will not be even greater misfortunes. This is an attempt to draw the line, to limit yourself, your impulses, to return to reason. They draw the line for each other, they forbid themselves from crossing this line, and trust that they can hold back. At the last moment, however, so characteristic of Natalya Petrovna, she destroys this line, erases it, she breaks it with one push, impulsively, forgetting about everything, and spitting at everyone.

Then comes the "contribution" of her husband, Islayev. All the other roles have been played. Now it is his turn. Moreover, if this solo is not heard, it means the concert is over before they announce the end.

This happens in many performances. However, if Islayev will *act*, if he will do his job, some of the impulses of Vera and Natalya Petrovna will remain. The last sharp impulses before the end.

Moreover, it will end with the role of Islayev, who suddenly takes everything upon himself, for the time has come when his wife needs to be protected. When it is necessary to force everyone to let her rest. And he will send everyone away. And he himself leaves to see off Rakitin. When everything calms down, Natalya Petrovna enters and quietly sits alone.

The performance ends, like *Othello*, with a long silence.

In almost all my productions, however, the characters appear to be reporting their troubles in the very first scene. Even the solemn wedding ceremony at the beginning of my production of Nikolai Gogol's *Marriage*, for example, expresses trouble, even though a church choir is singing beautifully.[97]

And in *Othello*, when Iago looks long and silently at his enemies seated in the distance, certainly we immediately understand that nothing good will come from this.

However, for *A Month in the Country*, by contrast, it is possible to provide an extremely pleasant beginning. A country estate shining in the sun, a boy playing with a hoop. A tutor and a governess. A teacher of French and Russian. Grandmother, aunt, mama. Elegant Rakitin. A kite with an unusual form, which can float up to the sky. All the characters involved in some type of cheerful activity. Laughter and exclamations of the boy are heard. In a word, an idyll, serene happiness, well-being. Graceful, beautiful, amicable.

Further, when Natalya Petrovna remains alone with Rakitin, and somewhere upstage the old people are randomly playing a game of cards, she should conduct the scene approximately like this: all of us are safe, but indeed, you, Rakitin, are in love with me, and you are a perceptive man, so can you guess what is *troubling* me?

In addition, laughing, he joins in this imaginary game, only he does not quite begin to search for the solution there. It is like the well-known children's game "cold-hot." "You're cold, cold," laughs Natalya Petrovna. "You are not very perceptive. Don't look for it there."

It is necessary to begin the performance on the note of "the charming gentry," but to end with the desperate note of *The Cherry Orchard*.

The So-Called Correct View

The ideological and artistic credo of each classic work is obviously contained inside it. It would be absurd, for example, to produce *The Storm* by Ostrovsky and interpret Marfa Kabanova as good and nice and Katerina as unattractive and silly.[98] In a sense, there is a limit to the interpretations of each play. However, the so-called correct view of older plays does not exclude the possibility of variants, depending on new actors, designers, and directors. Or the time and place of the production. These variants can strongly differ from the axiomatic interpretation, changing something in our view of the old play, expanding and enriching it. Despite the fact that some of the new variants will always come across not only serious but empty, all of us, it seems to me, should take care that the strictly axiomatic view of theatre has not triumphed.

However, sometimes people do not understand the nature of theatre. They become angry when the theatre thinks independently when dealing with classical works. They do not argue with the idea of independence as such, however, but with one or another performance, which, in their opinion, is the distortion of a classic. However, by doing so these people involuntarily put forward *their own* understanding, which quite often is simply traditional, habitual. Habitualness of this kind is easier to conceal behind words than when it has to be presented on stage. Sometimes it seems to those writing about art that they know the truth, but the theatre does not. Sometimes this happens, of course, but it is bad when, in a condemnation of one or another performance, the idea imperceptibly filters through that the theatre should produce *only* what is already known to the critics. Their own convictions are dearer to them than a sincere attempt to understand and feel someone else's creativity.

However, the theatre by its very nature is obliged to be a very lively institution, and not a peaceful, quiet place, like a museum. If this debate is won by the "strict" point of view, then in my opinion it will be very boring at the theatres. Only for a short period, however, because the nature of theatre will gain the upper hand all the same.

Othello

Maybe rehearsals of *Othello* should begin like this. Determine in general terms the structure of everything connected with Brabantio. Everything from the beginning up to the meeting in the Senate inclusively.

Define the major peaks of all the incidents, starting when the Senator is awakened, learns about the abduction of his daughter, and runs after her in pursuit. He wants to deal with the kidnappers himself, but he is called to the Senate, transfers his grievance there, and suddenly loses it.

Do not start with one peak but several high points toward which the action is striving, and when the action reaches one peak, it breaks off and strives further.

Iago needs Roderigo's help, and consequently it is necessary to dispel all his doubts. Nonetheless, all this is only a pathway for the main thing ahead.

They knock, shout, and call Brabantio from his house, but this too is only *for reference to the future*. Brabantio is awakened, he asks why these people knocked and shouted, he is angry and threatens to punish them. They persuade him to return to the house and see if Desdemona is there. However, once more all this is *on the way* toward something still to come.

Brabantio exits. Convinced that his daughter has been abducted, he is shaken, depressed, destroyed, his thoughts are confused, but all the same, although he is confused, he knows his purpose—pursuit.

Meanwhile, Iago is telling Othello how he stood up for him in the conflict with Brabantio. All this is in the course of the pursuit, however, which means it is swift enough.

Then Brabantio encounters Othello on the same street, and a minute of stoppage occurs when it seems, perhaps, that something essential might occur that will strongly change the course of events.

However, Cassio appears and reports about the war and the session of the Senate.

The action again develops swiftly.

The session is not a stoppage either, since the Senators are speculating about the intentions of the Turks, waiting for their military leader, who will study the war closely.

However, here something unforeseen occurs. The necessity to do something about the Turks interferes with Brabantio's complaint about the very same Othello, who at this moment must rescue the fatherland.

Nonetheless, this stop is relative, since the Senators can only be briefly distracted by outside affairs, and must try to settle them in the shortest period.

Even Othello's monologue, his huge monologue, in which he tells how Desdemona fell in love with him, this "star" monologue, which is always an effective *stop*, actually is only a path, moreover a difficult path. Since Othello must speak to the preoccupied Senators, who are constantly being distracted by the entrances and exits of the messengers. It is difficult to speak about love under such conditions. This is a compelled story, the story is a necessity on the way to something that, one way or another, must take place.

Everything is resolved positively for Othello because there is a war on, and Othello is *necessary*.

Then Brabantio surrenders, and his daughter and Othello leave for Cyprus.

Therefore, everything is in continuous movement, continuous additional aspirations, only with small, somewhat relative delays.

Now it will be necessary, taking notebooks in hand and rehearsing nothing yet, to feel only this *flow*, this push to the future, this *whole*.

The whole thing is like a long distance race in which Brabantio lags behind. Stumbling, he will fall somewhere in the first hundred meters, and the others—will run ahead.

It needs to be said that in this uncontrollable motion toward a tragic ending, on each page Shakespeare raises newer and newer obstacles, supposedly demanding stops or at least minimal highlighting. Yes, mostly *minimal*, for otherwise the complex structure of the play will begin to crumble and tire out.

Meanwhile, there are new places and new characters, now we are already on Cyprus, the holiday begins, and everyone drinks and has fun, while Iago accustoms Cassio to drinking in order to prepare for his dismissal.

There are so many opportunities for delays, for playing separate scenes, but even if done well, this type of playing will not bring beneficial enough. This is precisely a long distance race, only now we lose Cassio.

The most complex scene begins in the third act, when the issue of jealousy appears. The third, fourth, and fifth acts.

The path in these three long acts is long, yet even with the loss of hundreds of nuances, it is necessary to run through it *entirely*. Then the true high points will appear.

To show how Othello, after believing in the betrayal of his wife, finally reaches complete chaos, madness.

Overloading is the danger here. That is why everything must move *further and further* swiftly, toward something that *will happen,* something that is unavoidable in the end.

A true catastrophe will not occur if there is no *distance* covered. Without this distance, the catastrophe will be *forced.* However, if this distance is covered, the catastrophe becomes inevitable.

Frequently multiple murders pile up in Shakespeare. However, *over the distance,* everything, as in the momentum of a fatal battle, becomes inevitable.

In the intoxication of battle, even Iago forgets the *reasons.*

Over the distance, the intoxication of battle turns everyone into animals.

To come back to one's senses is difficult, a very strong impact is necessary.

An owner once boasted about his house, "If a crane is brought in here and hooked up to the roof, my house is built so strongly that the *whole* thing will rise, not one piece will fall to the ground."

Then I imagined how this small wooden house would rise up into the air, light as a bit of fluff.

However, if another house is lifted by the corner of its roof, the whole thing will begin to fall to pieces, everything will collapse into dust, boards will fall, and whole rooms will collapse. Even the furnace will fall out and crash to the ground.

First, however, the roof will be hooked up and collapse.

Meanwhile, the first house is pulled into the air in one piece. Everything there is so well fitted together that it is impossible to tear it apart.

Listening to the homeowner, of course, I doubted it would happen. After all, a house is not a toy. However, he very confidently expressed the idea that his house was meticulously built.

I repeatedly recalled this when, for example, I saw a certain performance and mentally lifted it up by one corner, and immediately whole scenes fell out, roles sprang out, even some sort of dust and the debris fell into fragments.

However, indeed, it is necessary to lift up certain scenes, even to lift up an entire act, to make sure it is well put together.

It is especially difficult to lift Shakespeare into the air so that no beams fall out, there are ultimately so many of these beams. Shakespeare, as they say, did not spare any building material.

Just try to lift him!

The entire story of jealousy comes unraveled in time and space if you are not super-attentive and if you do not nail this building together the way it is required.

A Month in the Country

In the beginning of the third act, Doctor Shpigelsky asks Rakitin to help him with the courtship of Bolshintsov and Vera. The doctor admits that if he succeeds he will receive the gift of a troika of horses from Bolshintsov.

It would be good to play the Doctor as a man who performs this matchmaking sincerely, and then here in the third act, suddenly, unexpectedly, to expose the underlying reason. But not to present the reason as a dirty trick, but as a consequence of the overwhelming desire of a poor man to obtain such a magnificent gift. In a word, the character of the doctor can be played one dimensionally, unmasked. However, it can also be done subtly, humanly.

Certainly, the main issue is not in that, however, but in Natalya Petrovna.

Rakitin tells Natalya Petrovna that yesterday, specifically at the end of the first act of our performance, she was unrecognizable. She laughed, jumped, and capered like a young girl. He speaks bitterly to her about this, and not only because he is in love with Natalya Petrovna himself, but because from his point of view yesterday's merriment was almost painful, tense. It was, as I already said, an incredibly forceful attempt to free herself from the feeling of old age and uselessness.

Now the excitement has passed and Natalya Petrovna is sad. Behind all this grief, however, is an opposite feeling. "*All this* needs to be ended," thinks Natalya Petrovna. "*It is necessary to do something unexpected again.*" Here is where the opposite feeling comes in.

This confusion is difficult to hold inside. She wants repentance, recognition of her own panic, someone's advice. This heavy burden needs to be unloaded. Shifted to someone else.

She exits quickly, thinking that Belyayev has come, and stops sharply, seeing it is Rakitin. At first, Natalya Petrovna does not hide her irritation from this unnecessary meeting with him. However, having offended Rakitin, she feels awkward and asks his pardon. Actually, he is the only person with whom she could be frank. For some minutes, she tries to hide her condition, but she cannot maintain it and tells him everything that she feels. She asks Rakitin not to turn away from her but to help her. Knowing that he loves her, she understands that this is cruel on her part, but at the same time, overflowing with her own troubles, she does not understand.

However, he is powerless to control himself. He says that he needs to collect himself a little. She asks him for help and becomes angry with him.

She meets Vera, still not knowing how to act. Whether she should continue the intrigue or stop it. Her behavior and mood suddenly and continuously change from any surprise, any word. She looks unwell. At first, she has seemingly decided to continue the matter she began, that is, to inform Vera that she has arranged for her marriage. However, even in this message she does not show great confidence in herself, she has slips of the tongue, she asks Vera to really understand her, and so forth.

When Vera becomes frightened and starts to cry, Natalya Petrovna also becomes frightened, she begins to comfort Vera, to kiss and embrace her. She suggests they should be like sisters so that they could be calm and frank with each other.

Moreover, Vera really calms down and even becomes interested in who this fiancé is; suddenly thinking that it might be Belyayev.

She begins to laugh loudly after learning that it is Bolshintsov. Her reaction is so sudden and frank that it forces Natalya Petrovna to break off the conversation, for is it possible to continue to speak about a fiancé who incites not even tears but laughter?

All the same, Natalya Petrovna would like to understand, is it only because of contempt for Bolshintsov that Vera does not wish to marry? What about Belyayev? Moreover, how does Belyayev feel about Vera? Natalya Petrovna cannot stop herself. From anger, she immediately changes to kindness, from kindness to anger. From genuine love to malice. All this is almost unconscious, however, a type of intoxication. Clearly, her behavior is dominated not by reason, but by emotion, passion, so much that it becomes pathetic to her. In addition, it is frightening to see her struggle with herself. After learning about the possible love between the two young people, she became so lost that she can hardly hear or see. She is feverish.

With Rakitin, she is frankly *shameless*. It makes no difference to her that her frankness causes Rakitin pain.

She begs for his help, and then after he refuses, she insults him.

Again, embracing him, she asks for his pardon.

Islayev, Natalya Petrovna's husband, finds them at just this moment. His reaction to their strange behavior should not be jealousy.

From his point of view, something serious has probably happened, he is concerned, his wife is crying, but she does not tell him the reason. Rakitin promises to explain everything a little later, and Islayev, loving and respecting Natalya Petrovna, is compelled to wait. How considerate of him to call her "Natasha."

It is necessary, by the way, to play this role as Natasha and not as Natalya Petrovna. It is necessary to play Natasha who does not wish to be Natalya Petrovna.

Then, in the conversation with Belyayev, she again creates a bunch of nonsense, completely confusing him and herself.

The second half of the play is not so difficult to analyze as the first. Because you have gradually grown accustomed to the idea that *they* are *not they*, but *you*.

Valentin has a story called "The Cemetery in Skulyany," in which he speaks about his great-grandfather, who lived in the days of Push- kin and is buried in the place where the hero of Pushkin's story "The Shot" was killed.[99] He says that he wrote the story based on old writ- ings found in his great-grandfather's archives. He begins the story, however, as though from his own persona. "I died," he writes, "from cholera on the banks of the River Prut in Skulyany, a historical place. My wife Maria Ivanovna is bustling about near me, together with some gypsy girls and our serfs."

For some time, writes about his great-grandfather's funeral as if it were his own, properly speaking. "Time has finally lost its authority over me. It flows in various directions, sometimes even in the opposite direction, from the future to the past."

"Who is the great-grandson and who is the great-grandfather?" he writes further on. "I have changed into him, and he into me, and both of us became a certain uniform essence. Our general existence was conducted according to new, undisclosed, unknown laws."

I think that Kataev described here precisely what happens (or should happen) with us concerning the classics.

I should become them and they become me, and we all become a certain uniform essence. Our general existence should now be carried out according to certain new, undisclosed, unknown laws.

It is probably necessary, however, to make a correction to this re- markable artistic image, which emphasizes the unity of the past and present.

An image is an image, but reality is reality, and I certainly will never become Doctor Shpigelsky and Doctor Shpigelsky does not be- come me. Even if he were my great-grandfather. In the process of analysis, however, if the analysis is only put together correctly, I really start to comprehend a person who is far different from me.

I say that the analysis should be correctly put together, but for many actors the preparation of a role is carried out according to some strange habits alien to my understanding. They imagine the role in the form of some sort of figurine and then try to represent this figurine. Some do this very well, others very badly, but even those who do it perfectly, all the same I do not like it, since no matter how much you contort yourself, and the outcome does not go beyond some sort of imitation of an animated doll.

Some actors *pretend* to be Doctor Shpigelsky, sometimes even remarkably well.

Pretending has advantages for certain actors. In their acting, there is always a huge quantity of components, details, trifles. Like Plyushkin, Gogol's miser in the novel *Dead Souls,* they collect small handfuls of riches, every small piece [until they collect the character together in their mind].[100]

However, I prefer another type or relationship with the character.

Not *miserliness*, but *blood.*

I prefer that the actor loses a multitude of even very useful details, just so he felt that it was precisely himself that "died in Skulyany," instead of his great-grandfather. The connection of one method with the other would be ideal, of course, but I do not even dream of such a possibility.

Perhaps it is necessary to choose between one method and the other.

By the way, Kataev sustains the story about his great-grandfather as himself only for two or three pages, and then begins to place the rest in inverted commas, slightly altering his great-grandfather's diary, apparently, and retaining himself only as the commentator. Apparently, it is not so easy to sustain the merger of oneself with one's own great-grandfather artfully.

Shpigelsky has a long monologue in the fourth act addressed to an elderly woman whom he asked to marry him. This is a very frank monologue. Shpigelsky speaks of certain things not often told to other people about themselves. More specifically, to be truthful in this way is peculiar only to people of a certain type. That is, to those generally disgusting people for whom there is always a difference between who they actually are and how they try to appear in the opinion of others. Yet this contradiction always burdens their souls, and, as often happens with Dostoyevsky's heroes, they search for an interlocutor whom they could confess to suddenly and stormily. Their confession is like an unexpected expulsion of air from a balloon. Naturally, actors can represent all this with wit; reproduce it with talent, highlighting all the tricks of such eruptions.

Even in this case, it is better for me to have the sensation of a blood relationship with a character whose [counterfeit] sincerity is alien to me; however, he should merge in some strange way with my sincerity, until it becomes difficult to understand where I am and where he is.

The outburst of this character can be alien to me as a human being, of course, but my craft, or more accurately, my personal control of it (if there is any), makes it possible for me to make some artful rearrangement, and then I can faithfully reveal myself in this monologue, even though it is Shpigelsky.

I am convinced that the psychological value of this artistic method is much more significant for the spectator than any other. ·

I have taken the example of Doctor Shpigelsky, yet everything is even more obvious when it is a question of Natalya Petrovna or Vera or even Rakitin, since these people are more familiar to us. They, and even Doctor Shpigelsky, must have the present day in them, and not some past pleasures, passions, and experiences. In addition, the hats and clothes of Turgenev's time should not interfere with the illustration of this contemporaneity.

"Who is the great-grandson and who is the great-grandfather?"

"I have turned into him and him into me, and both of us have become a certain uniform essence.

"Our general existence was conducted according to new, undisclosed, unknown laws."

The Cherry Orchard

The role of Lopakhin begins, so to speak, from a *memory*.

A slender young woman rescues him from a whipping by his father. He waits for this woman, who is now in trouble herself, so that he can rescue her from this trouble.

Since the sale of the cherry orchard is by no means a familiar topic for us nowadays, I visualize an entirely different picture as a working hypothesis.

A patient knows everything about her illness perfectly well. They try to give her advice. However, advice [of any kind] is ridiculous, like the advice that it would be possible to survive somehow, if, let us say, her nose changed places with her eye.

Lopakhin tries to force his way into their empty conversation, empty from his point of view, of course. A sick person be treated immediately and not talk about childhood, for example, or love for some bookcase or a little table. Lopakhin is not alien to a certain sentimentality, but after all, everything in it is own time.

Lopakhin must leave for Kharkov; the train will not wait. He forces his way into their conversation, first from a distance, then suddenly deciding to present the matter as a happy discovery, then insolently taking offence at their levity and lack of seriousness.

They laugh at him because for the moment they find escape in their laughter. It is not possible to be serious in their position. That would mean to believe everything immediately.

Then three weeks pass.

Ranevskaya no longer pretends that she does not hear Lopakhin. Moreover, there are no more traces of natural or deliberate carelessness [on her part]. There will be no more cherry orchard, and there will be no estate. The auction is already at hand. Now she asks for help. Only there must be no dachas and summer residents! This would be so vulgar! Maybe there is *another* way.

Again, I am not looking at the cherry orchard, but simply at a disease, let us say, leprosy. There is only one medicine, if indeed, there is any at all, but she does not like this medicine. There is no more time to think. Lopakhin is ready to collapse from powerlessness.

She says it seems like her home is collapsing.

Then a strange sound is heard, right out of the sky. It could be an eagle or an owl screeching, no one knows. A drunken man passes by, like a nightmare from an unknown world.

When their small island collapses, this [real] world will be completely revealed to them.

Peter Trofimov appears at the end of the first act. They have hidden him away from Ranevskaya in order not to remind her of her son, who was drowned here (Peter was the son's tutor). However, Peter cannot bear it and escapes from his hiding place. They rush to him, hold him back, but it is too late. Ranevskaya screams and begins to cry, then suddenly realizes that she will awaken Anya. She begins to ask Peter about himself, and Peter, delighted, begins to make fun of himself.

He appears again in the middle of the second act. Here Peter has a long monologue about the dreadful life of the intelligentsia, and remaining with Anya he again speaks long and in detail about the necessity to live somehow differently, not as they always lived and now live in this house.

This role was once played by Vassily Kachalov.[101] There are pictures of a twenty-something young man wearing glasses and the uniform jacket of a student. For Kachalov, *The Cherry Orchard* was a modern play. Trofimov speaks about the life of the intelligentsia, about their habits of drunkenness, their empty philosophizing, their inability to work, and about the manual laborers who sleep without mattresses, thirty or forty to a room. It is possible to imagine what such a monologue would have meant in a modern play. It is possible to imagine that it was addressed to the intelligentsia that were sitting in the theatre.

Then for the actor, the text was unquestionably not the only important thing. All the motives were important, all the springs. The springs of a concrete, immediate life. They investigated the text for a long time in the table period, [a rehearsal process] that virtually disappeared a long time ago.[102]

Not only was "dangerous" text spoken from the stage, of course, but also a living person stood there, with a specific concrete personality.

Now there are only photographs. Meanwhile, the play became history. Its [thematic] problems were replaced [by other ones]. Something remains, but something has also gone. Meanwhile, in many later performances Peter simply "pushed" straight through his speeches.

Sometimes it seems that Chekhov's alleged ridicule of Peter shows through. Because his speeches are rhetorical. Other times he is very intelligible and dramatic.

Not only Lopakhin, but Peter too aches for this home, though differently from Lopakhin.

All this nonsense about the cherry orchard and the dachas seems unworthy to him. Happiness, according to Peter of course, is not [found] in this. Not in the rescue of the orchard. It cannot happen. The way out is through some sort of different attitude to life, the way out is in a healthy, sensible view of things, not in business, but in good judgment. The way out means an end to this absurd, ridiculous, careless way of life. It is necessary to get busy with something serious, to work, to put one's soul into something.

Her lover, Paris, a funny and ridiculous brother—all this pitiful pride, everything must be given up. It is better to live without money, but with peace of mind. Indeed, Ranevskaya's conscience is tormented. Her life is so confused; she is so *exhausted*. What can help? What does Lopakhin offer? After all, this is business too: dachas and tourists. This will not make someone like Ranevskaya feel better and happier. It is necessary to throw everything away and live as [ordinary] people.

However, nobody wants to hear about this or about Lopakhin's dachas either. Lopakhin is shouting *in the void,* just as Trofimov is shouting, only from another direction.

Lopakhin is rich; Petya is poor, shabby. Chekhov both believed in him and did not. After all, what *will* happen is always a mystery. However, Chekhov believes in one thing: that Trofimov as well as Lopakhin are agonizingly searching for a way out. It is difficult, however, to be a prophet among one's own people. Peter is as tired of this role as *the prophet in his own country.* He is tired that people do not listen to each other, of their terrible carelessness, their empty conversations. Their attitude toward him is the same as toward Lopakhin. Lopakhin's truth is concrete, he has money, he has the force of a man, but Peter's position here is that of a small boy, a simpleton. Neither young nor old, he does not know how to love, his beard does not grow, and furthermore he is an eternal student. He gets through to Anya a little, but her mother only laughs and becomes angry. He is a "phrase maker," a talker, and a philosopher. In addition, it is necessary to rescue him from his awful nickname. They provoke him to say something clever, progressive. However, it is necessary to refuse, to get away from his imposed role as the clown. Although inside it is painful, and he wants to say something directly, to reach out to them. This is only momentary, however, and all the rest is a defense against their requests to "entertain."

A sufficiently complex design off stage, but on stage almost continuous rejection, reckless rejection throughout the entire long text. However, suddenly, involuntarily, something will explode in there, and then go back into hiding. The *tired philosopher.* He tells himself that he will not teach, that he does not want to, but all the same it bursts out, sufficiently crudely and sharply, and then it closes up again.

Like Lopakhin, he does not agree with *them,* but his plans are different, not materialistic, and in this lay the entire *dramatic nature* of his advice. Peter is like a teacher at school. Time passes and now you see this teacher is somewhat shabby and even ridiculous. We have a good history teacher, some girls will say, but they only laugh at him.

In addition, someone once even tripped him, and the teacher fell down.

Although if asked individually, everyone would say: We had a good teacher.

Through-Action

Why is this seemingly habitual retelling of the content always so important to me and what is this retelling, which at the same time is *not a retelling,* but my analysis of what happens, my attitude toward it? First, I need to begin to understand and feel the content, make it absolutely *mine,* to make it absolutely so that I could think that everything happening *to them* is happening *to me.* For me this retelling is already part of my interpretation, and then all the rest will *express* this interpretation. Only what is "all the rest"? Once I sat down and tried to describe what it is necessary to do with each dialogue in the play when you penetrate into its uniform core. It is as though this core penetrates all the dialogue so that no word remains detached from it. However, dialogue assumes the participation of at least two people, and the cores in the dialogue happen to at least two people as well. In addition, they are guided by pointers, so to speak, in different directions. Moreover, the entire matter lies in the opposite orientation of these cores, strictly speaking, because when you grasp this contrast and you finally comprehend the conflict, then the secondary conflict seems to subordinate itself to the main thing, and the dialogue begins to become elastic, no longer filled only with text, but with *action.*

I used this word "core" and thought there was no need for me to invent some definitions, like the fact that the cores must be found, since a better definition had already been devised a long time ago, and this definition is "through-action." It was devised by the same Stanislavsky that each generation knows increasingly less "personally," and whom, in my opinion, everyone will ultimately come to study more and more.

Because what is unimportant will be forgotten, and only what is very essential will remain in memory. Moreover, one of these very essential moments of memory about Stanislavsky will be his principle of "through-action."

You may think that because you know the terminology, you will know everything—but far from it!

It is still necessary to arrive at this core action in each episode with your own mind, your own intuition, because what many people present as the core action is only the external shell of the dialogue, nothing more.

Try to understand the scene between Vera and Belyayev, for example, in the fourth act of *A Month in the Country.* Belyayev must leave because Natalya Petrovna is jealous of him, and Vera, feeling it is her fault, comes to apologize to Belyayev. Then she reproaches

Belyayev for his lack of openness with her. She suspects that he has not been candid because he knew about her love for him. She tries to learn whether Natalya Petrovna has told him about her love. Beneath his indifferent answers, she comes to understand that Belyayev does not love her. She rejects his attempts to justify himself to her somehow. She blames only herself. And Natalya Petrovna. Not because she loves Belyayev, however, but because of her deceitfulness.

From the way I am now retelling the content of this scene, however, anyone could retell it, although in this retelling there is also a desire to retell in terms of *action*.

Unfortunately, however, all this has nothing to do with what is necessary. I say "unfortunately" because otherwise our work would be easy. Only think, just retell the content of the dialogue in terms of action! This is easily done by the actor, the director, and even the tenth grade student if you train him a little. The essence of an analysis that is actually useful, however, consists of a certain psychological discovery, an *explanation* of the very core of the scene, and the set of "actions" included in it. Until this discovery occurs, this multitude is only a collection of *confused scenes,* in which the actor will become lost in scores of back streets.

It is possible, however, to reach a truth of some sort in this case, only it is relative.

Therefore, Vera does one thing in the scene, then another, and a third, but where is that one thing, that core, which pierces through the entire scene? Moreover, here it is compulsory to speak not about craftsmanship, which is possible to learn to one degree or another, but about the ability to feel, the ability to understand the psychology of a person that is apparently very distant from you.

This skill can also be improved, however, only if one works at it, of course.

Vera comes to Belyayev after a recent explanation from Natalya Petrovna. Moreover, during this explanation, the main thing is that after this Vera has suddenly begun to see things clearly. Natalya Petrovna is such a surprising, beautiful, ideal woman, in whom Vera has found an upbringing, who is like a mother to her, who was represented as an example to her in every respect, who inspired not only true respect, but also true love—this woman has suddenly proved to be subject to passions, mean, deceitful, capable of crippling Vera's life because of her own feelings. On top of that, for whom? For a young man hardly older than Vera.

What's more, Vera must now marry a fifty-year-old man, disgusting and foolish besides.

Naturally, this moment of knowledge, *unexpected* knowledge, is a moment of *shock*.

Shocks are of various kinds, of course. Moreover, rebellion and confusion prevail at first for Vera.

Protest and anger completely overwhelm her. This protest, this disagreement, this violence desperately erupt from her. Vera is essentially neither subjugated nor obedient. In addition, her self-reproach from her past naive trustfulness toward Natalya Petrovna is unrestrained, not silent. This desperation must be loudly expressed to someone. However, to whom? Naturally, to the one who understands her and will share her suffering: Belyayev.

Specifically in this impulse, in this desire to let loose, is the main core of the entire scene. However, it is necessary not to become distracted by anything.

For some reason it often seems to us that the author writes out the lines slowly and accurately. Here Vera has said something, and here Belyayev has replied. Moreover, we play it "in sequence."

However, a good author, it seems to me, writes swiftly. Because it is necessary to have time to write down what lies ahead.

In addition, in this there is that sense of *through-ness* that comprises the entire charm of a thing.

Then, perhaps, the author will begin processing. He wrote it in fifteen seconds, but processed it perhaps for a month. The same is true for us. It is necessary to grasp the *motion*, the *general premise*, the *common objective* of all the emotions, and then to process it as much as you want, only not so much that you forget about this general premise.

The Most Important Thing

On television they showed some sort of average film with Laurence Olivier.[103] It is a pity that we see such acting only occasionally. Films like this should be shown in theatre schools, stopping the film at necessary places and then scrolling ahead in order to scrutinize *how it is done*.

Often the actor thinks he should play someone or something, and Laurence Olivier, of course, does not play himself. You will not perceive this, however, for he does not play *himself*, but *from himself*. This is a familiar aphorism, but not everyone understands it.

Here, in addition to the highest talent of submerging oneself into another's life, is the even more special technology of acting.

It is as though he does not quite linger on anything *to act*. His acting is penetrated by a single, swift, internal motion. Infinitely long and old-fashioned text is light and weightless on his tongue, as if he does not attach a decisive meaning to a line. If we spoke all these lines and checked up on each one of them, we would be probably become confused. However, Olivier knows the *one thing* that is hidden beneath five or ten lines, and he performs the dialogue guided only by this one thing.

His partner, Katherine Hepburn, does the same thing. Clarity comes from this, and the scene seems so simple, as if it is impossible to play it any other way. However, it only seems this way, for hearing the text, if you are a professional, you will easily perceive that this is a special *reading*, this is an ability to grasp the most important thing and subordinate everything it to. That is why the dialogue is so mobile and light, and everything in the scene pushes forward. However, if you think that in this acting they do not know what a *stoppage* is, you are mistaken! The focus is on the most necessary line, *the most necessary vision*, and they do all this so powerfully that once more, you are amazed at their accuracy, and you want to go back to this place again to scrutinize *how it is done*.

A Bad Rehearsal

What is a bad rehearsal? When the actors play something that is not in line with a precise, clear plan. Then everybody suddenly ceases to be intelligible. I do not blame the actors, but I begin to think that my own plan is incorrect. Rehearsal ends, but I remain for an hour or two afterward at the theatre. I mentally go over all the internal motions and transitions endlessly, I try to understand where the error is. It is hard to find with a tired brain, but I do not have the strength to force myself to go home and rest. Then I plod home with only one thought: that tomorrow should come sooner in order to correct something. Only it is still necessary to understand what to correct. I do not want to have dinner. You try to rush the time. What? It is still only six o'clock in the evening? How can I wait until morning? Thank God that in the evening there is a rehearsal of another performance. It is finished at ten. Now I only have to wait a little longer. By this time, the error is starting to emerge. Now it would be nice to have a good night's sleep. I set the alarm clock for 9:30 a.m. and take a sleeping pill. My son awakes at 7:00 a.m. and usually leaves quietly, but I am already awake and looking at the clock—6:45. Four whole hours until rehearsal, it is impossible to wait. My son comes in and sees me at the table. "Do you really think about your mistakes all the time?" he asks me in bewilderment. I admit that this is just how I am. I slowly start to iron a shirt, have a shave, etc. Everything done slowly, for these four hours must pass somehow.

But when I finally arrive at rehearsal, it is pleasant for me to pretend that I am calm, that there are no complex questions, and that yesterday's bad rehearsal was a trifle that can easily be corrected in ten minutes.

Those actors who do not know me well will easily believe this pretense.

"Detached" Chekhov...?

Everyone was captivated by the film *An Unfinished Piece for Player Piano,* adapted from Chekhov's fragmentary notes.[104] However, I watched it with mixed feelings.

Naturally, it was a good film, but why does my interest somehow flag after the middle? Apparently, because the director, maybe even Chekhov himself, observed all these people *from a detached point of view.* He felt sorry for them and despised them for their helplessness. The hero wanted to drown himself; he rushed from the bank into the river, but the water proved to be only knee-deep, and he only got soaked; and that is all. His wife embraces this "suicide," also standing knee-deep in the water, wraps him in a woman's shawl, she sincerely cries, but all this is rather pitiful, and he is a ridiculous milksop.

Moreover, here I thought (not only here, however, but much earlier too, since this moment was already at the end of the film) that if you looked at this *not from a detached point of view,* but *from within,* it would be a completely different story.

Suppose I decided to rush from the bank into the water to put an end to my life. If I am not drowned because the water is too shallow, then in any case I will be badly hurt, I will be bloody. In addition, this will not be "pathetic," but more likely, frightening.

When Chekhov first began to write, he looked at things entirely differently from the way he looked at them later on. Therefore, in *Platonov* [which was the basis of the film] there is none of the psychological penetration that is found in *Three Sisters.* In *Three Sisters,* there is no ironically detached point of view. This play is no longer about someone else, not about "others," but about "oneself." It is possible to ridicule oneself, of course. However, this ridicule is only an accompaniment to genuine, sincere, personal suffering.

They say that Chekhov frequently wrote about people who were incapable of action.

Platonov returns home at twilight in a dirty, wet raincoat. The veranda is closed... His loving woman waits for him and suggests that they should leave, but instead of rushing to her, he rushes to this veranda, into this closed door. The words she speaks are rather pompous and consequently a little humorous, and so it is possible to understand why Platonov does not throw caution to the wind and run away somewhere with this woman.

All this is correct, of course. All the same, some kind of involuntary irritation arises in you when you look at these stupid people. Not because they are stupid, for possibly you are no better than they are, but because if something similar happened to *you*, all this would be expressed with a somewhat different quality. Not so amusingly funny.

The doctor in the film talks about how frightening it is to travel to patients at night; he is afraid of the moment when there is a knock at the door, etc. A familiar Chekhovian motif. And here on the screen the doctor cries like a boy, talking about his fears. His dithering is very well played, however it is not played "about me," but about some other doctor whom I, the director or the actor, consider a ditherer.

However, what if you take yourself seriously?

I think about how I sometimes talk about the tortures of my own rehearsals, how I do not sleep at night after a bad rehearsal, how I frequently fear the following day and the next meeting with the actors. Would someone portraying me really begin to whine so pitifully? Then he simply does not know what it is like to be afraid of the next day and the next rehearsal.

However, are the tortures of that doctor really less than *mine*; are his fears less than mine? Yet they can be anything at all, but why not perceive them as my own? Indeed, at this point, the beginning of a specific creative view of the thing begins; the beginning one artistic direction or another emerges.

Balzac once said (I am not certain of the accuracy) that when he was writing about the broken arm of his hero, he kept reaching for his own elbow.

Yes, let the river only be knee-deep, but you got up with a bloody face and a broken hand, and this is by no means amusing. In addition, there can be a terrible shock in an *incomplete action*.

And the thought—that despite the unsuccessful attempt at action, life will go on as before—will not be diminished from the fact that there will be a strong shock in this *attempt*.

Podkolesin, in Gogol's play Marriage, also did not complete an action, he did not get married, but his *attempt* must be furious, divested of its notorious comicality, of its notorious imperfections. It is necessary to live life for Podkolesin, and not to depict some stranger's life with a certain share of sarcasm and a melodramatic nature.

This ability to see the *depth of things,* in my opinion, distinguishes great artists from those less great. In particular, it is what distinguishes the mature Chekhov from the less mature Chekhonte.[105] It is what distinguishes Tolstoy, Dostoyevsky, and Shakespeare from many other people.

It is possible to say about their characters: "Ah, they were so touchingly absurd, so pitiful." Moreover, in this approach there is also something instructive [about human nature].

Shouldn't Platonov's hopelessly wasted life move me with comparable force? However, I leave after the film feeling only squeamish pity, although I share the opinion that this is a very well made picture. In this case, I do not think it could have been made any differently. No, I am only *discussing* and even looking at my own work with a certain horror: is [what I perceive] different, or am I only dreaming? In reality, is my viewpoint the same?

Now I am directing *A Month in the Country.* Natalya Petrovna's action also did not take place. However, this must be such an attempt that even when it ends in failure, nevertheless it is necessary to perceive *what this futile attempt is in itself,* and what it costs.

Advice from a Writer

The writer Valentin Kataev and I were strolling along the path of a summer resort.[106] He said that in his old age he understood one truth.

If you are walking along a country path, you are thinking about a certain artist, and some thoughts come to you about this artist, then go home quickly and write about him and not about another artist, even if you were supposed to write specifically about that other artist today for one reason or another.

He said further that there is a "still-life" side and a narrative side.[107]

Skillful distribution of narrative and still life—it is necessary to study this your entire life.

The Cherry Orchard

In *The Cherry Orchard,* they all hear a strange sound, from right out of the sky, like the sound of a broken string. Lopakhin nervously suggests that possibly a bucket fell in a mineshaft somewhere far away.

Gaev, to soften the impression, then says the sound came from a bird, perhaps a heron. However, Trofimov adds that the sound came from an owl.

Clearly, for Peter that sound does not portend anything good. Only an oddball could suggest it was the cry of a bird. Then Peter angrily adds his sarcastic remark about an owl. It is a sneer at Gaev's comment. Gaev's starry-eyed idealism has no limits. Peter does not know the source of this sound, of course, however it is certainly not from a bird.

It is possible not to interpret the moment in this way, but any dialogue must be elastic from meaning. Meanwhile, so many [actors] chatter on stage for nothing...

Lopakhin explains how it is possible to divide the cherry orchard into dachas. However, Firs recalls that once people knew a beautiful method to dry cherries.

Ranevskaya: "Where is this method now?"

Firs replies that they forgot it.

There is so much meaning in all this, of course, that it seems you could pronounce the text anyway you like as long as it would be heard, and then the meaning would be intelligible to everyone. Most often, in fact, it happens otherwise. A certain life is present on stage, and the actors strive to retain it, but its meaning is incomprehensible. Yes, life flows, but *what* it is speaking about is not known.

Firs is deaf, but he hears with his eyes and skin. He hears and sees that everything turns to dust. He even knows that everything has turned upside down "from freedom" [i.e., since the peasants obtained their freedom from the landowners]. Before everything had its place, but now everything is "coming apart." Moreover, the tasty cherries are only a part of that whole picture. Lopakhin distracts them from Firs's idea. Firs senses this even if he does not hear it. His story about the cherries is an opposition to the *dachas*. That is why Gaev shouts: "Be quiet!" Not because the old man is interrupting with his worthless mumbling, but because in his apparent *vagueness* Firs inserts something of his own, turning them back to the past.

However, Firs only turns his head a little, and after a brief silence, stubbornly finishes talking about the former charm of the cherries, about the old method of drying and boiling.

—"Where is this method now?"

Firs replies *reproachfully*, "They forgot it!"

No one can return to what went before. Everyone betrayed the past, but not him. Unfortunately, he is powerless.

Lopakhin speaks about excellent nature, where a man should be a giant. Ranevskaya, speaking ironically about this idea, notes Yepikhodov entering. Someone says that the sun has set. Trofimov agrees. All this could be played, so to speak, purely for atmosphere, for everyday life. Evening, the setting sun, everyone quietly discussing one thing or another at the end of the day... However, I prefer to find dynamics and conflict in such moments. Internal dynamics arise from the differences among those who are talking. When Ranevskaya announces the entrance of Yepikhodov, there is an unconscious, almost instinctive repudiation of the "giant" that Lopakhin has just spoken about. After all, Lopakhin is always saying that Ranevskaya should not live as she does. He does not literally talk about this at this particular moment, but the inertia of disagreement nevertheless exists in it. He prattles about giants, and here is the reality—Yepikhodov enters. Reality can be unattractive, after all.

Gaev comes forward in support, saying that not only is Yepikhodov coming, but also *the sun has set,* which is much the same thing.

However, Trofimov does not simply confirm that the sun has set. His "Yes" is like a warning that "doomsday" is inevitable if all this absurdity continues.

All this happens swiftly and almost unconsciously for the characters, of course. I really like these active moments filled with conflicting ideas, even in those places that seem to be intended purely for "everyday life," for "atmosphere."

Old Dialogue and New Content

It is interesting to fill the old and long familiar dialogue of classical plays with new content! In Molière's play *Don Juan,* for example, Sganarelle asks Don Juan whether he has enjoyed his countless marriages. Don Juan answers with another question: "Could anything be more pleasant?"

Naturally, similar scraps of conversation are generally conducted largely from habit, much as tradition requires. Don Juan's answer is simply the bravado of a philanderer.

However, what if there is an opportunity to give Don Juan a rather complex character? Although who guarantees that Molière did not treat Don Juan with sufficient complexity in his own lifetime? Nevertheless, *tradition* more often simplifies him.

But if Don Juan is not simply a rake, but a person who has lost all hope of finding truth, then his answer to Sganarelle's question will not only be bravado alone. It will be just as serious as the question itself.

Is there any greater happiness than the daily amusements of love-making? As Don Juan, perhaps, I understand that frequent marriages are wicked from the point of view of morality, but can the same morality suggest to me another source of such happiness? I ask you about this, Sganarelle, because it torments me personally.

Sganarelle can only make an effort to reply, for he really does not know what would be better than *this*. He only knows it is a sin.

However, at this point Don Juan only brushes him aside. Things such as sin do not disturb him since he has asked an *essential* and *fundamental* question, and he received a positive answer, but with the reservation that although nothing is better than this, nevertheless it is a sin. Therefore, you [Don Juan] will fail from your own sins until they can think of something better!

A purely comic conversation acquires, so to speak, philosophical outlines, and perhaps the public will continue to laugh, but somewhat more intelligently.

Naturally, two lines of dialogue will not focus all the attention in the direction you would like, but the interpretation [of this moment] should penetrate the *entire* verbal fabric.

This interpretation must be *significant*, however, because otherwise it would be better if it penetrated nothing.

Furthermore, even if the interpretation itself is good, it must not be imposed on the text "intellectually." The entire essence lies in *emotional freedom* with a very precise meaning.

The Cherry Orchard

I am preparing for rehearsal after a one-year break, and I am trying to recall what our production of *The Cherry Orchard* was based on. I read the play, and the *basis* comes to the surface even clearer than before: all these people are in a state of anxiety. They are afraid to stop, afraid of a concrete word about *the real thing,* since nothing promised them a happy outcome.

Possibly before, in earlier performances, this anxiety was hidden in the subtext. However, outwardly it was a peaceful way of life, at least at the beginning of the play. In our production, we brought all their unrest to the surface. It grew and grew, become wider, reached a panic, almost to that mystical note when everyone heard a certain sound like a broken string. Like Ravel's "Bolero"—one melody expanded into a nightmare.

In the beginning, Lopakhin waits with Dunyasha for Ranevskaya's arrival. Their anxiety is uncovered, candid, because the train has not arrived on time, because Lopakhin does not know what kind of person he will encounter. The nervousness is transferred from one to the other. Our Yepikhodov not only dropped his flowers, but also even knocked down a table and broke a plate on one of the gravestones from anxiety. Any interpretation, of course, can border on vulgarity. Yet it is worthwhile to recall when you are waiting for something in real life, particularly when you are not expecting something good, when the emotional qualities are lively and sharp.

Then Ranevskaya arrived. Everyone bustled about, they hid, and they hid from something, they were afraid to name the misfortune in their eyes. Ranevskaya drank coffee as a narcotic, the conversations did not make sense, and everyone ran off somewhere, pushing aside Lopakhin with his business speeches. They opened their souls about trifles, made foolish mistakes, and were ashamed. Everything was light and rapid because they pretended that *this* is not what is important, what is important will happen later on, and then they ran away from the main thing again, until at last a drunken passer-by scattered everyone in terror. Trofimov remained behind, impotent with rage, repeating [his warnings] about carelessness.

Undoubtedly, *The Cherry Orchard* was a controversial production at the Taganka Theatre. Not least because Chekhov was being produced at an absolutely "un-Chekhovian" theatre. Here the characters are prosaic to the point of impudence. Their main weapon is ridicule. In addition, if they perform a drama, they are more likely to present it as genre piece. However, Chekhov's plays are subtle and graceful. In fact, to produce Chekhov at the Taganka means deliberately courting disaster.

Recently, however, Chekhov has not even been successful where refinement and lyricism were precisely the style of the particular theatre. Because this lyricism and poetry were performed partially from habit. It was no longer possible to feel the spirit. That is why the desire to produce Chekhov at the Taganka Theatre was no simple whim. I certainly knew that losses were inevitable. Those losses would be different, however, from those now evident at the Moscow Art Theatre, but this exchange of losses and even a certain exchange of advantages seemed useful.[108]

However, the controversy was not only in this. The controversy was in *what* to consider as the essence of *The Cherry Orchard*. It is pointless to argue about this, however, since everyone knows from school that it is about the passing of the nobility, etc. However, this meaning was apparently simple-minded habit as well.

The twist that was needed, of course, would be intelligible to some and unintelligible to others.

When *daring to do* such things, however, it is necessary to *take it to the limit. H*ere timidity would neither add anything nor take away anything [from the habitual point of view]. Everything [about the play] would turn out the same [as before]. It was necessary to make the familiar theme of the passing of the nobility *more comprehensive, more philosophical.* So that *real life* would not predominate, but a *problem.* The problem of the inevitable loss of one life and the passage to another. A drama of farewell to the past and a search for the new. However, for the characters in *The Cherry Orchard* these searches are only possible in a fumbling way. Because these characters, unfortunately, are very weak people. They are vulnerable because of a badly wasted life. They are careless, stubborn. They do not know how to close the door in a storm. Those who know, know only *half*; however, almost nobody wants to hear them. They are decent, these people, but at the same time spoiled. They are rather proud people, but at the same time pitiful.

The tragic meaning needs to be made somewhat grotesque.

Company Discussion of *The Cherry Orchard*

At the Taganka Theatre, there was a company discussion of *The Cherry Orchard.* The actors who were not involved in the work greeted the performance rather indifferently. In their opinion, it was dull in some places, unintelligible in others.

They said politely and abstractly that the general meaning was clear, but they could not discuss anything about this general meaning itself. What is it?

Only a writer, who was accidentally present during the discussion, said that life "sneers" at the characters [in our production], but they live and do not know their own destiny. And Chekhov is sad about this. This spectator, I thought, knows how to disregard the details, whether he likes them or not, and form a general impression in his mind.

"But all the same," he said, "it is not always possible to play the final result. Destiny is destiny, but people live, they aren't simply pawns, marionettes in some sort of prearranged construction, whereas the actors in the performance were more like marionettes than living people."

I replied that it is necessary to achieve *depth*, of course, but nowadays actors have almost forgotten how to achieve it.

Nowadays, thank God, the director and actor do try to seize some sort of core, but they put it into practice with complexity and torment. In Moscow, perhaps, there is only one Gaev: Innokenty Smoktunovsky.[109] The rest of the actors take only one feature of the character, if that. Where does Gaev come from at the Taganka?

An interpretation comes not only from contemporary *problems*, but also from contemporary *possibilities*. The director, like the sculptor, works with a certain material.

At the Taganka, we achieved a performance in which the general solution did not flow from three-dimensional living tissue, but from the fruit of some sort of artificial construction. This is true.

In my view, however, there is a certain merit in this. Obviously, the fact that human material is different today from what it was in Chekhov's time dictates not simply a historical, classical performance, but an experiment that brings an old play closer to today's voices, so to speak, both spiritually and physically. Then *The Cherry Orchard* becomes like a completely new play, and furthermore one that is wonderfully written.

Naturally, Chekhov scholars are irritated with this liberty, but they will have to get used to it, since a person of the 1880s will never be resurrected. True, certain talents will still be capable of penetrating into *that epoch* to a greater or lesser extent. Most likely, however, those talents will not only be able to penetrate into *that epoch*, but they will also be capable of expressing a contemporary attitude to old problems and situations.

Sophocles will never be presented as he was in his time. Nor will Chekhov be presented as he was in his time. Yes, and it is not even necessary.

All the same, it is still necessary to try to achieve depth. This is the point where the writer came forward with his discussion about marionettes, yet all the same, it is true.

However, what is meant by depth? Maybe it is the daring expression of a role, absolute possession of it. An ability to reveal yourself in it to the utmost. Stanislavsky was right when he thought up the well-known formula—"me" in the given circumstances. The given circumstances in the play remain the same, but the "me" eternally changes. If it really is "me," and not something only vaguely specific, then this "me" must be revealed, boldly interpreting everything around it in a new way.

Directing at Another Theatre

Working on *The Cherry Orchard* at the Taganka Theatre was hard. It is difficult to come into a theatre that has a completely different handwriting. Only the [reputation of the] many plays I have already produced allowed me to make something there that was *my own*.

If I were not well known to them from my other works, perhaps I would not be understood. Sometimes I felt as I did when I first started directing.

They have other habits at the Taganka Theatre, another type of rehearsal work, and a different stage. Their manner of acting is different.

They are criticized often about the abstract form of their staging, but in fact they are much more realists than many of us.

In general, this is a very interesting theme. At the Taganka Theatre, they are absolute realists, sometimes even rather primitively so.

It is a paradox, but to them I seem to be a "formalist."[110] My aesthetic sometimes seems to them "elusive," they are used to a more powerful, forthright aesthetic.

This is their aesthetic genre, I suppose. Moreover, *The Cherry Orchard*, in their opinion, is some sort of "abstract psychologism"

They are worried that my concept will be boring, will not be supported with enough perceptible concreteness. The actors worked wonderfully, but besides the actors occupied with the work, there are the other actors who are not yet occupied, and finally, as in every theatre, there are the "ideologues" of the theatre's artistic direction. Oh, do not fall into their hands. Away from their theatre they sometimes accept something else uncharacteristic of them, but at home give them only what they strongly stand for themselves, although probably there was a time when they had difficulty with this [aesthetic] as well. Then they became used to it, came to believe in their success, and now—there never was anything else!

Pardon me, but I recollect how Edward Gordon Craig once wanted to direct a performance at Stanislavsky's theatre.[111] And how this turned out. Continuing my amusing comparison, I may say that I felt more like Stanislavsky directing at Craig's theatre.

What was unique about that situation was that "Craig" for all his "screens," loved a richly psychological way of living, but

"Stanislavsky," for all his love of *psychologism*, was attracted to an incomprehensibly "Craig-like" abstract aesthetic.

In a word, you cannot figure it out!

I want to repeat, however, that my comparisons are meant to be humorous.

It was most difficult of all for the actors, because to survive *within the theatre* is often more difficult than to survive *before the public*. After all, it is necessary to get to this public through your co-workers without losing faith in what you are doing.

All the same, it seems that we have apparently gotten through to the public.

Now I am back home at the Malaya Bronnaya Theatre.

After you travel, you come back home...

Two Types of Playgoer

...Here is a conclusion I have come to. There is an audience impression that arises directly from what is happening on the stage or screen. On the screen someone is suffering, let us say and you suffer right along with him. On the other hand, someone is cheerful, and you become cheerful. However, there is also excitement that seems to go not from the stage to you, but from you to the stage. This excitement seems to arise within you, relatively independent from what was on the stage or screen.

Of course, a crying person on stage also forces you to begin to cry. All the same, you are deeply moved not only by him, but also from something that was born in you at this moment, slightly independent from him. Some parallel thought has flashed through your mind, or a personal feeling has arisen related to what is on stage, anyhow a stick has been tossed into the fire. In addition, from this feeling of *yours*, the experience arising in you has been doubled, so to speak, and you find yourself *especially* absorbed by the action.

It seems to me that audiences, generally speaking, can be divided into two categories. Some watch and listen wonderfully, they become excited and laugh, but they do not seem to be able to feel and think "parallel" to what's happening or maybe *counter* to it. Then the emotional wave that goes from them to the stage is much less. These spectators feel only to the extent that the material gives them food of one kind or another.

It is as though there is no space in their hearts for any "adjacent" mood that could add something to the simple, normal perception. Alternatively, this "adjacent" mood, on the contrary, only has the property of an "obstruction."

Someone seems to go parallel with the "feeling of the scene," while another anticipates it or is hopelessly late.

I am not saying these different groups are always stable. On the contrary, people in the auditorium seem to wander internally from group to group, depending not only on the performance, of course, but also on them. From how they themselves are living today, right now. Now, one person's soul feels something, while another's does not.

I say this not to condemn any of the groups. I am simply establishing the fact that this "stratification" of the audience is almost inevitable.

On the Way to Rehearsal

I arrived at the theatre in the morning, and my head was full of ideas. I am not guaranteeing they were all good ideas, but in any case, there were quite a few of them. We were rehearsing a contemporary play, it seemed sketchy, and we needed to find some clever key to extract the entire content. Until this day, we had not been able to find the way.

However, it seemed that I had thought of something the previous evening, and now it was only necessary to report it to the actors. I should say that to come with ideas is often more difficult than to come empty-handed. [When you come empty-handed] you are at peace with yourself, you don't become disturbed about possible rehearsal obstacles, and it doesn't seem to you that the day is too short, and that you won't have time to do what you planned.

This is a very unpleasant feeling: to carry something [in your mind] and know ahead of time that there will be obstacles, that perhaps someone will be sick, another will be late, and a third will not be in the mood. A stranger begins to make a noise somewhere [outside], and the time is already ending. Sometimes it begins to seem that it would be better to come empty-handed, as actors do so very often, by the way. How casually they arrive at the theatre in the morning. They are not carrying any burden that needs to be put down exactly in the right place. They sit, they chatter, and wait for someone to create their scene for them.

However, there are other types of actors too, of course. (I have written this sentence as insurance in case someone suddenly takes offence.)

Therefore, I went to the theatre in the morning with ideas. There were many people at the cloakroom, including a good friend who came just to see me. He came to tell me that somewhere on his trip he met a person who was at the premier of our production of *The Cherry Orchard*. The essence of his evaluation of the play consisted of this: The director, he said, had placed a cemetery on stage and implied in this that all delicate feelings were already dead, and in our time, only coarse feelings remained. Our epoch is apparently without delicate feelings. This [performance is intended as] a slander against our epoch.

It was ridiculous, of course, but I was terribly upset. In the morning, you should not be distracted by something unrelated to your work. For a half hour of work will surely be wasted. However, people frequently run up to you before rehearsal precisely with something to upset you. You arrive and hear the voice of the stage-door watchman: "First find the theatre manager, he was looking for you." You go in and they tell you about a meeting where they treated you badly. It is necessary to learn about this, but it would be better *after* work. On the other hand, maybe I am just too sensitive? I do not think so. I have not asked other directors, but I have frequently seen actors after an unpleasant conversation—they go on stage and poorly grasp what they are doing.

It is probably the same, however, in any profession.

However, perhaps other professions do not depend on a person's mood as much as ours does. And here I am walking onto the stage with this irritation about *The Cherry Orchard*.

A certain actor, of course, was late. An actress got sick, and the theatre manager asked for someone else to play her part, and asked me to help her out. I felt my mood collapse like the heaviness after a heart attack.

By this time, my mood could be aroused only with an extreme effort of will. However, where will you find this will? "Why," I thought, "did that spectator think that I was burying all delicate feelings? He might just as well have said that I had sunk a ship in the Bermuda Triangle." However, why couldn't I simply laugh about this? Because I knew from experience what sometimes happens because of these foolish [audience] responses.

Meanwhile, the work went on, I followed the scene at hand and even tried to grasp the error, and I grasped it and corrected it. However, when rehearsal was finished, I thought that the morning's frustration was absolutely nonsense. It is a pity that this simple thought did not occur to me sooner.

The World Has Changed

Rubens painted a woman *one way* and Picasso *another way*. However, does the fact that Picasso used certain broken lines to paint a woman mean that he values and loves nature less than Rubens did? The world has simply changed, life has changed, and the artistic means of expressing this life have changed.

A coach harnessed to a troika is not like an airplane, but both these "subjects" arise from the same striving for faster travel.

Hamlet

Among the interpretations of *Hamlet* is apparently the type that only shows Hamlet's struggle for the throne. Shakespeare probably has many plays about this subject. Nevertheless, no other plays seem to be precisely what *Hamlet* is about.

The struggle for the throne is at least clear [in his other plays], but in some *Hamlet* productions—most, in fact—a complex canvas obscures precisely such clarity. True, everything in *Hamlet* is moving, moving... Perhaps I do not know one performance where I could remember very well what this play is about. Although, during the performance of one or another *Hamlet*, there were moments when it seemed to me that I grasped a certain latent meaning, but then a stream of all-too-familiar action overwhelmed me, and, owing to familiarity and habit, this stream no longer said anything. Since everything was known, and since there was so much of everything in each of these performances, I personally did not have time to concentrate and really grasp any special thread.

All sorts of generally obvious ideas also become clear, possibly, but these generally accepted ideas are vigorously erased by repetition, and new paint probably does not "lie" easily on top of the old. At this point, it turns out neither one thing nor the other.

To begin with, let us push off in the opposite direction; let us say that there is no sort of struggle here for a throne, for power. Here the brother of a king kills the king because of a woman who is the wife of that king, so that he can become king and take her as his wife. Her son, having arrived and expecting to see grief and mourning, sees love and celebration. To him it seems unbelievable. It is hard for him to believe how all this can be *true*.

His activity is more accurately that of striving to understand something, to *realize*, to *accept*.

Once admitting this, however, he becomes a part of this world, but he came from another world.

His uncle and mother do not grieve for the father at all. Then the Ghost appears with terrible news. In the house where everything was so clear before, nothing is any longer understood. It is time to go out of your mind!

Usually in performance, *Hamlet* is afraid to be silent, he does not know which lines of verse are most relevant, and he whips himself up as a coachman whips a horse to become more spirited. He is ready to choke from anger, he protests, he cries, he screams. Isn't this too early though? Indeed, this canvas is too prepared, too well known in advance. Nothing will be revealed to anyone.

For nothing has been revealed *anew* to the actor. However, that is precisely the point. He knew his mother and father, this father and this excellent mother, and now he sees that *both are different*. Should he be angry? However, perhaps it is too early? After all, this is terrible news, and furthermore everything is *news*, everything is in a new light, as though he arrived not at home but on Mars. He sees, he does not believe, he wants to think there has been a mistake. He is not used to being angry; for this is the first time he has seen the house like this. Maybe he is going out of his mind?

Specific personal circumstances are necessary, and then the general ideas will come, but if they are still in pre-finished form—it is not worth a thing.

Response to *The Cherry Orchard*

I was interested in one common response to our production of *The Cherry Orchard*.

"There is a Society for Wildlife Conservation," I heard, "and it should also be necessary to establish a Society for Preservation of the Classics."

I will digress from this concrete situation for a moment and turn to Shakespeare. Try to imagine how many interpretations of *Othello* or *King Lear* there have been over the last four hundred years. There is, however, no Society for the Preservation of Shakespeare. How come? Did Shakespeare win or lose? Has any one interpretation shaken some truth or done any damage to Shakespeare?

Have any of Shakespeare's plays ever become inferior from the performance of, let us say, the 854th experiment?

No, not one Shakespearean play has become inferior from this experiment or from any another.

These plays sit quietly on a shelf by themselves, and anybody who wishes can turn to the *words* any time. He can turn to them enriched by many *disagreements* and *agreements* or simply like a schoolboy. It is hardly necessary to prove that an approach built on extensive experience is *better*. However, very many adults look at the classics like schoolboys, that is, they remember what the teacher said, but they are indifferent, let's say, to *The Inspector General* or *King Lear*.

Now let us turn to Ostrovsky for a moment, and we will decide whether it is better for him that his plays have not received as many *different* interpretations as Shakespeare's have.

No, it is not better. His plays are rarely produced. There are no new interpretations to amaze us, no new discoveries.

True, Shakespeare already has more than 400 years, and there has been more time for fruitful experimentation. However, a Society for the Preservation of Ostrovsky is more feasible than a Society for the Preservation of Shakespeare, if such a thing even existed, which is why I wonder whether the next three hundred years will pass successfully enough?

Now, I should say here that I understand the question about establishing a Society for Preservation of the Classics was not meant literally, but figuratively.

Instead of arguing about these figurative suggestions, wouldn't it be better to say a few words about *Chekhov himself* in these discussions? To discuss some particle of what has been revealed to him about Chekhov in recent years. Then to consider one performance or another quietly, seriously analyzing what it was about.

Few people will do this, of course, for being clever people, they understand perfectly well the force of their figurative suggestions and the weakness of any literal ideas they could state about Chekhov. After all, to say something constructive it is necessary for these people to study anew, research deeply, and express something *personal*, but there are so many daily obligations that you won't really sit down to read a Chekhov play again. It is necessary to be satisfied with what you knew once, though you have completely forgotten it.

We would like to reveal precisely to this sort of person something based on what we study today, breathe today, and live today. Just this. We would like him to believe, at least, that not everything he sees in our performance is done from ignorance of what *he knows,* but because of our present-day study and experience.

He can disagree with us, but why [does he] appeal for *protection*? Does he know what would happen if this protection were really put into action?

First, the director (I am not referring to myself, but to directors in general) will begin to grow timid, as timid as he was many years ago [in Stalin's time]. Meanwhile, a timid artist is like a physicist that is afraid to go into a laboratory.

Say what you like, but discoveries are most often made by people that are not timid. It would be bad for Picasso and Modigliani if someone had thought up a society to protect human faces from their "distorted" reproduction by artists. I am saying that such "figurative" societies really existed [in the Stalin era], however, and what "advantages" they brought are all too well known.[112]

A diligent member of a society such as this can mess things up more than any "plunderer." That is why it seems to me it would be better to place all the thoughts about the subject on the altar of dispute. These thoughts must give birth to reciprocal creativity, instead of extinguishing it. The dull retelling the old truths does not benefit the living material of the theatre.

Whenever I read an article about some sort of "protection," for example, I immediately search for *the assumptions behind it.*

However, when the assumptions are weak from too little knowledge of the subject, this is even worse plundering than an experiment that has not succeeded at all.

On the other hand, maybe I am only grumbling again. If so—it is foolish.

Lightness

In a conversation with the actor Smoktunovsky, he indicated that recently he'd become tired, exhausted, because directors require him to force, and perform, and rehearse to the limit, they require you to spill out all your passion, everything you've got, etc.[113]

Finally comes the destruction and impoverishment of the organism, and you feel disemboweled. He says that he envies the French (speaking in this case about the recent tour of Jean-Louis Barrault's theatre to Moscow), where the most dramatic situations are played lightly.[114] Where the actor plays so that you do not feel his limits. It is necessary, Smoktunovsky believes, to learn to express the sharpest experiences lightly.

I listened and I agreed, although I belong to that group of directors who require force.

I think these demands for the utmost self-expression are a consequence of the high point of craftsmanship in previous years, of coldness and indifference in the actor's playing. Craftsmanship still exists to some extent, however, but for those who have left behind the school of extreme scenic expressiveness, naturally the moment of new craftsmanship should come when it would be possible to express drama lightly, not hysterically.

Even in a play like *Othello,* I think it is good to achieve this lightness, even airiness, without which you simply will not be able to "digest" Shakespeare.

Nevertheless, French is for the French, but, after all, there are other schools. I will not dare to judge our own, but let us look at the Americans. Do they express the strongest passions by acting lightly? Perhaps no. Even in film, where it is possible to work with less expressiveness than in the theatre because only individual *shots* are filmed, the American actor pours himself out to the limit. I recollect even Marlon Brando.[115]

There are not only different schools, however, but also different individualities. In addition, one general rule, perhaps, is not necessary for all. As for myself, I now consider it necessary to find a *light* means for expressing the heaviest scenic moments. Therefore, I agree with Smoktunovsky.

Othello

I am writing to put my thoughts in order after a bad rehearsal.

1. The beginning of our second act (Shakespeare's third, fourth, and fifth acts).

Cassio runs off after seeing Othello. Othello sits down at the table to work. His back is visible in the rear of the stage.

Iago is on the ramp, he looks for a long time at Othello's back, takes out a knife, measures it apparently as a joke, runs at top speed, throws up his hand with the knife, laughs at himself, and turns back.

Desdemona enters, wishing to tease Othello. He hears steps, he turns around, she is frightened, and they both laugh. They joke. She plays the master. He plays jealous. However, he becomes serious when the conversation turns to Cassio's pardon. She is angry and wants to leave. He catches up with her and promises to do everything [she asks].

For a long time after she leaves, Othello sits in silence.

2. He returns to work again. His *back.* Iago looks at his back as before.

Iago's first questions are those of a person determined to get to the point. Othello is bewildered. He speaks to his aide about the ambiguity of his words. About his unnecessary mysteriousness.

Here Iago has a large piece involving a *refusal to speak*, with its own development. Moreover, even when he says something clearly and wants Othello to hear what he's talking about, Iago makes it appear as though he's purposely refusing to speak, refusing to reveal any of his secret suspicions.

Although his discussion has already dealt with the subject of jealousy, Othello sincerely did not understand Iago. He thought that perhaps Iago knows something about a military plot. However, how is jealously involved here? Othello leaves angrily, breaking off the conversation.

3. Iago makes use of Othello's exit. He says he did not want to speak, but since Othello is so impatient with innuendos, the way to the truth has now been cleared for Iago, and he will say it. It is necessary to be able to play the transition to his decision to tell the "the truth" after a long period of generally refusing to report anything.

At this point, the first actual pause occurs.

At this point, Othello finally *hears* Iago and understands what he is talking about. Stunned, he appears again and approaches Iago. Iago does not want to look into his eyes, wonderfully playing modesty. After all, it is a question of the disloyalty of Othello's wife.

"Dost thou say so!" says Othello after a long silence.

This line is prepared by a whole pause; however, it is not enough only to speak it, it is necessary to act it, this line should pour out, break loose. The discussion deals with those fears that were deeply hidden within Othello, and here they are being justified. Incredible pain breaks out in this line, although Othello tries to control himself.

Furthermore, Iago must observe extraordinary tact, he pretends that he has already said it, he does not come out with any moralizing, but on the contrary, once more he seems to refuse to continue the conversation, for everything is clear.

Othello must cut Iago short, even seeming to show that everything actually is clear to him and listening any further would be offensive.

However, when Iago wants to leave, Othello stops him. He painfully pronounces the words that are hateful to him, about Iago *spying* on Desdemona. Iago has waited for this.

4. Othello does not speak his lines about being *black* and *growing old* while he is alone, but as an *outburst*, turning these words to Iago

as a friend. This is the acknowledgment of his secret premonitions about the possible infidelity of his wife.

Maybe Iago has already left, however.

5. Desdemona enters. Othello covers his face with his hands, and Iago, if he is still here, remains as though protecting him from the traitress.

Desdemona senses a secret and anxiously questions Othello, trying to understand what happened.

Othello can say the line "I am to blame" in another way, not in the literal sense of being sorry that specific moment.

He seems to ask her to forgive him for forcing her to suffer with him, for being *black* and *old*. Desdemona decides that he has become ill, and runs for a cloth or medicine, for something that could help.

He stands for a long time with the damp cloth she placed on his forehead, then he removes it, and laying it aside, he departs, afraid to look at his wife.

Desdemona is disturbed about the *vagueness* of what has happened, and follows him.

6. It is probably necessary that the scene where Emilia finds the handkerchief should not begin at once, but after a small respite from the previous atmosphere, since there was so much tension the audience will not have time to turn their attention completely in a new direction.

It is necessary to find the *beginning* for a new scene that does not hang on the tail of the previous one.

Emilia sees something lying on the floor from afar. Approaching it, she takes up the handkerchief. The process of realizing the success of what she has found should come naturally, even using up some time.

After all, Iago asked her to steal precisely this handkerchief. In addition, here lies the handkerchief that Iago asked her to steal! He will be so pleased! What a surprise it will be for him!

However, at this moment Iago is occupied with something else, he does not react to the surprise, and his wife irritates him with the irrelevance of her lingering here. It is necessary to play the entire process of this assessment accurately, with all its twists. This must be a small and complete masterpiece of handling dialogue.

Emilia has a surprise. Iago does not understand at first. Emilia is hurt that her husband does not accept her, even when she has a *surprise*. Finally, he realizes what the issue properly is, but instead of gratitude, he begins to warn her that it will be bad for her if she tells anybody about it. Then Emilia begins to ask him not to use this find for something bad. He pushes her out. And at this point, he is ready to meet the incoming Moor.

7. Othello's second major scene with Iago begins. It is dangerous to play Othello's frustration *in general,* his torment *in general,* etc. Then everything will soon become boring, since it will be monotonous.

It is necessary to find concreteness here, specifics, and the precise point of the disease that has already begun.

It lies in the fact that Othello departed with the feeling that he had fallen into some sort of trap, a torture chamber, and it is *Iago's fault.*

What is it necessary to do now? Strangely enough, in this scene his whole temperament is not directed against his wife, but *against Iago.* His entire rage is directed at Iago. It is necessary to express something to Iago. So that he knows what he has done. Who asked him to reveal this truth? The truth is not necessary.

Iago reacts stormily to this denial of the need for the truth. Iago perceives Othello's words as though they were a denial of their mutual ideal of service to the truth.

The one who is truthful is now opposed to the truth. And the liar is in favor of it.

8. The transition of Othello from his previous scene to the monologue of his farewell to the past.

It is *impossible* to say farewell for the last time.

Otherwise, what is to be done in the following moments of actual farewell? It is necessary to *adjust* to the fact that everything beautiful he lived is already behind him. It is a subtle section, and it is necessary to find the path, the rhythm, and the meaning of the passage.

9. Then a new path.

It suddenly occurs to Othello that Iago is crafty. Then he strikes Iago, warning him that this blow is a *small* thing, but if Iago is lying to him, then he will be threatened with something much *greater.*

Iago berates himself for being a naive fool to tell the truth to his chief.

In addition, the simple-hearted Moor again begins to question.

In a flash, like a boxer, Iago sees that his enemy has exposed himself, and he delivers his blows. He talks about *proofs.*

That is all! There are no more doubts. Now Othello bids farewell to the past for the last time.

Both swear revenge.

Perspiring from stress, tired like after heavy work, Iago remains on stage alone, he rests.

10. After a lighting quick respite, a new heavy scene follows; indeed each scene of Shakespeare is like an avalanche. However, to avoid tiring out the public from monotony, everything must be calculated with a high degree of sensitivity.

Next, Desdemona, who left Othello in the last scene in a condition that seemed to her like the oncoming of illness, now runs to him to learn how he feels. Othello, however, does not look ill any more.

Something very different begins to disturb Desdemona.

Othello carries on a conversation with her in a manner unknown to her before. He seems to hint at something, something he wants to say is secretly insulting. He says that her hands are moist, a sign of an unfaithful nature, etc.

He behaves toward Desdemona in a way that no longer indicates an illness, but her husband shows a certain character trait unknown to her before. An unpleasant feature. A tyrant, is that it?

She responds to him lightly, but with a certain resistance.

For Othello, meanwhile, her resistance is open proof of her faithlessness.

11. As a result, this scene looks even more mysterious for Desdemona than the one before, when Othello seemed to be ill. He has changed so much in such a short time that his appearance is the only evidence that it is Othello really standing before her.

This difficulty of Desdemona's effort *to understand the mystery* should be scenically interesting, disturbing.

Iago translates the mystery in a more realistic direction: it only means that something has happened along military lines, he says to her.

Moreover, Desdemona frantically grasps this version. In it is her rescue.

Her happiness at overcoming the deadlock of incomprehension can be played sharply, fearlessly.

After the gloom of uncertainty, it suddenly seems to Desdemona that there is a solution. She comes to believe that this solution is right.

12. For the sake of a small respite, there is a scene with Bianca, which nevertheless is necessary to accurately point up everything about the handkerchief. Furthermore, to build up the relationship between Bianca and Cassio.

13. Now comes one of the most difficult moments in the act, for since the act depends on the second half, new means are necessary for maintaining attention, the development of the action, so that there will be sufficient tension.

Othello and Iago appear again. This is their third scene.

Othello almost *runs away from Iago*. He wants to be saved from [hearing] any [damaging] new information. Iago overtakes him with his messages, and leads up to the faint.

This needs to like a *whirlwind*—up to the faint, and then—a stop.

Iago calls Cassio to look at Othello lying in a faint.

14. Then a new whirlwind—to hide the Moor in a trap and force him to *eavesdrop*.

Here it is necessary to release the entire contents of rhythm and form into the action, for if everything hinges on the game alone, I am afraid the action will be *repetitious*.

It is necessary to maintain the terrible *rhythm* before the arrival of Lodovico, and then strongly to suspend, to push in everything deeply, until the slap across Desdemona's face.

15. If this scene is conducted at the necessary pitch of intensity, then the last quarter of the act can be played less theatrically, more humanly, intimately, with a gradual forcing of the tragedy until the end.

Afterthoughts about *Othello*

I want to write down some words quickly, since the summer has ended and the days of hell have begun. *Othello* has already opened, and the different opinions are tearing me up. The type of opinion I would like to hear about our performances seldom pleases me. The basic aversion [this time] is about Othello's role. (Although for the sake of fairness, I should say that Othello's role was not always criticized. I also encountered those who understood this interpretation and agreed with it.)

Naturally, the basic objections were along the lines that our Othello was too "ordinary." There was insufficient nobility in him, beginning with his external appearance, but "even" internally, such as there is in Shakespeare.

One could argue, of course, whether the issue is the nobility of our Othello or the grandeur Shakespeare's Othello himself. But all the same, I would lose this argument, even if I was right, for there will be so many opponents of this interpretation of the text that even Shakespeare would retreat before the grandeur of their fabrications. Moreover, a theoretical idea, not proven on the stage, not influenced properly by emotion or even by awareness of the audience, has little standing. I will only explain again how Iago speaks of Othello as an unpolished "nomad." On one hand, completely civilized people are completely different, and on the other hand, with a tender soul—but a nomad. Naturally, this very simple person must be sincerely noble, but specifically sincere, and nothing else. I recognize, however, that our actor probably does not entirely convey enough nobility, and so the concept of Othello's "ordinariness" is easily subject to doubt.

Despite everything, those less numerous opinions are still dear to me in which I feel an understanding of our perceptions of this play, which consists of the fact that in this play the simple mechanics of the destruction of a pure but sometimes weak person should be revealed before our eyes. This play examines the mechanics of the evil that destroys people such as Othello.

In my view, the entire point lies in this, although each critic will have his own point of view, which, of course, he will present as the commonly held one and the only one.

My point of view is not unique, but to me it is precious.

It is well known that Othello is trustful, but why does he trust Iago, and not Desdemona or Cassio? I already addressed this question earlier.

Why is he trustful of those who are evil and mistrustful of those who are *good*? Is it possible that Desdemona and Cassio with all their appeal are [nonetheless] incapable of such trust? Indeed, their innocence is obvious, even if we only judge by their appearance. Is Othello really so blind that he is incapable of doubting the honesty of his lieutenant, who comes running each time with obviously implausible proofs? Really, this cursed handkerchief could solve the whole thing, but why don't Desdemona's eyes mean anything to Othello? Doesn't the truly sincere suffering of Cassio and Desdemona prove their innocence to him? Why is he so one-sided in his trustfulness?

Could it be this is not actually trustfulness, but simply crude and foolish jealousy, which many have wanted with such force for many centuries to transform into something nobler and more precious?

Then, it very well might be anything, since Shakespeare himself never explained his meaning. The stories, presented on paper, without his commentaries, will always be a certain riddle. Let it not be an absolute, but a relative riddle.

All the same, I am inclined to agree that the matter is precisely in his trustfulness, and in his trustfulness precisely of evil, and not good.

But why?

Because there is this crucial, almost innate feeling of uncertainty, a feeling of inferiority in comparison with other people whose skin is of a different color. After all, he has to live *among them.* In addition, he has fallen in love with a woman precisely from this other world. However, this love is already unstable by its very nature. He is *different* from her. Moreover, his subconscious conviction of evil instead of good coming from this is the basis of his one-sided trustfulness, of his suffering and the suffering of others who genuinely love him. It is the same basis on which Iago conceives his terrible game. He plays on what he knows: the world is divided into them and us, and this division is rooted in the hearts of many people, and to destroy people it is enough to touch this sick place in their heart.

However, how should this seemingly clear idea be expressed on stage with absolute lucidity in the entire structure of the performance and in each nuance of the actors' work? How can this become the property of *all* the spectators, without exception, and not just those who wish to accept us with open readiness?!

Once there were actors like Pavel Mochalov.[116]

There was calculation in the way they shocked audiences with their acting. It could be any performance you like, but the whole content of the play was sustained for the sake of a few minutes of shock from the tragedian.

Perhaps because the type of actor changed or simply because the questions became different, in any case now we hope for more than passion from a tragedian. Besides, who could shock us with the power of his passion today? Whomever you name will be deficient in this respect.

In the West, where there is Marlon Brando or Laurence Olivier, for instance, productions are not built on the actor's passion, but on a more *complex* basis. Laurence Olivier, for example, did not want to undertake the role of Othello for a long time because he did not think he could portray a contemporary black man.

A new point of view, a new interpretation of old, familiar approaches seems to be the leading tendency now.

The winners are those who find a contemporary form and content for old plays by using feelings very close to those of today.

Naturally, even then, both passion and spirit are necessary, for without them Shakespeare would not be Shakespeare, but the quality of these passions also seems to acquire new, contemporary highlights. Or should acquire them.

That is why, when approaching a Shakespearean production, it is no longer possible to do so with a feeling of heaviness, with a feeling that it is necessary to overstrain. With a feeling that it is necessary to carry a heavy load.

Even in the preparations before opening a play, it is no longer possible to be *afraid* of the future presentation, no longer possible to be *frightened* inside by it. Some [still] say, for example, my God, another one of those *heavy* plays today, the type that wears everyone out physically but whose results will be minimal compared with the physical load. However, you cannot approach a play with such thoughts and feelings.

Shakespeare apparently needs to be restrained with today's means, with your present-day skills, today's viewpoints, and today's style of talent.

If you do not succeed in restraining him, then Shakespeare himself forces you down and buries you. Then neither the actors nor the audience feels anything except fatigue.

That is why it is necessary to remember at least two tasks. First, that our present-day interpretations of a play must be extremely clear to everyone.

So that we feel the concept not merely speculatively, but *with the whole person.*

And second, that the clarity of this conception must be expressed *lightly*, not overstrained, so that the entire structure and performance of the play convey happiness and pleasure both to the audience and the actor himself, despite the tragic content of the play.

Now it is probably necessary to say something in more detail about these two tasks, about the interpretation and lightness of the means of communication.

We more or less remove from [the characterization of] Othello the customary coating of exclusiveness, heroics, and a starring role.

Yes, we say he is a general, a commander, the super-classical creation of a genius writer from a previous era—all this is true, but for us in a specific performance he is nevertheless a completely simple, normal, good person, kind, dismayingly trustful, in some ways even an ordinary intellectual. For our idea consists of showing how intrigue brings down not some general, but an artless, good person, how this intrigue twists and destroys him.

We transform the exceptional, one-of-a-kind characters and incidents into a more ordinary plan in order to remove the audience's impression that this is only ancient history, when certain ancient Turks were at war with equally ancient Cyprus.

No, in spite of the entire historical authenticity, before us is a completely intelligible man, who is honest, who loves, who is naively openhearted and pure, and in this open-heartedness is his nobility. However, beside him is another man, extremely worldly, realistic, seeming to know the price of everything worldly, and therefore *cynical*.

This second person is corrupted by life. He has lost faith in it, in himself, and in success. He is filled only with the cynical desire to destroy everyone and to bring everyone down to his level. "I am manure, but everyone else should be manure as well."

However, he is a subordinate; he is at the bottom. It means he needs to conceal. It is necessary to *decompose* the world, bring it down to his level. To bring the decomposition down to the level in which he finds himself. No one should be *higher*.

Stature offends mediocrity.

It is necessary to torment, to make happy people into manure. Yet *secretly*, of course.

This is the sense of the interpretation—the horror of *base intrigue*. Not mental, but animal, carnal.

Othello needs to be reduced to manure, reduced to his level. Iago needs to prove to himself that his level is the natural level, and there must be no other. It is necessary to grind up and destroy a good man, to drown him in Iago's swamp, to assault him.

Dying is not so terrible for Iago. Massacre, bloody destruction—it is his element. He lives in it and is ready to rot in it, just so others would not be [better than he would].

Therefore, it is about the horror of this *collision*, about the horror of such an intrigue...

I feel it is necessary to make one reservation here, however. With all the normalcy and "anti-exclusiveness" of Othello, nevertheless he should be an *outstanding* man, for otherwise everything becomes incomprehensible. Let him be no "ancient" general, but essentially a man, a man in whom there is surprising content. So that the new viewpoint has not led simply to the creation of a good-for-nothing.

It is necessary to avoid normal careless imprecision, ordinariness; simple *anti-traditionalism* is still only the negative side of the issue, it is still necessary to add something to this tradition, to *create* something different.

In addition, Iago is not only *evil*, not only the engine of the intrigue. He is three-dimensional. A *human being. Living flesh. A philosophy.* So that what the collision was about will be clear.

Furthermore, lightness, rhythmic playing, *effortlessness.*

When an idea becomes flesh, it is not necessary to be *pushed*. Violence such as this is only the other side of empty content.

Precision, concreteness of idea, and lightness.

Olivier said that it would be bad if the Moor had a tenor voice, for Othello should at least be a baritone. When everyone returned to rehearsal after a holiday, Olivier's voice was an octave lower.

Olivier practiced! I read this and thought: Could this simply be an English fairy tale?

...Ease—this is what should be the property of even the most tragic theatrical work. Effort, heaviness is capable of destroying any good thoughts and good feelings. Especially in Shakespeare. He is immense. Either you restrain him, or he will crush you. It is impossible to master him by pushing on regardless of obstacles, subordinate to all his demands—tearing up your heart at every turn. You will overstrain, but despite everything, you will not master him. It is necessary to weep, to fight, to fall on the ground, of course, but only with enormous *calculation*. In addition, part of this calculation is the most precise rhythm. No dragging out, otherwise everything will be too long. All the transitions from one state to another—quick as lightning. Drama must rush at you, not drip through like water in a clogged up sink.

Yes, Shakespeare is a storm, but not a black cloud hanging overhead all day. He is compulsory movement, development, change. He is something constantly living, mobile, changeable, not a stagnant swamp. Isn't it true that when a storm breaks out, and lightning flashes, and thunder roars, there is a certain ease in all this? Nature does not strain to force clouds together and hammer thunder from them. It is effortless. A gust of wind shifts enormous masses of clouds like bits of fluff, lightning hangs in the air for a single instant of illumination, and then is no more. It is necessary to manage Shakespeare as the wind manages the clouds. Either it is necessary to drive away these clouds entirely and then the pure open sky will be revealed, or to arrange a storm, a thunderstorm, so that the bolt of lightning will strike exactly there, where it must.

You say this is difficult? However, is it easy for athletes to work on the [gymnastic] bars? What they can do nowadays on those bars! The dexterity of a chimpanzee jumping from branch to branch or the ease of a bird—nothing compares with the dexterity and ease of present-day athletes. And in the theatre there should be the same dexterity and ease. However, imagine a Neanderthal watching modern artistic gymnastics. Imagine *that* rough face and body, *those* hands, next to *the athlete's* dexterous and clever refinement, and you will understand the difference between old rough acting, and what it must become to-day.

A Month in the Country

In *A Month in the Country,* it is awful if we assume that we are beyond the scope of a "love story," but we do not escape from this framework itself.

In the first two acts, while the theme is hidden, everything seems mysterious and promising.

But further on, where the theme starts to open up, there is a danger of remaining within the limits of a love story. However, even if we really do remain within the limits of this love story, then it is necessary to develop Natalya Petrovna's relations with the student much more. We rejected such a direction, however, and assumed that there was a possibility of larger meaning in this *supposed* love story.

Nevertheless, this still needs to be *accomplished*, this *larger* meaning achieved, otherwise it will not be one thing or the other.

Even with a simple love story, there are things that thus far are still not intelligible enough.

Eventually it turns out that Belyayev also loves Natalya Petrovna as she does him. This can appear in a boyish way, no more. He had fun and more fun, then he suddenly felt something vague, and his heart sank.

That is supposedly how it is written. Something sudden and unforeseen simply happened. However, this can hardly be interesting without some additional meaning. Indeed, a latent interest in this must be present from the very beginning. In addition, his feeling is not simply for a woman, but for some unknown world of beauty. This world attracts him, only he thinks that he is not good enough for it. Moreover, suddenly it turns out that it is possible. In addition, at the same time entirely impossible. Then this is drama. Now he will return to his own dreary students, whom he speaks about so ironically. In addition, that is all. Indeed, for him this break is no less painful than

Peter Trofimov's break with the cherry orchard. For Peter there is something after the cherry orchard, while for Belyayev there is nothing.

However, often it turns out that this cheerful boy only became entangled, and then he leaped to his freedom in time. There is no sort of second plan that would make his story richer or deeper.

In the first half, not only playfulness is necessary, perhaps, but also a latent second plan, he is secretly growing accustomed to a different and attractive life. Perhaps this is the motive for his attention to Vera. Because of his fleetingly half-conscious yet deeply felt problems regarding Natalya Petrovna. Perhaps because of a wish to make [a gift of some] fireworks for her [enjoyment].

Now a scene comes that is simply a conversation between Rakitin and a frivolous and cheerful youth. Actually, this is probably two different worlds. Belyayev is a playmate for Vera, but as for himself, he is more complex. And for us. Then as a result, there will be a comprehension of what was already latent in him.

In fact, this is an entire class history, so to speak. His history is precisely the same as Natalya Petrovna's—the history of the impossibility of living a life not his own. To lose the childishness in this role is not so terrible as to lose the *larger meaning* behind his childishness.

Then finally, if everything is correct, the remark that Belyayev has only one jacket will also merge with the course of things, instead of being simply a line of dialogue. In addition, when he decides to leave, it is not only liberation, but also a unique *loss*. As when it is sometimes necessary to tear something from your own *flesh*. It is not as though he simply took off a jacket that did not belong to him and then departed.

His farewell speech is a complex and inconsistent monologue, with as much feeling of the necessity to leave as there is sorrow that it has to be done. After all, where he is going to is not so wonderful. It is more beautiful for him to remain here, not only for the sake of love, but also for the sake of knowing certain people with high ideas.

It is possible to play the superficial plot of this role dashingly, but it is also possible to penetrate somewhere further, so that his longing for Natalya Petrovna would be no less [interesting] than her longing for him.

It is necessary to find all the signposts in the development of this internal line, from the first entrance, through all the possible further nuances, to the basic scenes. Not only her yearning for a different life, but also his.

Why do we consider that Belyayev is only joking when he talks about his small childhood cottage, that Vera is superior to his sister, that he is an orphan, etc.? Why do we concentrate so little on the moment when he suddenly understands that Vera is in love with him, that this has angered Natalya Petrovna, and that there is some kind of hidden meaning in this interrelationship?

Further, is it really so easy for him to free himself from this lovely estate? And not only for financial reasons.

The scene when Natalya Petrovna reproaches him, he tries to leave, but remains—this is probably more difficult than we normally make it, for here is the latent yearning of two people for a different way of life, and not just an amusing turn of the plot. This scene can be splendid in its rhythm and form, but its entire content must be sound.

Then in a monologue of his, he feels that something has happened. All this should emerge logically, and what it is based on must not be unexpected.

In a word, it is necessary to check and recheck the content of this role. It is written in a way that is not easily comprehensible to today's audience, and so our interpretation needs certainty. Much depends on that, on how precise it is.

Now for Natalya Petrovna and Rakitin. It seems that everything necessary is planned, yet we have this fear that we are still showing less than we mean to. We reject the simple course: a woman falls in love with a younger man simply because he is younger than she is. We want to say that this is the result of her entire life, a display of her disturbed character, her revolt against the constraints of her past, beginning with her childhood and continuing to the present time. To her, as Denmark seems to Hamlet, it is a prison, while to others it is not. To her it seems that they are pursuing her, observing her. She wants freedom and peace of mind, but she does not know what they are. Should she run away from the life that troubles her, or on the other hand, try to overcome her almost painful impulses. She examines herself, seeks the advice of others, she reflects, she argues, she protests, she restrains. She seems to be learning how to live independently; she rejects the routine way of things, and at the same time doubts that it should be rejected.

This is the beginning of the disintegration of certain fundamentals, doubt about the past and the present and ignorance of the future.

To play it, it is not necessary to extract the meaning from the text vocally, but on the contrary, to conceal it, while *understanding* it.

In addition, Rakitin's path is always to make sure that this does not remain within the [traditional] framework of "unrequited love."

Theirs is the theme of becoming part of the "rear guard," the theme of growing old. They are both caught at the moment when their view of the world is shifting, and they are trying to come to terms with it. His monologues are not simply those of a jealous or offended man. These are attempts to comprehend what has *changed* in the world. This is a play about the fact that something has changed in the world. It is as though they have felt the trembling of an earthquake for the first time, yet not knowing from history that this is what it is.

Yes, of course, theirs are all general conversations outwardly. However, if the play is not impregnated with all this, our experience of reading Turgenev with today's eyes will appear compromised. We will depart from what was once the good the old theatre, yet we will not arrive at something new.

However now, when everything has already been said, it is necessary to pass on to what is perhaps the most difficult [issue]. The issue is that even though it may seem as though the content has been well understood, nevertheless it needs to be expressed not only by pronouncing the meaning of the text, but in something more complex. It must be demonstrated in the construction of a role, by a precise internal design together with complete lightness in pronunciation of the text.

The attempt to master the content should not be limited simply to *rational* acting. It must be related to something different, something that I will now try to explain. It is necessary to express the theme not simply with the aid of words—something should happen to people right before our eyes that reveals the meaning of this important theme.

It must be an incident that grabs us not only through reason, but also through [something] that suggests the theme to the audience emotionally.

In the third and fourth acts, the entire shift occurring in the characters must [actually] *happen*. It must appear not only in their conversations, not merely as a verbal explanation of the theme. This must be specifically an *earthquake*, a *tornado*, a *whirlwind*, which detaches all these people from habitude, and makes them for some period completely unrecognizable.

For the complete period of two acts, the third and fourth, and then from the moment of the second entrance of her husband (when he notices Natalya Petrovna with Rakitin for the second time), humility must begin in Rakitin. In the fifth act, Natalya Petrovna again disturbs him, when she tries, through a conversation about painting, to continue her *personal connection* with Belyayev, and then revolts after Belyayev's departure. If all this is done strongly, then her moments of explicit, enforced solitude, her giving up, will be even more expressive by contrast. However, even in complete loneliness (in her last scene, after everyone leaves), she must forcefully resist despair. She also tries not to surrender to loneliness, and that is why this sounds even more tragic.

Unexpressed Talent

A young man asked me to allow his wife, an actress, to try out for a part.

The next day a tall young woman came in, slender, with very distinctive features. Blushing from nervousness. It was immediately apparent that she was gifted, but it would be difficult for her to get into the theatre because of her distinctive appearance. Her appearance has to intrigue someone. Someone must be interested in this young actress, and then perhaps something will come of it. However, how could someone become interested her here, amid all this commotion, this flood of [everyday] affairs, when you hardly even have time to understand your own actors. I asked her what she wanted to show me. She replied, "The Proposal." "Anything else?" I asked. She was silent for a while, and then answered sharply, "That's enough!"

I laughed because her faith in herself was attractive to me, because in this faith there is already something of talent. "Why haven't you found a position before now?" I asked.

She answered sharply, slightly blushing: "I have a big nose."

If it were up to me, I would have accepted her immediately, but after that, the usual postponement of auditions occurred, and then the lack of [available] openings, and then everything subsided. She was not the first on the list or the last.

I often think how many people there are with strong, unexpressed talent in them, but which also perishes in them, since more than talent is needed in order to express it. An entire chain of conditions is necessary. Meanwhile this feeling of inexpressiveness tears even a very young person to pieces. More accurately, this strong feeling *in itself* gradually burns out in them, and is laid to rest.

How many people there are with such a current inside themselves! Frequently they write letters, even without a return address, only to pour out some of their feelings, their thoughts, which will not let them rest. There is usually something *unexpressed* in a person, something unspent, an untouched reserve of feelings, a stock of good motives. In one, it is expressed through work, in another through love, in a third through something else. And the fourth cannot express it in any way.

Then they want at least to write a letter.

Yes, I understand this.

Even George Bernard Shaw, who lived such a stormy life, found expression in letters.[117]

Uncle Vanya

For some reason, we are in the habit of thinking that Shakespeare wrote tragedies and Chekhov wrote about melancholy. Although this has been repeatedly disproved, all the same many people continue to think this way in their souls.

Performances and films confirm that many think precisely *this way*. Whether these performances and films are lyrical or poetic, I cannot say. Actually, they are only melancholic.

Lost rhythm, a depressed suffering intelligentsia, boring provincial life, etc., in the same spirit.

Meanwhile, I am increasingly convinced that there is no such lyricism in these plays. There is absolutely no "sleepy trance" in them. These plays are *tragic* in the true meaning of the word, with all the necessary consequences.

Where are all the "halftones and pauses" and "sadness," when almost from the first words the feelings of the characters are revealed with such fury, with such frankness and passion?

Honestly, *Uncle Vanya* is no less tragic than *Hamlet*, not only in its essence, but also in its means of expression—yes, its means of expression![118]

The theme of despair from the consciousness of an unfulfilled life is expressed here in maximum colors, so strongly and directly that its boldness and clarity concede nothing to any play of Shakespeare's.

The only difference is that one is the past and the other is modern life, that is all.

I am not convinced (Oh, horrors!) that Nemirovich-Danchenko was right in saying that the fates of Chekhov's characters are decided when they are having dinner, for example, or when they are simply sitting peacefully at the table. In *Uncle Vanya*, it is not true, for there everything is stripped bare and tragically exposed.

Every generation has its own Chekhov, however, just as it has its own Shakespeare. Moreover, it is ridiculous to dispute the achievements of the past. However, today it seems to me that Chekhov should be produced *openly tragically*.

It is not necessary to disguise supposedly latent dramas with ordinary life, but it is necessary to present them without any sort of "covering" of ordinary life, precisely as it is written in the play. Take [the character of] Uncle Vanya, for example.

How openly Uncle Vanya reveals his love for Yelena Andreyevna.

How openly Doctor Astrov falls in love.

How openly Sonya suffers.

Moreover, how openly even Professor Serebryakov expresses his despair, in which he suddenly begins to realize his old age, feebleness, and debility.

What a strong play! Accompanied by such open groans and cries. Then finally, a shot!

What a nervous pitch of desperation.

How horrible to have a young wife and feel yourself growing old, and living to become a burden to her. Moreover, not simply suffer from all this quietly, but arrange a mutiny against yourself, against everyone, against old age. It can be a foolish mutiny, but it is an open Shakespearean mutiny.

Moreover, how awful, to be honest, to have an old husband, without loving him, when beside you is Astrov, who loves you and calls you to him. What torture is involved in her aspiration to remain honest.

Is everything here really hidden in the subtext, hidden behind everyday life?

Obviously not! No less exposed than in *Hamlet* or *Richard III*.

However, no one wants to reach this fever pitch in a Chekhovian play. They are afraid. Afraid of being reproached that this is *not Chekhov*.

However, what would physicists do if they were afraid, for example, to touch an atom! If they only obeyed the previous scientists and only thought about the laws of the past. However, truly, I do not know this subject.

As far as *Uncle Vanya* is concerned, I am convinced that there is not a crumb of boredom or whining, no nights of lyrical conversation, but there is a fatal battle to make something different of one's life. A fatal battle and fatal *defeat*.

And the only pause occurs after everyone has left. *It did not happen!*

However, until then, energy, violence, sharp outcries, frankness, but everything as in Chekhov, *out of place, discordant,* with tragic force—shots wide of their mark.

This must be a strong performance, vivid, sharp.

Reading *Uncle Vanya,* I thought what a storm was concealed in the writer's nature. Inside his ailing organism was strong passion, passion for life, for action, for health, for love. However, he lived estranged, generally closed off, and this passion was often splashed out on paper in the form of *weeping, groaning,* and *wailing.*

In the first act, Doctor Astrov complains that life has drained him, that he has become an eccentric, wants nothing, and loves nobody.

Vanya yawns, enters with a sleepy, wrinkled face. For the entire act, he groans that he is melancholy and bored.

Everyone speaks about everything directly, not hiding anything, but then where is the subtext, that subtext which is apparently is so important in Chekhov?

It could be that this is nonsense—that it is necessary to act both this yawning and these eccentricities resulting from boredom. And they quietly drink vodka and grumble... That is how they usually play it, meanwhile chattering something about subtext. However, where is it and what does it consist of?

Indeed, this boredom and melancholy are so obvious. However, the key is exactly in the fact that they are not bored today.

Indeed, they behave in the customary manner. Everything is the way they say it is, however *not today.*

For [today] there is *Yelena Andreyevna.*

My God, who has not experienced this lift, this enthusiasm, love or simply excitement, from being next to someone like her?

The subtext is the fact that Astrov and Vanya understand: today they are terribly excited about something. And not only today. It beckons, it disturbs. Then suddenly an interest appears, and let it stay hidden, however the entire essence lies *in this.*

It is one thing to argue about melancholy *in a void.* It is another thing when this *arrival* happens, the appearance of a woman, the aroma of her, and the novelty of these sensations. Especially for people like them, who have lived for years without love.

They are instantly revived; they are excited, disturbed, they expect something, and all their complaining today is just for show, although there is truth in it.

Both of them are waiting for her to arrive. Where is she? Here she comes; there she goes... They even compete, but it must be hidden from our eyes, almost hidden to be exact, but their *enthusiasm* is the subtext, and in this subtext is the entire drama, for it, this enthusiasm, is fated to collapse. Then at this point, melancholy appears; only it is much more terrible than before.

In contrast to this enthusiasm of Vanya and Astrov is the night scene with the Professor, Yelena Andreyevna's husband.

He is, on the contrary, frustrated, in decline, though not passively frustrated, not melancholy and capricious, but actively attacking despair from old age and illness, from his sudden realization of the void.

He is irritated, malicious, fierce, and angry. He finds fault, demands, and protests. He shouts, he *scares everyone away,* some sort of nightmare, and that is not all.

Let him behave this way and that way, worse than Vanya or Astrov, but he is not behaving hypocritically, he is simply unrestrained in his illness and suffering, no less than the others are. He also needs kindness, but he looks at things sensibly enough, on this night, at least now. Only the old woman, Marina, will comfort him and embrace him, and then having calmed down, he goes to his room and goes to sleep.

Yelena Andreyevna suffers alone in silence for a while, hiding her despair behind apathy, behind calmness, behind apparent sleepiness.

However, when her husband shouts, when the other men compete before her, she alone knows: her position is hopeless. It is much more terrible than theirs is.

After all, Vanya and Astrov hope for something, something has excited them, if only her. Her husband's night illness will pass, and [in the end] he will take care of his affairs, even though they are stupid, foolish affairs, still he believes in them occasionally.

She will be faithful to him, but there are no affairs for her to care for, and [she has] the feeling that everything has been over for her for a long time; she seems to be buried alive.

Moreover, Vanya is openly pursuing her, but she does not like him, and she becomes bored when he speaks to her about his love.

Meanwhile this same night the somewhat drunken Vanya becomes extremely frank. Why is he growing old? Why is everything in the past? This wild theme resounds not in muted tones or in the subtext, but with Shakespearean fury. In addition, it is revealed, so to speak, with "impudent" candidness. A man barely able to struggle against hysterics, and drunk besides.

However, the subtext, perhaps, is only in that Yelena Andreyevna is *unattainable.*

His whole life was now tied up in this knot. In the morning, he calmed himself down with some hope, swaggered, but at night, everything presents itself more severely, soberly. Moreover, at this point, there is almost an open attack of despair.

Chekhov did not have an easy life if he was capable of writing such stories... After all, when a good author writes about someone, he unfailingly writes about himself as well, even if only in some small degree.

Chekhov was ill and did not drink. However, Vanya has gotten drunk at night, and Astrov is also a little drunk, moreover he is still lively, still with some sort of hope. After all, he did not come over here for the professor, but for her; and doesn't he actually feel a little pleased?

Astrov opens the cabinet, reaches for the vodka, and reproaches something, insults something, but once more, there is subtext: this is not simply grumbling, on the contrary, it is a certain flight, indeed a false flight, momentary, and then everything will become intelligible. Now, he poured himself a small glass, drank something, and ate, almost not seeing whom he is speaking to, he speaks with pleasure, although he is angry.

Sonya sees, however, that he is in good spirits, this happens so rarely, he is so fine, talented, especially when he is in good spirits, and she would like to think that his good spirits relate to her a little. She serves him, has a little snack too, and even dares to tell him something about love, only indirectly, but he is far away, though next to her, and absolutely does not hear her.

Then it remains only for the poor woman to confess something friend to friend, but here also is lack of coordination.

No one knows how to describe the tragedy of incoordination as furiously as Chekhov does. Everyone speaks frankly, openly, apparently directly—and such disorder.

Next morning, Vanya has washed up, calmed down, and is even a little cheerful. He arranges something in the drawing room so that "Herr Professor" can report his news.

The third act even begins in a light way.

No, not lightly, perhaps, but at least *lively*. People are not typically in one mood for a long time. More accurately, they try to struggle with themselves. Now the experiences of the previous night are hidden away somewhere. Whether they are hidden deeply or not, they are still hidden.

Let Vanya speak once more to Yelena Andreyevna about his love, but now apparently with humor. As a peace offering, he even goes off for some autumnal roses.

However, Sonya has already spoken openly about her love and now wants at least a small change; she wants to learn something, at least some sort of truth. And here Yelena Andreyevna undertakes to learn it. However, this blasted subtext (!) is present once more, since she seemingly goes on to learn about Sonya, but again thinking only about herself. Astrov excites her, and only honesty and duty interfere with her freedom. Her strong inclination to love is hidden under a mask of apathy, sleepiness. She barely manages to control herself, she would like to conceal it, but somehow to bring up the theme of *love*, yet Astrov, after carrying out her request, tells her something about *forests*. Although he is not interested in this subject now, and his story is continually interrupted by silences that become terrible to both of them. Each one is afraid to make an incorrect step, but Astrov suddenly guesses Yelena Andreyevna's poorly hidden weakness, and their entire hidden attraction to each other has become obvious. Astrov embraces her, she is frightened, she wants to leave, and she is terrified that everything has turned out this way. It is [become] disgraceful now for Sonya.

At the high point of their embrace, Vanya comes in with the flowers.

For a long time, he remains externally calm, only understanding with difficulty precisely what "Herr Professor" has come here to report.

Now that storm of passion breaks out once more.

I remember in the film version how Smoktunovsky played the scene where Uncle Vanya shoots at Professor Serebryakov with a certain irony. As if he were ashamed of the openness of a feeling that in Shakespeare would be considered the norm.[119]

Sometimes we will think up any excuse in order to leave a little something on the side.

It often seems to us that Chekhov is ironic in similar places. At this point, it is said, they shoot at each other. Wow! How excited they have become! However, no, it is necessary to approach this drama the same way, for example, that we experience the suffering in *King Lear*. However, *we do not experience it this way,* and we substitute real meaning for *rhetoric*. Because not everyone wants to pour out his heart.

Nor can everyone.

Then, as so often happens in Chekhov's plays, a *departure* begins, a *farewell*. And the loneliness of those who remain. To evaluate the calm is possible only after the storm, however, when the debris is strewn around and the wind has died down.

Coda

There is a place in Fellini's film *The Clowns* where the clowning reaches its highest point.[120]

The orchestra thunders, the clowns dance madly, the light reflects off the trumpets in the orchestra.

Moreover, to crown it all, a clown flies up to the top of the tent and spins around up there among a collection of paper streamers. And suddenly the orchestra is silent, and everything stops in a second. Only this clown remains spinning by inertia under the cupola. And in the silence, only the rustling of the paper streamers from this clown is heard. However, as his movements grow slower and slower, he finally becomes entangled in the streamers, and simply hangs there, absurdly suspended.

Below, the arena is already empty, and only the refuse remains left over after the celebration.

Alone, one old clown with a drawn face smiles pitifully. Feeling uneasy and shrugging his shoulders, he says uncertainly, "I liked it…"

Photographs

Figure 1. *Othello*, Olga Yakovleva as Desdemona.

Figure 2. *Othello*, Nikolai Volkov as Othello and Lev Durov as Iago.

Figure 3. *Othello*, Nikolai Volkov as Othello and Olga Yakovleva as Desdemona.

Figure 4. *Othello*, Lev Durov as Iago.

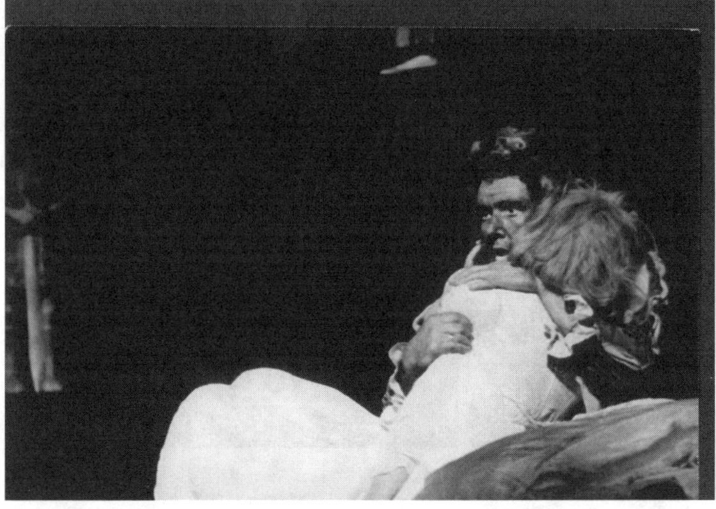

Figure 5. *Othello*, Nikolai Volkov as Othello and Olga Yakovleva as Desdemona.

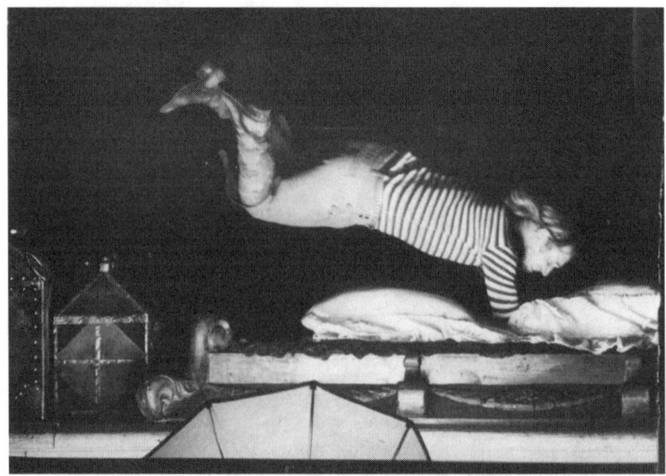

Figure 6. *Othello*, Lev Durov as Iago.

Figure 7. *A Month in the Country*, Olga Yakovleva as Natalya Petrovna and Anna Kamenkova as Vera.

Figure 8. *A Month in the Country*, Oleg Vavilov as Rakitin and Olga Yakovleva as Natalya Petrovna.

Figure 9. *A Month in the Country*, Olga Yakovleva as Natalya Petrovna.

Figure 10. *A Month in the Country*, scenery by Dmitry Krymov

Figure 11. *A Month in the Country*, members of the company

Figure 12. *A Month in the Country*, I. Shalbatas as Belyayev.

Figure 13. *A Month in the Country*, Anna Kamenkova as Vera.

Figure 14. *The Cherry Orchard*, Alla Demidova as Ranevskaya.

Figure 15. *The Cherry Orchard,* Alla Demidova as Ranevskaya and Vladimir Vysotsky as Lopakhin, with members of the company.

Figure 16. Anatoly Efros at rehearsal

Figure 17. Anatoly Efros at rehearsal

Chronology

<table>
<tr><td>1925</td><td>Anatoly Efros is born July 3 in Kharkov, Ukraine.</td></tr>
<tr><td>1941–45</td><td>Efros works as lathe operator in an aviation factory in Perm, Siberia.</td></tr>
<tr><td>1946–47</td><td>Efros studies acting at the Mossoviet Theatre Studio.</td></tr>
<tr><td>1947–50</td><td>Efros transfers to the directing program at the Lunacharsky State Institute for Theatre Arts (GITIS).</td></tr>
<tr><td>1950</td><td>Efros graduates from GITIS.</td></tr>
<tr><td>1951</td><td>Prague Remains With Me by Kiril Buryakovsky, adapted from Notes from the Gallows by Julius Fucik, Transport Workers Theatre (GITIS graduation project).
Come to Zvonkovoie by Alexander Korneichuk, Ostrovsky Theatre.</td></tr>
<tr><td>1952</td><td>Efros joins the directing staff of the Ryazan Dramatic Theatre.
The Dog in the Manger by Lope de Vega, Ryazan Dramatic Theatre.
Lyubov Yaravaya by Konstantin Trenyov, Ryazan Dramatic Theatre.
Love at Dawn by Yaroslav Galan, Ryazan Dramatic Theatre.
The Ardent Heart by Alexander Ostrovsky, Ryazan Dramatic Theatre.</td></tr>
<tr><td>1953</td><td>Efros marries Natasha Krymova.
Girls are Beauties by Andrei Simukov, Ryazan Dramatic Theatre.
When the Spears Are Broken by Nikolai Pogodin, Ryazan Dramatic Theatre.
Stones in the Liver by Andrei Makayenok, Ryazan Dramatic Theatre.
The Stepmother by Honoré de Balzac, Ryazan Dramatic Theatre.</td></tr>
<tr><td>1954</td><td>Efros joins directing staff of the Central Children's Theatre
Efros's son Dmitry is born.
Someone Else's Role by Sergei Mikhalkov, Central Children's Theatre.
Good Luck! by Viktor Rozov, Central Children's Theatre.</td></tr>
<tr><td>1955</td><td>Three Who Went to Tselina (with Maria Knebel) by Nikolai Pogodin, Central Children's Theatre.</td></tr>
<tr><td>1956</td><td>A Fairy Tale about Fairy Tales by A. Zak and I. Kuznetsov, Central Children's Theatre.</td></tr>
<tr><td>1957</td><td>Hedda Gabler by Henrik Ibsen, Film Actor's Theatre Studio.
Boris Godunov by Alexander Pushkin, Central Children's Theatre.
In Search of Happiness by Viktor Rozov, Central Children's Theatre.</td></tr>
<tr><td>1958</td><td>Anyone by Eduardo de Filippo, Sovremennik Theatre.</td></tr>
</table>

Free Masters by Zinaida Danovskaya, Central Children's Theatre.

The Dreams of Simone Mashar by Bertolt Brecht, Yermolova Theatre.

Kolka, My Friend! by Alexander Khmelik, Central Children's Theatre.

1960   Publication of *The Director's Work on the Production,* Moscow: Central Publishing House of the USSR.

Unequal Battle by Viktor Rozov, Central Children's Theatre.

Guests and at Home by Alexander Volodin, Yermolova Theatre.

Former Boys by Nikolai Ivanter, Central Children's Theatre.

1961   *The Noisy Day,* from *In Search of Happiness* by Viktor Rozov, Mosfilm.

1962   *Before Supper* by Viktor Rozov, Central Children's Theatre.

Leap Year by Valentina Panova, Mosfilm.

1963   *Marriage* by Nikolai Gogol, Central Children's Theatre.

Two on the Steppe by Alexander Kazakevich, Mosfilm.

1964   *Them and Us* by Nina Dolinina, Central Children's Theatre.

Efros is appointed Artistic Director of the Lenkom Theatre.

Wedding Day by Viktor Rozov, Lenkom Theatre.

104 Pages about Love by Edward Radzinsky, Lenkom Theatre.

1965   *My Poor Marat* by Alexei Arbuzov, Lenkom Theatre.

Shooting a Film by Edward Radzinsky, Lenkom Theatre.

Everyone Gets What He Deserves (with Lev Durov) by Samuel Alyoshin, Lenkom Theatre.

Efros suffers a heart attack.

1966   *The Seagull* by Anton Chekhov, Lenkom Theatre.

Judicial Chronicle (with Alexei Adoskin) by Yuri Volchek, Lenkom Theatre.

Molière, or The Cabal of Hypocrites by Mikhail Bulgakov, Lenkom Theatre.

Efros is dismissed from the Lenkom Theatre for "ideological deficiencies."

1967   Efros joins directing staff of the Malaya Bronnaya Theatre.

Three Sisters by Anton Chekhov, Malaya Bronnaya Theatre.

1968   *Kalabashkin the Seducer* by Edward Radzinsky, Malaya Bronnaya Theatre.

Platon Krechet by Alexander Korneichuk, Malaya Bronnaya Theatre.

1969   *The Happy Days of an Unhappy Man* by Alexei Arbuzov, Malaya Bronnaya Theatre.

The Rest Is Silence by Vladimir Delmar, Mossoviet Theatre.

1970   *Romeo and Juliet* by William Shakespeare, Malaya Bronnaya Theatre.

Tales of the Old Arbat by Alexei Arbuzov, Malaya Bronnaya Theatre.

1971   *The Outsider* by Ignatii Dvoretsky, Malaya Bronnaya Theatre.

Boris Godunov by Alexander Pushkin, Central Television.

Marat, Lika, and Leonidik by Alexei Arbuzov, Central Television.

1972   *Brother Alyosha* by Viktor Rozov, from *The Brothers Karamazov* by Fyodor Dostoyevsky, Malaya Bronnaya Theatre.

Platon Krechet by Alexander Korneichuk, Central Television.

1973   *The Situation* by Viktor Rozov, Malaya Bronnaya Theatre.

Don Juan by Molière, Malaya Bronnaya Theatre.

A Few Words in Honor of Monsieur de Molière, from the biographical novella *The Life of Monsieur de Molière* by Mikhail Bulgakov and *Don Juan* by Molière, Central Television.

The Shot by Alexander Pushkin, All-Union Radio.

1974   *The Campsite* by Edward Radzinsky, Mossoviet Theatre.

Tanya by Alexei Arbuzov, Central Television.

The Outsider by Ignatii Dvoretsky, Central Television.

1975   *Marriage* by Nikolai Gogol, Malaya Bronnaya Theatre.

The Evacuation Train by Mikhail Roshin, Moscow Art Theatre.

The Cherry Orchard by Anton Chekhov, Taganka Theatre

Fired and Replaced (with Lev Durov) by Yuri Volchek, Malaya Bronnaya Theatre.

Pages from Pechorin's Journal, from *A Hero of Our Time* by Mikhail Lermontov, Central Television.

Publication of *The Joy of Rehearsal*, Moscow: Iskusstvo.

Efros suffers another heart attack.

1976   *Othello* by William Shakespeare, Malaya Bronnaya Theatre.

Martin Eden, from the story by Jack London, All-Union Radio.

Fantasy, from the story "Spring Water" by Ivan Turgenev, Central Television.

Dear Liar by Jerome Kilty, Central Television.

1977   *A Month in the Country* by Ivan Turgenev, Malaya Bronnaya Theatre.

Thursday and Never Again by Alexander Bitov, Mosfilm.

1978   *The Veranda in the Woods* by Ignatii Dvoretsky, Malaya Bronnaya Theatre.

Marriage by Nikolai Gogol, Edinburgh Festival.

Marriage by Nikolai Gogol, Guthrie Theatre, Minneapolis (American cast).

The Stranger by Alexander Blok, All-Union Radio.

Islands in the Stream, from the novel by Ernest Hemingway, Central Television.

1979   *Don Juan, Continued* by Edward Radzinsky, Malaya Bronnaya Theatre.

The Rest is Silence by Vladimir Delmar, Central Television.

Little Tragedies by Alexander Pushkin, All-Union Radio.

Molière by Mikhail Bulgakov, Guthrie Theatre, Minneapolis (American cast).

Publication of *Profession: Director*, Moscow: Iskusstvo.

1980   *The Road* by V. Balysnii, from the novel *Dead Souls* and the letters of Nikolai Gogol, Malaya Bronnaya Theatre.

Summer and Smoke by Tennessee Williams, Malaya Bronnaya Theatre.

Marriage and *A Month in the Country*, Grand Prize, Duisburg Theatre Festival, Duisburg, Federal Republic of Germany.

1981   *The Cherry Orchard* by Anton Chekhov, Toen Theatre, Tokyo, Japan (Japanese cast).

Memoirs by Alexei Arbuzov, Malaya Bronnaya Theatre.

Tartuffe by Molière, Moscow Art Theatre.

Mr. Dom's Idea by Fernand Crommelynck, GITIS.

The Life of Molière by Mikhail Bulgakov, All-Union Radio.

1982   *Three Sisters* by Anton Chekhov, Malaya Bronnaya Theatre

The Living Corpse by Leo Tolstoy, Moscow Art Theatre.

Natasha, from *A Month in the Country* by Ivan Turgenev, Toen Theatre, Tokyo, Japan (Japanese cast).

The Stone Guest by Alexander Pushkin, All-Union Radio.

1983   *Napoleon I* by Ferdinand Bruckner, Malaya Bronnaya Theatre.

The Cherry Orchard by Anton Chekhov, National Theatre, Helsinki.

The Tempest by William Shakespeare, Pushkin Museum, Festival of December Nights.

Mozart and Salieri by Alexander Pushkin, All-Union Radio.

A Month in the Country by Ivan Turgenev, Central Television.

Romeo and Juliet by William Shakespeare, Central Television.

1984   *The Theatre Director* by Ignatii Dvoretsky, Malaya Bronnaya Theatre.

Efros is appointed Artistic Director of the Taganka Theatre.

At the Bottom (aka *The Lower Depths*) by Maxim Gorky, Taganka Theatre.

1985   *War's Unwomanly Face*, from the novel by Sergei Alexeivich, Taganka Theatre.

A Lovely Sunday for a Picnic by Tennessee Williams, Taganka Theatre.

The Cherry Orchard and *At the Bottom*, Grand Prize, Belgrade International Theatre Festival, Belgrade, Yugoslavia.

Publication of *Theatre Novel Continued*, Moscow: Iskusstvo.

1986   *One-and-a-Half Square Meters*, from the story by Boris Mozhayev, Taganka Theatre.

The Misanthrope by Molière, Taganka Theatre.

1987   Efros dies of a heart attack at his apartment on January 13.

Members of the Society of Cactuses by Ignatii Dvoretsky and *Hedda Gabler* by Henrik Ibsen, Taganka Theatre, uncompleted performances.

1992   Efros exhibition at the Bakhrushin Theatre Museum, Moscow.

1993   Efros Theatre Conference, Russian Theatre Agency, St. Petersburg.

Publication of collected edition of Efros's books, including the posthumous text *The Fourth Book*, Moscow: Russian Theatre Fund.

2000   Publication of *The Theatre of Anatoly Efros: Recollections and Articles*, Moscow: Actor-Director Theatre Publishers.

Publication of *Occupation: Director* (selected passages from *Theatre Novel Continued* and *The Fourth Book*), Moscow: Vagrius.

2006   Publication of *The Joy of Rehearsal*, Trans. James Thomas, New York: Peter Lang.

Notes

1. Anatoly Efros, *The Joy of Rehearsal,* Trans. James Thomas (New York: Peter Lang, 2006).

2. This passage deals with Efros's voluntary departure from the Central Children's Theatre in 1964, when he accepted the promotion to Artistic Director of the Lenkom Theatre. It also refers to his involuntary departure from the Lenkom Theatre three years later, when he was dismissed from as Artistic Director and consigned to the directing staff of the Malaya Bronnaya Theatre. Efros is writing about himself, of course, but the "necessity for change" is aimed as well at the reactionary establishment that clandestinely orchestrated his dismissal.

3. Michael Alexandrovich Ulyanov (b. 1927), actor-director-screenwriter, graduate of the Schukin School of the Vakhantangov Theatre (1950), National Actor of the USSR and other awards, Artistic Director of the Vakhtangov Theatre.

4. *Dear Liar* (1970) by Jerome Kilty (b. 1922), adapted from the correspondence of George Bernard Shaw and actress Mrs. Patrick Campbell. Produced at MAT in 1966.

5. Josef Rayevsky (1900–72), actor, director, teacher, and member of Stanislavsky's Second Studio.

6. Anatoly Ktorov (1898–1980), actor, MAT debut 1933. Angelina Stepanova (1905–60), actress, MAT debut 1924.

7. Dmitri (Mitya) is Fyodor Karamazov's eldest son in Fyodor Dostoyevsky's novel, *The Brothers* Karamazov (1880).

8. Viktor Rozov (1913–2004), whose coming-of-age plays for youth were popular in Russia during the Thaw. Efros directed several at the Central Children's Theatre and later, including *Good Luck!* (1954) and *In Search of Happiness* (1957), which created wide interest in the Moscow theatre world and among the general public, and helped to establish Efros's reputation as a director.

9. Alexei Arbuzov (1908–96), Soviet-era playwright whose plays extended the Marxist boundaries of doctrinaire Socialist Realism. Efros directed his plays *My Poor Marat* at the Lenkom Theatre (1965) and *The Happy Days of an Unhappy Man*

at the Malaya Bronnaya Theatre (1969). Ignatii Dvoretsky (1919–87), author and playwright whose works dealt with the ethical and businesses concerns of modern managers and executives. At the Malaya Bronnaya Theatre, Efros directed *The Outsider* (1971, and Central Television 1974), *The Veranda in the Woods* (1978), and *The Theatre Director* (1984). Another play by Dvoretsky, *Members of the Society of Cactuses,* was in preparation at the Taganka Theatre when Efros died.

10. Constantin Stanislavsky, *Stanislavsky Produces "Othello,"* Trans. Helen Nowak, (London: Geoffrey Bles, 1948). Compiled from instructions Stanislavsky sent from Nice to the Moscow Art Theatre in 1929. In the translator's note for Stanislavsky's third acting book, *Creating a Role,* Hapgood says that toward the end of his life Stanislavsky spoke of re-writing all his acting books and centering them on *Othello.* "He felt this play would be accessible to students of many nationalities, especially English-speaking ones. Indeed at this very time in France, he was sending back to Moscow suggestions for the production of *Othello,* the direction of which he was forced to relinquish because of his serious illness in 1928. These suggestions are the basis for *Stanislavsky Produces "Othello,"* a director's promptbook, with his instructions published opposite the text of the play, a volume of enormous value as a demonstration of how this great director worked on a play." From *Creating a Role,* Trans. Elizabeth Reynolds Hapgood, (New York: Theatre Arts Books, 1961), ix–x. A comparison of Stanislavsky and Efros's work on this play provides a valuable illustration of the latter's late-modernist point of view about interpretation and performance of the classics.

11. See *Stanislavsky Produces "Othello,"* 46.

12. In 1975, Oleg Yefremov, then Artistic Director of the Moscow Art Theatre, invited Efros to direct *The Evacuation Train* by Mikhail Roshin as part of the official observances marking the thirtieth anniversary of the end of the Great Patriotic War (WW II).

13. In the Soviet era, terms such as "decadent," "formalist," and "subjective" were said to reflect a dangerously unwanted interest in inner psychology at the expense of the collective, and form over content.

14. Vassily Kachalov (1875–1948), one of the leading actors of the original Moscow Art Theatre. Yevgeny Yevstingeyev (1926–1992), stage and film actor, leading actor at the Moscow Art Theatre beginning in 1975, before which he acted at the Sovremennik Theatre.

15. Efros makes an audacious assertion here, but a balanced assessment of theatre history in the modern era—that is, the era of the director—will show that he is essentially correct.

16. Ivan Moskvin (1874–1946) was a leading member of the original MAT company. Among his his roles were Tsar Fyodor, the title character in Alexei Tolstoy's play *Tsar Fyodor Ivanovich* (1898); Ilyusha Snegiryov (aka Mochalka [Woody]) in the MAT dramatization of Dostoyevsky's novel *The Brothers Karamazov* (1910); Yepikhodov in *The Cherry Orchard* (1904); and Fedya Protasov in Leo Tolstoy's play *The Living Corpse* (1911).

17. Nikolai Khmelyev (1901–45), was a member of the MAT Second Studio (1919–26), the second generation MAT company (1926–37), and was Artistic Director of the Yermolova Theatre (1937–45). For Moskvin, see n. 16.

18. See Chronology for 1975.

19. Maly [Small] Theatre, est. 1756, named the "second university" after Moscow University owing to its influence on Russian society and culture.

20. A line by Konstantin Treplev from *The Seagull,* in which he complains to his uncle about the outmoded conventions in the theatre of his day.

21. Efros's reference here is to Treplev's line from Chekhov's play *The Seagull.*

22. Lev Durov (b. 1931) is an actor who worked with Efros throughout much of his career.

23. Efros instilled his plays with a special type of physical liveliness that illustrated the inner lives of characters through virtually continuous stage movement. He called this process "psychophysics," and he based it on his belief that theatre should be like dance, with the same plasticity of movement and physicalized expression of relationships among the characters. He believed that every inner thought and feeling should be expressed by external means. As a consequence, his performances were constantly in motion, often to the point where the staging seemed almost to fall apart. Psychophysics also extended to scenery that was abstract and unlocalized, which encouraged freedom of movement within a carefully structured environment. Efros's staging was compared to chemistry's "Brownian motion," the random motion of small particles suspended in a gas or liquid, just as his actors seemed to be suspended in the space of the stage. He liked to compare the freedom apparent in his staging with the role of improvisation in jazz, which depends on freedom within the mutually self-imposed limits of the basic melody.

24. *The Ardent Heart* (1869) by Alexander Ostrovsky (1823–1886) was one of Stanislavsky's many notable successes at the Moscow Art Theatre (1926).

25. Yuri Lyubimov directed a modern-dress *Hamlet* at the Taganka Theatre in 1974, for which David Borovsky designed a huge woven curtain that swept dynamically across the entire stage to accompany scene changes.

26. Amadeo Modigliani (1884–1920), Italian painter and scrultor.

27. See n. 16.

28. Efros directed Molière's *Don Juan* at the Malaya Bronnaya Theatre in 1973, in which he emphasized the ethical assumptions of Don Juan's world. See *The Joy of Rehearsal*, passim.

29. Efros directed *A Month in the Country* (1850) by Ivan Turgenev at the Malaya Bronnaya Theatre (1977). "At the provincial estate of the practical landowner Arkady Islayev, his wife Natalya (Natasha) Petrovna regrets her more exciting past and is fearfully conscious of her waning charms. Bored by the languid and polite attentions of her husband's friend Mikhail Rakitin, Natasha is roused to fresh love when the lively young Aleksei Belyayev arrives as tutor for her son. Aleksei is equally prepared to flirt either with the twenty-nine-year-old Natasha or with her seventeen-year-old ward Vera (Verochka); but Natasha's jealousy and passion drive him back to Moscow. Rakitin, despite Islayev's pleading, also leaves. The observant and cynical Dr. Ignatii Shpigelsky, the only one who has been getting what he wants, teaches the clumsy old neighboring landowner

Afanasy Bolshintsov how to propose and pushes the now bitter and lonely Vera, who had bloomed beneath the tutor's attentions, into the old man's arms. Natasha is left frustrated, lonelier and more bored than before." Plot summary from Joseph Shipley, *Crown Guide to the World's Great Plays,* (New York: Crown Publishers, 1984), 782-83.

30. Stanislavsky directed *A Month in the Country* at MAT in 1909.

31. Efros is referring to his difficult years as Artistic Director of the Lenkom Theatre (1964–67). See *The Joy of Rehearsal,* Introduction, passim.

32. See Dmitry Krymov's setting, Figure 10.

33. The reference is to Stanislavsk'ys description of Turgenev's style as "psychological lacework" in the 1909 production at MAT.

34. It is not exactly clear which director Efros is referring to here, but very likely it is Yuri Lyubimov, whose stagings have sometimes been considered extravagantly expressive.

35. A poetic epigraph by poet Boris Pasternak (1890–1960), who is best known in the West as the author of Doctor Zhivago (1958).

36. *Hamlet* 1.2.148.

37. From Alexander Pushkin's poem "Gypsies" (1824).

38. Efros is referring to Stanislavsky's rehearsal innovation known as Active Analysis (sometimes mistakenly referred to as the Method of Physical Actions), which he used in his own rehearsals and actively promoted to others. See *The Joy of Rehearsal,* passim. See also Bella Merlin, *Beyond Stanislavsky* (London: Nick Hern, 2001) and *Konstantin Stanislavsky* (London: Routledge, 2003); Robert Leach, *Stanislavsky and Meyerhold* (Bern: Peter Lang, 2003); Constantin Stanislavski, *Creating a Role,* Trans. Elizabeth Reynolds Hapgood (New York: Theatre Arts Books, 1961) and *Stanislavsky Produces "Othello,"* Trans. Helen Nowak (London: Geoffrey Bles, 1948); Vasily Toporkov, *Stanislavski in Rehearsal: The Final Years,* Trans. Christine Edwards (New York: Theatre Arts Books, 1979); and Sharon Carnicke, *Stanislavsky in Focus* (Amsterdam: Harwood, 1998), among others.

39. *Othello*, 2.3 passim.

40. Jean Louis Barrault (1910–1994), French actor, director, and producer, who was especially noted for his work in poetic mime. *The Book of Christophe Colomb* (1933), a verse drama by Paul Claudel (1868–1955).

41. In 1890, Chekhov traveled to the Russian penal colonies on remote Sakhalin Island off the coast of Siberia, later publishing the treatise "The Island: A Journey to Sakhalin" (1893–94), which helped to implement social reform there.

42. Maxim Gorky (1868–1936), Soviet writer and activist, best known in the West for his play *The Lower Depths* (1902). Lydia Avilov was Chekhov's companiont for ten years, 1889–1899. See Lydia Avilov, *Chekhov in My Life,* Trans. David Magarshack (New York: Harcourt Brace, 1950).

43. Inna Solovyova (b. 1927), is "one of Russia's most prominent theatre historians and critics with particular expertise in the history of the Moscow Art Theatre." See Robert Leach, ed., *A History of Russian Theatre* (London: Cambridge, 1999), for which she was an important contributor.

44. Boris Semyonov-Pishchik, eccentric landowner in Chekhov's play *The Cherry Orchard*.

45. Olga Knipper-Chekhov (1868–1959), wife of Anton Chekhov and leading member of the original MAT company.

46. I have found no record of Nemirovich-Danchenko ever directing *A Month in the Country*. See *Moskovsky Kkhudozhesvenny Teatr: sto let* (*Moscow Art Theatre: One Hundred Years*), Ed. Anatoly Smeliansky et al, vol. 2, Moskva: Izdaltyelsvo "Moskovsky Khudozhesvenny Teatr," 1998.

47. Alexander Kugel (1864–1928), critic and publicist, editor of the influential pre-revolutionary journal Theater and Art, associated primarily with the Maly Theatre and noted for his sarcastic tone.

48. Nadezhda "Nadia" Rusheva (1952–1969), daughter of a scenic designer and a ballerina, who died unexpectedly at the age of seventeen and left behind thousands of strikingly modern graphic works.

49. *Resurrection* (1899) was Tolstoy's last major novel. Nekhludoff, a Russian nobleman serving on a jury, discovers that the young girl on trial, Katusha, is someone he once seduced and abandoned and that he is responsible for reducing her to a life of crime. He sets out to redeem her and himself in the process.

50. *Othello*, 4.1. passim.

51. In Russia, it is proper form to address others by their first and middle names. Thus, Anatoly Vasilevich Efros would be "Anatoly Vasilevich."

52. *Othello*, 1.3 passim.

53. *The Marriage of Figaro* (1794) by Pierre Augustin Caron de Beaumarchais (1732–1799), directed by Stanislavsky at the Moscow Art Theatre (1927).

54. See n. 9.

55. *Woe from Wit* (1823) by Alexander Griboyedov (1795–1829), a verse satire on wealthy Moscow society.

56. *Othello*, 1.2.

57. Yuri Lyubimov became artistic director of the Taganka Theatre in 1964. His directing style is based on the principles of Eugene Vakhatngov, Bertolt Brecht, and Vsevelod Meyerhold, whose portraits hang prominently in the theatre's lobby. (Soviet authorities insisted that Stanislavsky's portrait should be included as well.) Efros's production of *The Cherry Orchard* premiered at the Taganka Theatre in 1975. See Laurence Senelick, *The Chekhov Theatre: A Century of the Plays in Performance* (Cambridge: Cambridge University Press, 1997), 219–23.

58. Alla Demidova (b. 1936), leading actress at the Taganka Theatre. Vladimir Vysotsky (1938–1982), actor, lyricist, and poet-folksinger, affiliated with the Taganka Theatre. David Borovsky (1934–2006), leading Russian scenic designer of the post-war era, mainly affiliated with the Taganka Theatre, though he often worked internationally as well. Borovsky was essentially Yuri Lyubimov's co-author in famous Taganka productions. Valery Leventhal (b. 1938), chief scenic designer of the Bolshoi Theatre.

59. Borovsky was noted for the use of raw materials in his scenic designs.

60. Georgii Alexandrovich Tovstonogov (1915–1989), Russian director, head of the Bolshoi Academic Theatre of St. Petersburg, which now bears his name. Along

with Efros and Yuri Lyubimov, one of the three leading directors of the post-war period.

61. See Active Analysis, n. 38.

62. See n. 10.

63. Alexander Yakovlevich Golovin (1863–1930), painter, graphic artist, sculptor and MAT scenic designer, also designed many productions for Sergei Diaghilev.

64. See n. 25.

65. Jean Gabin (1904–76), French film actor in the 1930s–60s, known for portraying hidden strength, working-class intelligence, and tragic romanticism. Gabin played Jean Valjean in the 1958 French film of Les Miserables (aka in Soviet Russia, The Mighty of This World).

66. Stage adaptation of *The Idiot* by Fyodor Dostoyevsky, Starring Innokenty Smoktunovsky and directed by Georgii Tovstonogov at the Bolshoi Dramatic Theatre in St. Petersburg in 1957. See n. 50.

67. Peter Brook's production of *King Lear*, starring Paul Scofield, premiered in 1962 and toured several European capitals including Moscow the next year. The scenery consisted of rusty, geometrical metal shapes, and Lear was characterized as a wandering vagabond in a bleak landscape suggestive of the absurdist universe of Samuel Beckett. See Charles Marowitz, "Lear Log," in *Peter Brook: A Theatrical Casebook,* Ed. David Williams, (London: Methuen, 1988), 6–22.

68. *The Sorrows of Young Werther* (1774) by Johann Wolfgang Von Goethe. Classic story of Werther, a young man seeking the ideal in an art he cannot master and in a woman he cannot win.

69. Bulgakov died in 1940. Efros may be referring to his own son, Dmitry, who was born in 1954?

70. See n. 4.

71. Anatoly Ktorov (1898–1980), film and stage actor, joined the Moscow Art Theatre in 1933.

72. Nikolai Volkov (1934–2004), leading actor at the Malaya Bronnaya Theatre, worked for many years with Efros, including the role in *Othello*.

73. Dmitry Krymov (b. 1954), artist, scenic designer, and director.

74. *Othello*, starring Laurence Oliver, directed by John Dexter with Maggie Smith and Frank Finlay at the National Theatre (1964).

75. See n. 25, 57, 58.

76. Mikhail Morozov (1897–1952), noted Shakespeare scholar and translator. Available in English is his *Shakespeare on the Soviet Stage,* Trans. David Magarshack (London: Soviet News, 1947).

77. Alexander Ostuzhev (1874–1953), actor who excelled in tragic roles. His Othello was a person of refined culture and feelings, an interpretation which probably influenced Efros's thinking about the play.

78. Akaky Khorova (1895–1972), Georgian actor who excelled in the role of Othello, among many others.

79. *Hamlet*, starring Paul Scofield and directed by Peter Brook (1955). Its twelve performances at the Moscow Art Theatre were the first appearance of a British company in Russia since the Revolution. Brook's spare scenic environment was a

surprise to many who were accustomed to the heavily laden Russian scenic tradition. Moreover, Russian Hamlets traditionally were neurasthenic Romantic types, while Scofield's was active, non-neurotic, and ready to purge the kingdom of evil. What struck Russians most, though, was the play's abstract, minimalist staging.

80. *Boris Godunov* (1831), historical tragedy by Alexander Pushkin (1799–1837). Boris Godunov ruled as Tsar from 1598 to 1605. Pushkin's play comprises twenty-four blank-verse scenes. Efros directed the play at the Central Children's Theatre in 1957 and for Central Television in 1971.

81. Boyars were members of a class of higher Russian nobility that, until the time of Peter I, headed the civil and military administration of the country and participated in an early form of parliament.

82. *Tsar Fyodor Ivanovich* (1868) by Alexei Tolstoy (1883–1945), poet, writer, and dramatist. His play was the first production of the newly established Moscow Art Theatre in 1898.

83. The "Time of Troubles" was a period of political crisis in Russia, which followed the demise of the Rurik dynasty (1598) and ended with the establishment of the Romanov dynasty (1613).

84. "Tales of Belkin" (1830), Alexander Pushkin's first major collection of prose fiction.

85. *Ivan the Terrible* (1938), the last work of the film director Sergei Eisenstein (1898–1948).

86. *The Young Guard* (1945), a novel by Soviet writer Alexander Fadayev (1901–1956) about young communist heroes in World War II.

87. See n. 8.

88. In this section Efros is again referring to the rehearsal process known as Active Analysis. See n. 38.

89. See Active Analysis, n. 38.

90. Mikhail Bulgakov (1891–1940), Russian novelist and playwright, best known in the West for his novel *The Master and Margarita* (1940). *Black Snow: A Theatrical Novel* (1929) is a fictionalized account of Bulgakov's difficult years as resident playwright at MAT. See Anatoly Smeliansky, *Is Comrade Bulgakov Dead?: Mikhail Bulgakov at the Moscow Art* Theatre, London: Routledge, 1993.

91. See n. 38.

92. See n. 38.

93. *The Lower Depths* (lit. *At the Bottom*, 1902) by Soviet writer and dramatist Maxim Gorky (1868–1936), subtitled "Scenes from Russian Life," depicts a group of lower-class Russians in a lodging house in the city of Volga.

94. See Chronology for 1973.

95. Fyodor Shalyapin (1873-1928) is considered one of the greatest performers in the hisory of opera. He was greatly admired by Stanislavsky for single-handedly creating the realistic acting style in opera. Boris Godunov in Mussorgsky's opera of the same name (1868-72) was his most famous role.

96. Efros directed *Summer and Smoke* (1948) by Tennessee Williams at the Malaya Bronnaya Theatre in 1980.

97. For Efros's thoughts about Gogol's play *Marriage*, see The Joy of Rehearsal, 154 ff.

98. *The Storm* (1860) by Alexander Ostrovsky (1823–1886), shows the jealousy-induced hatred of a domestic tyrant, Madame Kabanova, directed toward her unfortunate daughter-in-law, Katerina.

99. Valentin Kataev (1897–1986), Soviet-Russian novelist, originator of "mauvist" ("bad-ist") writing style, which Efros frankly emulated in his own writing. See *The Joy of Rehearsal,* Translator's Preface.

100. *Dead Souls* (1842), novel by Nikolai Gogol (1809–52).

101. See n. 14.

102. See Active Analysis, n. 38.

103. *Love Among the Ruins* (1975 television film), directed by George Cukor, starring Laurence Olivier and Katherine Hepburn, winner of 6 Emmy Awards, Los Angeles Film Critics Award, and Peabody Award.

104. *An Unfinished Piece for Player Piano* (1977), film directed by Nikita Milhalkov, adapted from a fragment believed to be Chekhov's unfinished, first full-length play Platonov (1881). A teacher and a doctor undergo various stages of nervous collapse from realization of the failure of their youthful dreams. In 1984 Michael Frayn rewrote the play for the London National Theatre and titled it Wild Honey.

105. Chekhonte was the pen name Chekhov used in his early writings.

106. See n. 97.

107. In terms of theatre, "narrative" may be compared to plot, and "still life" compared to character or thematic development. Efros is alluding here to the delicate balance between plot momentum on one hand, and character or theme development on the other.

108. The neo-Stalinist Moscow Art Theatre was is a state of creative stagnation and bloated officialdom at the time, but eventually returned to its original ideals when Oleg Yefremov became Artistic Director in 1970. Improvement accelerated after the company split in 1987, at which time Yefremov and his followers remained at the original venue (the Chekhov Moscow Art Theatre), while the rest of the company moved to a new venue (the Gorky Moscow Art Theatre).

109. Innokenty Smoktunovsky (1925–1994), stage and film actor, graduate of the Krasnoyarsk Drama Theatre (1946), leading actor of MAT (1976–94), State Prize of USSR, National Artist of USSR.

110. See n. 13.

111. Edward Gordon Craig directed his famous and controversial production of *Hamlet* at the Moscow Art Theatre in 1912.

112. Efros is probably referring to the artist's "unions" formed during the Soviet era, which were calculated to ensure the promotion of Soviet-Marxist dogma in the form of Socialist Realism.

113. See n. 65, 107.

114. See n. 40.

115. Efros is probably referring to Marlon Brando's theatrically-inclined performances in *A Streetcar Named Desire* (1951) and *On the Waterfront* (1954), that is, prior to his notably restrained performances in *The Godfather* (1972) and later films.

116. Pavel Mochalov (1800–1848), said to be the greatest tragedian of the Russian Romantic style.

117. See n. 4.

118. *Uncle Vanya* was the only major play of Chekhov's that Efros did not have an opportunity to direct.

119. *Uncle Vanya* (1971 film), directed by Andrei Konchalovsky and starring Innokenty Smoktunovsky.

120. *The Clowns* (1971) by Federico Fellini, originally made for Italy's RAI-TV. The film portrays clowns and clowning by exploring some of Europe's greatest circuses and their best acts, while underscording the theme of life as a spiritual circus procession. Efros devotes several lengthy sections to an appreciation of Fellini's artistry in the Russian edition of this book.

Bibliography

English

Beumers, Birgit. *Yuri Lyubimov at the Taganka Theatre, 1964–1994.* Amsterdam: Harwood, 1997.

Dixon, Ross. "Slaughtering Sacred Seagulls: An Analysis of Anatoly Efros's Production of *The Seagull* at the Lenkom Theatre in 1967," *Irish Slavonic Studies* (2001): n.p.

Efros, Anatoly. "Energy, Enervation, and the Mathematics of Intrigue: Anatoly Efros in Conversation with Spencer Golub," *Theatre Quarterly* 7.26 (1977): 28–33.

———. "Directing Victor Rozov's Plays: The 'Thaw' and the Young Audience." *Through the Magic Curtain: Theatre for Children, Adolescents and Youth in the U.S.S.R.: 27 Authoritative Essays.* Eds. Miriam Morton, Natalya Sats and N. Krymova, New Orleans: Anchorage, 1979, 137–40.

———. *The Joy of Rehearsal.* Trans. James Thomas. New York: Peter Lang, 2006.

———. "What Is Hecuba to Them? Nikolai Gogol's *Marriage* at the Guthrie Theatre." Trans. James Thomas. *Theatre Topics* 3.2 (1993): 177–95.

Gershkovich, Aleksandr Abramovich. *The Theater of Yuri Lyubimov: Art and Politics at the Taganka Theater in Moscow.* New York: Paragon House, 1989.

Golub, Spencer. "Acting on the Run: Efros and the Contemporary Soviet Theatre." *Theatre Quarterly* 7.26 (1977): 18–28.

Lamont, Rosette. "The Taganka of Anatoly Efros." *Performing Arts Journal* 10.3 (1977): 96–101.

Leach, Robert, Victor Borovsky and Andy Davies, eds. *A History of Russian Theatre.* Cambridge: Cambridge University, 1999.

Olkhovich, Elena. "Produced Abroad." *Soviet Literature* 4.433 (1984): 206–8.

Senelick, Laurence, ed. *Wandering Stars: Russian Emigre Theater, 1905–1940.* Iowa City: University of Iowa, 1992.

———. "Chekhov on Stage." *A Chekhov Companion.* Ed. Toby W. Clyman. Westport, CT: Greenwood, 1985, 209–232.

———. "Directors' Chekhov." *The Cambridge Companion to Chekhov.* Eds. Vera Gottlieb and Paul Allain. Cambridge: Cambridge University, 2000, 176–200.

———. *The Chekhov Theatre: A Century of the Plays in Performance.* Cambridge: Cambridge University, 1997.

Shevstova, Maria. "Anatolij Efros Directs Chekhov's *The Cherry Orchard* and Gogol's *Marriage.*" *Theatre Quarterly* 7.26 (1977): 34–46.

———. *The Theatre Practice of Anatoly Efros, a Contemporary Soviet Director*. Devon, Eng.: Department of Theatre Dartington College of Arts, 1978.

Slonim, Marc. *Soviet Russian Literature: Writers and Problems, 1917–1977*. New York: Oxford University, 1977.

Smeliansky, Anatoly and Patrick Miles. *The Russian Theatre after Stalin*. Cambridge, England: Cambridge University, 1999.

Solovyova, Inna, and Jean Benedetti. "The Theatre and Socialist Realism, 1929–1953." *A History of Russian Theatre*. Eds. Robert Leach, Victor Borovsky and Andy Davies: Cambridge: Cambridge University, 1999, 325–57.

Wilson, Kyle. "Splinters of a Shattered Mirror: Experimentation and Innovation in Contemporary Soviet Theatre." *Transformations in Modern European Drama*. Ed. Ian Donaldson. Atlantic Highlands, NJ: Humanities, 1983, 99–118.

Russian

Efros, Anatolii. Kniga Chetvertaia (The Fourth Book). Fond Russkii Teatr. Moskva: Panas, 1993.

———. Prodolzhenie Teatralnova Romana (Theatre Novel Continued). Fond Russkii Teatr. Moskva: Panas, 1993 (1985).

———. Professia: Rezhisser (Profession: Director). Fond Russkii Teatr. Moskva: Panac, 1993 (1976).

———. Rabota Rezhissera Nad Spektaklem (The Director's Work on the Performance). Moskva: Tsentral'nyi dom narodnogo tvorchestva, 1960.

———. Repetitsia–Liubov Moìa (Rehearsal Is My Love, a.k.a. The Joy of Rehearsal). Fond Russki Teatr. Moskva: Panas, 1993 (1975).

Fridshtein, Iu. G. Anatolii Efros–Poet Teatra (Anatoly Efros: Poet of the Theatre). Moskva: Mezhdunarodnyi kommercheskii soiuz, 1993.

Kochetov, V. P., ed. Anatolii Efros–Professia: Rezhisser (Anatoly Efros-Profession: Director). Moskva: Vagrius, 2000.

Krymko, F. M. and E. M Tinyanova, eds., Anatolii Vasilevich Efros: Bibliograficheskii Ukazatel' (Anatoly Vaslyevich Efros: Bibliograhical Guide). Moskva: Tsentral'naya Nauchnaya Biblioteka. 1992.

Kuzicheva, A. P. "Repetiruet A. V. Efros: Tri Sestry" ("Anatoly Efros Rehearses Three Sisters"). Chekoviana: "Tri Sestry"–100 Let (Chekhov: 100 years of 'Three Sisters'). Eds. M. O. Goriacheva, V. B. , and A. P. Chudakov. Moskva: Nauka, 2002, 259–93.

Markov, Pavel. "Ob Anatolii Efrose" ("About Anatoly Efros"). O Teatr (On The Theatre). Moskva: Isskustvo, 1977, 4: 556–68.

Nikolskaya, Sonya T. Zhivoi Teatr A. Efrosa (The Living Theatre of Anatoly Efros). Moskva: Philologicheskii Fakultet MGU, 1995.

Shak-Azizova, T. K. "Anatolii Efros: Linia Zhizni" ("Anatoly Efros: The Contour of a Life"). Liudi I Sud'by Xx Vek. Moskva: OGI, 2002. 206–16.

Tsitriniak, Grigorii. "Ia–Za Takoi Teatr" ("I Am For Such a Theatre"). Literaturnaia Gazeta 38.5208 (1988): 8.

Zaionts, M. G., ed. Teatr Anatolia Efrosa: Vospominania, Ctati' (The Theatre of Anatoly Efros: Recollections, Articles). Moskva: Artist-rezhisser-teatr, 2000.

Zolotukhin, Valeri. Moi Efros: Dnevniki (My Efros: A Diary). Kiev: KMTIS Poezia, 1997.

Index